History
OF THE
Town of Weston
Massachusetts

1630–1890

Daniel S. Lamson

HERITAGE BOOKS
2024

HERITAGE BOOKS
AN IMPRINT OF HERITAGE BOOKS, INC.

Books, CDs, and more—Worldwide

For our listing of thousands of titles see our website
at
www.HeritageBooks.com

A Facsimile Reprint
Published 2024 by
HERITAGE BOOKS, INC.
Publishing Division
5810 Ruatan Street
Berwyn Heights, MD 20740

Originally published:
Boston
Press of Geo. H. Ellis Co.
1913

— Publisher's Notice —
In reprints such as this, it is often not possible to remove
blemishes from the original. We feel the contents of this
book warrant its reissue despite these blemishes and
hope you will agree and read it with pleasure.

International Standard Book Number
Paperbound: 978-0-7884-2985-9

CONTENTS.

CHAPTER		PAGE
I.	Ecclesiastical Origin of the Town	1
II.	General Description and Military Organization	18
III.	Civil and Ecclesiastical Organization and French and Indian Wars	27
IV.	The Old Town Records	39
V.	Thrifty Finance of ye Fathers (Rates, Taxes, Bounties, etc.)	56
VI.	Weston in the Revolution	67
VII.	In the Wake of the Revolution	102
VIII.	A Record of Forty Quiet Years	118
IX.	The Story of the Town from Year to Year	130
X.	War Veterans, Railroads, etc.	137
XI.	Business Interests of the Town	152
XII.	Schools and Teachers	165
XIII.	Evangelical Churches in Weston	173
XIV.	The Medical Profession	182
XV.	The Taverns	186

APPENDICES.

I.	Rev. Samuel Kendal's Letter of Acceptance	195
II.	Rev. Joseph Field's Letter of Acceptance	197
III.	Seating the Meeting-house	201
IV.	Town Clerks	202
V.	Town Treasurers	203
VI.	Representatives	204
VII.	Selectmen	206
VIII.	The Separation from Watertown as a Precinct	210
IX.	Location and Present Ownership of Historic Buildings and Places mentioned in this History	212

EDITOR'S PREFACE.

It is scarcely a debatable question, in the opinion of the writer of these lines, as to whether this or any other town history is worth writing and publishing. The story of any town is worth telling, and the story of any man's life is worth narrating, either briefly or at length. So, when requested to edit this History of the Town of Weston by the late Colonel Daniel S. Lamson, I was glad to address myself to the task of getting the manuscript into shape and seeing it through the press. In these annals of a quiet neighborhood and these outlines of homely but strong and sturdy lives, the good colonel has limned for us, with praiseworthy toil and zeal, many a pleasant little sketch of scenes in the past life of Weston. His work is meritorious for its graphic anecdotes, its annals of the church and of the town meetings, and especially for its full account of Weston in the Revolution, and for its pronounced patriotic tone throughout.

Such features of the work as the description of the grand wagon-freight routes from the North to the South along the coast and paralleling the Alleghany Range in the days before railroads; of the farmer-lads' wagon-freighting of wood to Boston from far New Hampshire and Vermont; or of the great trunk stage-road between Boston and New York which passed through Weston, the logical results thereof being visits to the town by Presidents Washington and Adams, events upon which the citizens prided themselves not a little,—these things, including minute accounts of the schools and of the business enterprises of the community, are interesting reading and cheer one's way through the dryer details. I take it that the latter are not intended for consecutive reading at all, but for consultation or peeping into on rainy days when the mood serves. In other words, a town history is, to a large extent at least, a reference book, however interesting it may be.

And how, then, do our ancestors look to us? What is the verdict on them? For my part, aside from that matter of offering a bounty for the destruction of crows, jays, and red-winged blackbirds (see Chapter V.), I find little or nothing in the history of Weston and its inhabitants in which we may not take pride. They had perhaps a little too close a grip on the gear, which is the familiar New England trait. But in that matter of the birds they were not at all to blame, because a fuller knowledge had not yet taught them that the birds put vastly more into one's pocketbook than they take out.

It would require a Velasquez or a Carlyle to give us an immortal portrait gallery of the men and women of early days, for they had strong and heroic lineaments and were worthy of the most gifted pen and pencil. And yet what finer characters can you find in the annals of New England than those of the early ministers of this parish as depicted by Lamson, Russell, Hornbrooke, and Putnam, and other writers on the church and town? And who can do full justice to the plain homespun lives of the laity? We all know them,—those sturdy, God-fearing, rugged-featured, strong-willed farmers and merchants; those patient, sweet-souled New England mothers. They are nearly an extinct race now. But, having known and respected them, we think the greatest genius in the world could hardly have chronicled worthily their lives.

I happen to have just been reading the story of a community as different from that of Weston, Massachusetts, as it is possible to conceive,—the story of the Italian hill-town Perugia. There is a terrible fascination in the blood-bespattered annals of its two thousand years of struggle and war, the insane feuds of its rival families, its Baglioni and its Oddi, the endless pageants, rejoicings, wailings, slaughters, and conflagrations of the turbulent populace and nobility, and a nameless charm, too, in the environing landscape of the warm Southland, where, alas! ever "the tender red roses of the hedges tossed above the helmets and glowed between the lowered lances," and the foliage of the trees waved in the twilight "only to show the flames of burning cities on the horizon through the tracery of their stems," and the "twisted olive trunks hid only the ambushes of treachery." Well, out of all that internecine passion and pain and splendid war there has resulted to the weal of mankind only a few great paintings and a massive and picturesque mediæval city still standing to shelter its inhabitants and give pleasure to tourists. Good art may have been in the past the concomitant or resultant of war. But it is not necessarily so. Again, there is something greater than art in the world, and that is noble character developed through the quiet, peaceful work of useful lives built into the fibre of the race. For my part I am prouder to be descended, as I am, from such plain Scotch-English stock as produced a Carlyle and a Lincoln than if I were sprung from the proudest high-stomached steel-clad brabbler lord of the Middle Age or any age. And so, doubtless, are the citizens of the fair and fertile hill-town of Massachusetts, the story of which is told in this volume.

As to the accuracy of Colonel Lamson's History of Weston, all has been done that could be done to authenticate and correct the data without expending upon them an amount of research that would have been almost equivalent to rewriting the whole book. The proofs have passed under the critical eye of several persons. The transcript of the Act of Incorporation of the town (see page 18) has been, with scrupulous care, collated with the crumbling old record of Acts and Resolves in the State House at Boston, and other similar collations have been made, while in Appendix VIII. is given a transcript from the State Records of the legislative Resolve setting off the town as a precinct. It may also be stated that, although Colonel Lamson's chronicle of the town's history ended with the year 1890, yet in a number of instances we have added statistics that bring the record down to 1910 and 1912.

Finally, the editor cannot but express his regret that Colonel Lamson himself had not lived to see his work through the press. For we all feel that he would have afforded no exception to the well-known law that the turning of manuscript into the printed page is always accompanied by innumerable corrections and betterments. We have done our best to do this work for him. The task was not altogether an easy one. Hence over our shortcomings would it be too much to ask that kindly charity draw the veil of silence? W. S. K.

BELMONT, MASS., February 24, 1913.

HISTORY OF THE TOWN OF WESTON

I.

Ecclesiastical Origin of the Town.

1630–1712.

At the second Court of Assistants, held at Charlestown, September 7, 1630, it was ordered "That Trimount be called Boston; Matapan should be called Dorchester; and the town upon Charles River, Watertown" (Prince's Chronological History of New England, pp. 248, 249).

The exact period when what is called Weston began to be settled is not known. It must have been at an early period of the Watertown settlement, for there are still standing houses or parts of houses which were erected a hundred and fifty years ago. June 26, 1637, "A grant of the remote or West Pine Meadows were divided and alloted out to all the Townsmen then inhabiting Watertown, being 114 in number, allowing one acre for each person, and likewise for cattle, valued at £20 the head, beginning next the Plain meadow, and to go on until lots are ended" (Watertown Records). These meadows were probably in the south and south-eastern part of Weston. In July, 1638, it was ordered

> that all the land lying beyond the Plowlands [lots in the further plain] and the lots granted extending west of Stoney Brook, having the great dividents on the one side [north] and Charles River and Dedham bounds on the other side [south], and the Farm lands at the further end [west] of it, shall be for a common for cattle, to the use of the Freemen of the Town and their heirs forever, and not to be alienated without the consent of every freeman and their heirs forever.

This is the first instance upon record where the term "Farm lands" is applied to Weston. The earliest proprietors of land in

Weston in 1642 are Bryan Pendleton, Daniel Pattrick, Simon Eire, John Stowers, Abraham Browne, John Whitney, Edward How, Jeremiah Norcross, and Thomas Mayhew. From 1647 to 1663 there was much dissatisfaction and contention about the early allotments of the Remote Meadows in Lieu of Township, and of the Farm Lands; and in 1663 this portion of the town was resurveyed and plotted by Captain John Sherman. It contained 1,102 acres, bounded on the south by Dedham, west by Natick and Sudbury, and on the other side by the Farm Lands. This district is frequently referred to in early deeds as "the land of Contention."

In ecclesiastical affairs what is now Weston was connected with Watertown about sixty-eight years, and in civil concerns about eighty-three years.* The inhabitants of the Farms, and those in the remote westerly part of Watertown, went to worship in the easterly part of Watertown, at a house situated in the vicinity of the old burying-place. The first church in Massachusetts was planted at Salem; the second, at Charlestown, including Boston; the third, at Dorchester; the fourth, at Roxbury; the fifth, at Lynn; and the sixth, at Watertown. On July 30, 1630, at Watertown, forty men subscribed a church covenant, and from that date seem to have been considered a distinct church. It would appear from Governor Winthrop's Journal that the Watertown church had a prior existence to the one at Charlestown, and was second only to that at Salem.

In 1692 began the contention in Watertown growing out of the location of the new meeting-house considered "most convenient to the bulk of the inhabitants." There was great opposition to a

---

* A history of Weston from the date of its separation from Watertown in 1698, as a distinct precinct, must necessarily commence with a history of its church. There are no records of the town other than those of the church for a period of fourteen years. In the early settlements of New England the church was the nucleus of organization, the bond which held together the scattered population of the rural districts, around which the people gathered and formed that essentially New England form of government which we call the Town Meeting. It was through the action of the town meetings that the democracy of New England was developed and brought the population of the towns to take personal action in all that pertained to the common interests. They voted to levy taxes on themselves and to dispose of their own money, they kept control upon money appropriations and watched carefully their expenditure. It was through the agency of town meetings and the public spirit they developed that the country was successfully carried through the Revolutionary War, and they became ultimately the framework of our general government. No better test of their efficiency can be found than in the successful maintenance of personal liberty and the Constitution against the assaults upon them at the time of our Civil War.

change in their place of worship, and in this dilemma the Selectmen agreed to refer the matter to the governor, Sir William Phipps, and his council. This mode of bringing the disputes of a town to an issue by referring them to the chief magistrate of the State would be deemed singular at the present day, but at that early period was not uncommon. The committee appointed by the governor to take the matter into consideration consisted of William Stoughton, John Phillips, James Russell, Samuel Sewall, and Joseph Lynde. They made their report in May, 1693. The Selectmen not being satisfied with some of the provisions of the report of the committee, it was subsequently revised in 1694. The report was still unsatisfactory to the townspeople, and a protest was placed on record, signed by one hundred citizens, of which thirty-three were inhabitants of the Farmers' District, later known as Weston.

The dissensions growing out of the new meeting-house location continued for some years; and as early as 1694 that part of Watertown now known as Weston appears to have had separate interests of its own in ecclesiastical matters. On October 2, 1694, "our neighbors the farmers [the name given to the settlers west of the present boundary of Watertown] being upon endeavours to have a Meeting house among themselves the town consents that they may come as far as Beaver Brook, upon the road leading to Sudbury; to the end there may be peace and settlement amongst us." Beaver Brook still retains its old name to remind us of this boundary. It passes the main road at the lower part of Waltham Plain. The origin of the name will be seen in the following extract from Winthrop's Journal, under date of January 27, 1632:—

The Governor and some company with him went up Charles River, about eight miles above Watertown, and named the first brook, on the north side of the river, Beaver Brook, because the beavers had shorn down great trees there, and made divers dams across the brook. Thence they went to a great rock upon which stood a high stone, cleft asunder, that four men might go through, which they called Adam's chair, because the youngest of their company was Adam Winthrop. Thence they came to another brook, greater than the former, which they called Masters Brook, because the eldest of their company was one John Masters.

This is the present Stony Brook, which forms the boundary between Waltham and Weston. The high hill which Winthrop mentions west of Mount Feake is, undoubtedly, Sanderson's Hill in Weston, upon which during the Revolution the beacon light was established, Jonas Sanderson being its keeper. General Sullivan speaks of this beacon light in his Memoirs as the connecting light, uniting his command in Rhode Island with Boston. The town of Watertown included what is now Waltham, Weston, Lincoln, and a part of Concord.

In 1697 Mr. Angier became the pastor of the West Precinct of Watertown. But as early as 1694 the inhabitants of the Farmers' Precinct, to the number of one hundred and eighteen, petitioned to be set off into a separate precinct, alleging the great distance to the church and protesting against being obliged to go so far from home. The prayer of the petitioners was not granted at once,—in fact, not until after a period of three years. Justice Sewall, who presided over the conference, states in his Diary that so great was the contention that he had to pray hard to keep the contending parties from coming to blows. Weston became a separate precinct in 1698; but on January 1, 1697, they were exempted from ministerial rates in Watertown, though not in legal form until a year later. After the incorporation of Weston in 1712 (up to which period it had been called the "westerly," "more westerly," and "most westerly" precinct of Watertown) the middle part acquired the name of the West Precinct, or Watertown West, and was incorporated as a town by the name of Waltham in 1737, or twenty-five years after the incorporation of Weston. It would seem that the inhabitants of the Farms were in earnest in their determination to be separated from Watertown, and probably feared that Watertown would not consent to the prayer of the petitioners, for in August, 1695, money was contributed by sundry persons for the purpose of preferring a petition to the General Court to that end. No record of any such petition, however, can be found. Some doubts arising about the eastern boundary of the precinct (see Appendix IX.), the General Court in May, 1699, passed an order, viz.:—

The bounds of said precinct shall extend from Charles River to Stony Brook Bridge, and from the said Bridge up the Brook Northerly to Robert Harrington's farm; and the brook to be the Boundary; Including the said Farm, and comprehending all the Farms, and Farm Lands to the lines of Cambridge and Concord; and from thence all Watertown lands to their utmost Southward and Westward Bounds.

The same bounds, in the same words, are defined in the act of incorporation of the town.

January 9, 1695, the inhabitants of what is now Weston agreed to build a meeting-house, thirty feet square, on land of Nathaniel Coolidge, Sr. In March, 1715, the deed of this land was passed to the church by Jonathan Coolidge, son of Nathaniel. This church was never completed, but services were held in it in 1700. It was styled the Farmers' Meeting-house. It was begun by subscription and afterwards carried on at the expense of the precinct. Meetings were held November 8 and November 15, 1698, officers of the precinct were chosen, and provision made to complete the church begun in 1695. On August 25, September 15, and November 16, 1699, still further measures were taken to finish the meeting-house. February 14, 1700, the precinct voted to have a minister to preach in the meeting-house, to begin the second Sabbath of the ensuing March. Thus it appears that the small house begun in 1695 was not so far completed as to be occupied till March, 1700. On March 5, 1700, money was granted to support preaching, and grants continued to be made from time to time for this purpose. A committee was chosen September 13, 1700, to apply for advice, as to the choice of a minister, to the Rev. President Mather of Harvard College. The committee consisted of Rev. Mr. Angier, Mr. Brattle, and Mr. Gibbs, and they were asked to make a report. Mr. Thomas Symmes was chosen, but no mention is made of him in the records. It is to be presumed he declined the call. Mr. Mors would seem to have been the choice of the Precinct Committee, as in December, 1701, it was voted that Mr. Mors should continue in order for a settlement. July 2, 1702, they gave him a call to settle in the ministry, the vote of the church being thirty for and twelve against him. In September, 1702, they renewed the call and granted him an annual salary, also engaging to build him a house forty by twenty feet. This house stood on the present site of the house of Deacon White. In 1704 the house was put into the possession of

Mr. Mors and a grant of money made to enable him to finish it. In this year difficulties arose respecting Mr. Mors's settlement in the ministry, but there is no record of what the difficulties were. In the controversy between the precinct and Mr. Mors, whatever might be the grounds of it, there appears to have been considerable irritation, and his opposers were thought to have been at fault. Mr. Mors had steadfast friends, who were zealous for his settlement; but they agreed to relinquish their object, and unite in the choice of another man, if the precinct would join in calling in mediators who would attempt a reconciliation between Mr. Mors and his opponents. Justice Sewall (Memoirs, vol. ii. p. 156), under date of March 6, 1706, speaks of a council held at the house of Mr. Willard, and they advise that after a month Mr. Joseph Mors should cease to preach at Watertown Farms. He left in the spring of 1706, and was afterwards settled in Stoughton, now Canton. A committee was appointed to treat with him for the purchase of his house and land, for the use of the ministry, but no agreement was reached until 1707, when he conveyed the premises to the Precinct Committee, as will be found in Registry of Deeds, lib. 14, fol. 646. The committee consisted of Thomas Wilson, Captain Josiah Jones, Captain Francis Fullam, Lieutenant John Brewer. These premises were assigned to Rev. William Williams, April 28, 1714 (lib. 22, fol. 211). In 1706 the precinct was presented at the Court of Sessions for not having a settled minister. A committee was appointed to answer the presentment at Charlestown.

February 11, 1707, the precinct chose Mr. Nathaniel Gookin to be their minister, but he did not accept the call. The precinct was again presented, May 9, 1707. In June, 1707, a petition was prepared to be presented to the Court at Concord, assigning reasons for not having a settled minister. The petitioners say "once more we humbly pray that the Honourable Court would not put Mr. Joseph Mors into the work of the ministry in our precinct." They were fearful the Court would place Mr. Mors here and not by their own election. July 16, 1707, they chose Mr. Thomas Tufts, but he declined the call in September. January 14, 1708, they agreed to keep a day of fasting and prayer. In February, 1708, the people gave Mr. William Williams a call.

Mr. Williams accepted in August, 1709, and he was ordained November 2, 1709, eleven years after the Farms had become a distinct precinct. It would appear that the church had no regular organization until 1710, when two deacons were chosen. They were Captain Josiah Jones and John Parkhurst. The membership consisted of nineteen males,—nine from other churches and ten who were not communicants. The following are the names of those who gathered with the church: Nathaniel Coolidge, Thomas Flagg, John Livermore, Francis Fullam, Abel Allen, Joseph Lowell, John Parkhurst, Ebenezer Allen, Francis Peirce.

The ten others were Joseph Jones, Thomas Wright, Joseph Allen, Josiah Jones, Jr., Joseph Woolson, Joseph Livermore, Joseph Allen, Jr., Josiah Livermore, Samuel Severns, George Robinson.

It would seem from the following that, although Mr. Williams was only ordained in November, 1709, he held a conference at his "lodgings" as early as October 12 of that year, and began at that date the organization of the church in Weston. The covenant then subscribed by the inhabitants who gathered with this church is so very interesting that its introduction here will not be out of place. It would also seem that twelve years after the signing of the covenant, March 12, 1721, a "Profession of Faith" was also signed by the young people of the parish, or what should properly be called a renewal of baptismal vows and promises. This last covenant is still more interesting, as it gives us an idea of the strong abiding faith which characterized our forefathers, but which in too many instances in this our day has given place to laxity and indifference in those things which our sires held in such love and veneration.

Says Mr. Williams: "October 12, 1709, was the day appointed (by the members of the Parish) to meet and confer together (at my lodgings) where they expressed their charity towards each other, and that there was no discord between them, or any thing that should hinder their Communion and fellowship. Some time was spent in reading the *Confession of Faith* put forth by the last Synod of churches held in Boston in New England, to which they assented, and in praying for the Divine Blessing. The covenant was read and subscribed by them all."

THE COVENANT.

We do under an abiding sense of our unworthiness of such a favour and unfitness for such a blessing, yet apprehending ourselves to be called of God to put ourselves into a way of Church communion, and to seek the settlement of all the Gospel Institutions among us, do therefore in order thereto, and for better promoting thereof as much as in us lies, knowing how prone we are to err, abjuring all confidence in ourselves, and relying on the Lord Jesus Christ for help, Covenant as follows:—

First, having perused the *Confession of Faith* put forth by the last Synod of Churches, held in Boston in New England, we do heartily close in with it for the substance of it, and promise to stand by maintaining, and if need be contend for ye Faith therein delivered to the People of God, and if any one of us shall go about to undermine it we will bear a due testimony against them. We do all combine to walk together as a particular Church of Christ, according to all those Holy rules of ye Gospel prescribed to such a society, so far as God has revealed, or shall reveal his mind to us in this respect. We do accordingly recognize the Covenant of Grace, in which we do professedly acknowledge ourselves bound, rooted to ye fear and service of the only true God our Supreme Lord, and to ye Lord Jesus Christ the High Priest, Prophet and King of his Church unto the conduct of whose Spirit we submit ourselves, and on whom alone we rely for pardon, grace and glory: to whom we bind ourselves in an everlasting Covenant never to be broken. We likewise give up ourselves one unto another in the Lord, resolving by his help to cleave to each other, as fellow-members of one body in brotherly love and holy watchfulness over one another, for mutual edification, and to submit ourselves to all the Holy administrations appointed by him who is the head of the Church, dispensed according to the rules of the Gospel, and to give our constant attendance on all the public ordinances of Christ's Institutions, walking orderly as becometh saints.

We do all acknowledge our Posterity to be included with us in the Gospel Covenant, and blessing God for so rich a favour do promise to bring them up in the nurture and admonition of ye Lord, with greatest care. Further we promise to be careful to ye utmost, to procure the settlement and continuance among us of all ye offices and officers appointed by Christ, the Chief Shepherd, for the edification of his Church: and accordingly to do our duty faithfully for their maintenance and encouragement, and to carry it towards them as becomes us. Finally we do acknowledge, and promise to preserve communion with the faithful Churches of Christ, for the giving and receiving mutual Counsel and assistance, in all cases wherein it shall be needful. Now the good Lord be merciful unto us, and as he hath put it into our hearts thus to devote ourselves to him, let him pity and pardon our frailties, humble us out of all carnal confidence, and keep it for ever more upon our hearts to be faithful to himself, and one to another, for his praise and our Eternal comfort, for Christ Jesus sake, to whom be Glory for ever and ever. Amen.

A FORM OF YE COVENANT ASSENTED TO BY YE YOUNG PEOPLE, MARCH 12, 1721.

You do thankfully acknowledge ye Divine goodness towards you, that you have been by ye act of your parents dedicated to God in your Baptism and by their pious care educated in ye Christian religion, do now willingly ratify their act, and solemnly choose ye Lord, Father, Son and Holy Ghost into ye profession of whose name you have been baptised, for your God and portion. And professing a serious belief of ye holy Scriptures as ye word of God, you resolve by his grace to take them for ye Rule of your lives: to guide and govern both your faith and practice, renouncing all you know to be contrary to his revealed will. You depend on the Lord Jesus Christ the mediator of ye Covenant for righteousness and strength—that you may be pardoned and accepted with God, and may be enabled to walk in sincere obedience before him. You do also subject yourselves to ye Government of Christ in his Church, and to ye regular administration of it in this Church while his Providence shall continue you here.

In March, 1720, the following young persons owned the covenant and became members of the church: Isaac Harrington, Joseph Livermore, Joseph Woolson, Josiah Jones, Robert Allen, John Allen, Ebenezer Felch, Josiah Brewer, John Hastings, Joshua Bigelow, Jonathan Bullard, Benjamin Rand, Isaac Allen, Jonas Allen, Elezebeth Spring, Zedakiah Allen, Benjamin Brown, Jr., Francis Allen, Thankful Harrington, Mary Woolson, Hannah Woolson, Patience Allen, Prudence Allen, Elezebeth Hastings, Mary Livermore, Elezebeth Allen, Ruth Allen, Anna Brown, Mary Spring, Mehitable, wife of Dr. Warren.

In January, 1715, at a church meeting it was voted that on communion day the contributions, or collection, shall in future be made previous to the blessing. Also voted that each communicant contribute a sum not less than ten cents at each communion.

On March 30, 1710, money was granted to finish the meetinghouse, by which we learn that the small meeting-house, thirty feet square, in Parkhurst Meadow, begun in 1695, had not been completed in fifteen years. In 1718 a motion was brought forward to build a new meeting-house, but the matter was then deferred. However, it was probably begun soon after, as, by a record extant of a town meeting held October 23, 1721, it was voted "to appropriate their proportion of the bills of credit issued by the General Court, and that they will forthwith proceed to cover and close in ye meeting house with the materials that are provided by the Committee." This committee consisted of Benjamin Brown, Benoni Gearfield, Ebenezer Allen, Joseph Allen, and James Jones. At this meeting it was also "Voted to grant the Rev. Mr. William Williams ye sum of seventy and four Pounds for his salary, for his labor in the Gospel Ministry amongst us for the present year, and six pounds for cutting and carting his fire wood ye present year." The location of the new church was upon that ground now called the Common, and not upon the land granted to the church by Nathaniel Coolidge in 1715.

In what year the new church was completed is not recorded. It is probable that at the time of Mr. Williams's pastorate there were no pews in the church, only benches, the men ranged on one side, the women on the other, the boys being kept by themselves, in charge of a constable. Pews were introduced much later, and were built one or two at a time, at the expense of individuals, upon obtaining permission from the Selectmen or more frequently by a vote in town meeting.

Mr. Williams continued in the ministry in this church until October, 1750, covering a period of forty-one years, and was then dismissed by a mutual council. No reasons are given on the parish records for this action. He remained a parishioner after his dismissal, assisted his successors, and for a time was schoolmaster of the town. He died in Weston, March 6, 1760, aged seventy-two years, and lies buried in our old burying-ground. Mr. Williams's wife, Hannah Williams, died in Weston, Sunday, December 29, 1745, aged fifty-eight years. Mr. Williams preached her funeral sermon, which is still extant. Four of Mr. Williams's sermons were published in book form as early as 1741. One of these, on "The Nature of Saving Faith," delivered in Mr. John Cotton's church in Newton, is still preserved. One of his sermons, on "The Prodigal Daughter," is illustrated, and is a most extraordinary production. In this publication is given what is supposed to be a picture of Mr. Williams delivering the sermon from the pulpit. Altogether it would seem that Mr. Williams was a man of no ordinary ability and energy.

At a meeting of the church held April 27, 1726, it was voted as the general sentiment that "turning ye back towards the minister to gaze abroad, and laying down ye head upon ye arms, in a sleepy position, in ye time of public worship, are postures irreverent and indecent, and which ought to be reformed where any are faulty therein, and carefully avoided."

In 1800 the church of 1721 underwent thorough repair. A steeple and two porches were added, and a new bell procured of Paul Revere, for which the sum of $443.12 was paid by subscription of the people. Mr. Kendal makes no mention of the original bell in his centennial sermon. It weighed only one hundred and sixty-four pounds, and was probably brought down from Canada in one of the expeditions against the French and Indians. It was a bell probably belonging to some chapel or convent. Mr. Revere purchased the bell at the time he sold the new bell, and paid $72.88 for it. The history of this old bell would be interesting to us to-day. There are persons still living who can remember the old church with its high-backed pews, sounding-board, and pulpit. There was an air of solemn dignity, an emphasis of religious fervor, which this old church typified, that impressed the beholder with a reverence its successor never succeeded in doing. The destruction of this old landmark, built of solid oak, and replaced by a monstrosity which only a nineteenth-century architect could devise, shows both lack of reverence and the decay of faith,—a marked trait of our times. When this church of 1721 was taken down in 1840, it was one hundred and eighteen years old. The church of 1840 was erected a little east of the old one, on land given for that purpose by Mrs. Clarissa Smith.

Rev. Samuel Woodward succeeded Mr. Williams, September 25, 1751, and died October 5, 1782, at the age of fifty-six years and in the thirty-first year of his ministry. He was greatly beloved by his people and his brethren of the clergy. His company was sought and enjoyed by all classes, old and young, the serious and the gay.

At a town meeting held February 24, 1783, Rev. Dr. Samuel Kendal received forty-three votes against nineteen opposing votes for his settlement in the gospel ministry as successor to Mr. Woodward. It was also voted "to grant £200 as an encouragement for his settling with us." And at an adjourned meeting held August 11, 1783, Mr. Kendal's answer was received and read in open town meeting. Mr. Kendal's letter is a long one and somewhat peculiar. His acceptance is conditioned upon an increase in the salary offered (£80), and the town voted him an additional £10 and an additional five cords of wood. The letter will be found interesting, and can be found in full in Appendix I. Mr. Kendal was ordained November 5, 1783. It is rather curious in this connection to note that eleven of those who voted adversely to the settlement of Mr. Kendal entered a protest against the proceedings which led to his settlement. The protest was placed on the records, but received no other attention. Mr. Kendal continued as pastor of the church for thirty years, and during this long period was kept from his pulpit but one Sunday, either by sickness or inclemency of the weather.

It is to Mr. Kendal's centennial sermon, delivered in 1812, that we owe what little we have of the past history of the town from the time of its incorporation. The loss of all the precinct and town records down to 1754 renders this sermon a most valuable document. Three ministers ordained in Weston had filled the pastoral office for over a century. Including the first eighteen years of the parish, 694 persons had been admitted to church fellowship,—namely, 425 under Mr. Williams, 163 under Mr. Woodward, 106 under Dr. Kendal. There were 2,569 baptisms, —1,082 in Mr. Williams's time, 18 between his dismissal and Mr. Woodward's ordination, 922 by Mr. Woodward, 15 between his decease and Mr. Kendal's induction to office, and 532 by Mr. Kendal. Ten deacons were chosen, as follows: Captain Josiah Jones, 1710; John Parkhurst, 1710; Benjamin Brown, 1715; Ensign John Warren, 1733; Thomas Upham, 1767; Thomas Russell, 1767; Samuel Fiske, 1780; Isaac Hobbs, 1780; Nathan Warren, 1808; Thomas Bigelow, 1808.

The population of the town was a little over 1,000. In 1895

it was 1,710.* Mr. Kendal gives the bill of mortality for thirty years, from 1783 to 1812. Before that time there were no means of computing. During these thirty years there were 396 deaths, making the annual average 13.5, or 66 in five years. Of the 396 who died, 90 arrived at the age of seventy and upwards. Out of the 90 that lived to this age, 52 attained to their eightieth year, giving more than 1 in 8 that reached fourscore years. Of the 52 that arrived at this age, 27 lived to be eighty-seven and upwards, giving 1 in 14⅔ that attained to advanced years. Twelve lived to be ninety and upwards, making 1 in 33 of this very great age. Three lived to be ninety-five and upwards, giving 1 in 132. One lived to be a hundred and two years old. This was Mary Hastings, widow of Mr. John Hastings, who died at the age of eighty-eight years. This bill of mortality shows Weston to be as healthy a spot as any in the world.

When Mr. Kendal was called to this parish, he made a condition that he should receive £100 a year. Mr. Woodward had received £80, and Mr. Williams £74. It was represented to him that the times were very hard, as indeed they were, there being no money in the country and the Continental money hardly worth the paper it was printed on. Although the people had added £10 and five cords of wood to the salary paid Mr. Woodward, Mr. Kendal wrote them a letter addressed as follows:—

My Christian Fathers, Brothers and Friends, . . . As the times are peculiarly difficult by reason of very heavy taxes, I do freely give up what you have now added for three years, so that until after three years are expired I shall expect no more than £80 and fifteen cords of wood annually. [Mr. Kendal well says] that since our ancestors landed on these shores, the wilderness has bloomed as the rose, and the desert become a fruitful field. The haunts of wild beasts or of savage tribes have become populous cities, villages or towns. Where nothing met the eye but nature in her rudest dress, where nothing saluted the ear but the yell of savages and the howling of beasts of prey, these spacious temples are erected to the living God, and the blessings of civilization enjoyed.

Mr. Kendal gives a list of the young men, natives of the town, who had received a collegiate education,—20 at Cambridge and 1 at Providence at the close of the centennial period: William

*Cf. p. 20, line 3.

Williams, 1729; Nathan Fiske, 1754; Daniel Jones, 1759; Phineas Whitney, 1759; Daniel Stimpson, 1759; Ephraim Woolson, 1760; Samuel Savage, 1766; Isaac Bigelow, 1769; Stephen Jones, 1775; Samuel Woodward, 1776; Abraham Bigelow, 1782; Thaddeus Fiske, 1785; Ebenezer Starr, 1789; Silas Warren, 1795; Isaac Allen, 1798; Isaac Fiske, 1798; Charles Train, 1805; Benjamin Rand, 1808; Alpheus Bigelow, 1810; Abraham Harrington, 1812; Isaac Fiske, 1812 (Providence).

Mr. Kendal married Abigail, daughter of Rev. Samuel Woodward, in 1786. She died in 1793, and he married her sister Miranda Woodward in 1794. A newspaper of the day speaks of the marriage, "and the mark of joy and approbation at this alliance manifested by the people of the town, rarely incidental to such an event." Mr. Kendal purchased for £490 3d. the estate of Mr. Benjamin Peirce, who before his death kept a tavern on the site now owned by Mr. Francis B. Sears. In 1791 the house was destroyed by fire, the family moving into the house of the widow Woodward, now that of Mrs. Dickson, which house Mr. Woodward built in 1753. Young collegians who were suspended for a longer or shorter term for breaches of college discipline were sent to rusticate with Dr. Kendal, who kept them up in their studies and classes, imparting moral stamina as well. Many men who have become famous in the different walks of life passed terms of rustication under Dr. Kendal's roof, among these the venerable Dr. Bigelow, who was one of the most noted physicians of his day. His name may still be seen on a pane of window glass in one of the rooms. Dr. Kendal prepared young Alvan Lamson for college, who later became a noted divine. In 1814 Dr. Kendal died. A long notice of his death appeared at the time in a Boston paper:—

On the 15th inst. departed this life the Rev. Samuel Kendal, pastor of the church in Weston. A man highly esteemed in life, and deeply lamented in death. Few characters, more deserving of respectful attention, have been found and exhibited in our country. In 1782 he received the honors of Harvard University and becoming settled as pastor over the respectable town of Weston he became at once the guide and father of his people. The degree of Doctor of Divinity was bestowed upon him by the University of New Haven in 1806.

THE ELLIS PLACE, CENTRAL AVENUE.

Formerly owned and occupied by Hon. James Lloyd, at one time United States senator from Massachusetts. In 1822 it was bought and occupied by John Mark Gourgas, of a notable Huguenot family. It is now owned by the heirs of Mrs. Lucinda A. Ellis.

THE OLD DR. KENDAL HOUSE, CENTRAL AVENUE.

Built by Rev. Dr. Samuel Kendal in 1795 from hand-hewn timber, given by Dr. Kendal's parishioners, and hand-made nails. Later Mr. Alpheus Cutter owned the place, and it is claimed that here he made the first cotton batting in this country, and then cotton cloth, later moving to Waltham and starting the industry there. Mr. Luke Brooks bought the place about 1840 and remodelled the house. In 1861 it was sold to Mr. George Sparhawk, and is still owned by his daughter, Mrs. Francis B. Sears. The house was destroyed by fire February 25, 1906.

After the death of Dr. Kendal, Joseph Allen, a student at Cambridge under the elder Ware, was invited to fill the vacant pulpit as a candidate for a settlement; but he declined, and the town voted on December 27, 1814, to give Mr. Joseph Field, Jr., an invitation to settle in the ministry (three only voting against him), and "that his sallary shall be $800 annually." Mr. Field's answer to the invitation was read in town meeting January 9, 1815, and will be found in Appendix II. These letters of the several pastors require no apology for their insertion in these pages. When we consider that the pastorate of this church has been held for nearly two centuries by only four ministers, and that Mr. Field held the position for over half a century, we see that he cannot but have left in the memory of the inhabitants a grateful sense of his many virtues and his marked ability. Mr. Field was ordained February 1, 1815, President Kirkland of Harvard College preaching the sermon. The thermometer on that day was eight degrees below zero, and the refreshments provided for the occasion by the people froze on the tables, the fruit being hard as stones. In 1865, at the completion of the half-century of his pastorate, his age and increasing infirmities compelled him to relinquish his duties. In compliance, however, with the wishes of his parishioners he continued to remain their senior pastor. He held this position at the time of his death, which occurred November 5, 1869, at the age of eighty-one years. The semi-centennial anniversary of Mr. Field, just alluded to, was attended by a large concourse of his brethren of the clergy throughout the county, as well as by others to the number of about three hundred souls. He delivered a valedictory discourse from Acts vi. 4, "The Ministry of the Word." His remarks were made with great feeling and with that peculiar emphasis which those who sat under him in earlier days will recall. Many were moved to tears as their aged pastor rehearsed his life and Christian ministry among them. The deacons chosen since his ordination in 1815 were as follows: Mr. Isaac Hobbs, Mr. Abraham Hews, Mr. Samuel Hews, Mr. Marshall Hews. He stated that he had solemnized over 200 marriages and 180 baptisms. Over 100 had been admitted to the church, and 480 deaths had occurred, many of those who had died being very aged. He stated that the venerable father of Dr. Kendal, his predecessor, lived to the age of ninety-nine years. Rev. Dr. Sears followed Dr. Field in an address to the people. The hospitalities tendered the guests on this occasion were of that liberal character for which the town has always been celebrated. With Dr. Field, it may be said, was first introduced into this parish what is now styled Unitarianism, in contradistinction to the old-time Congregationalism of the early fathers.

Rev. Dr. Edmund H. Sears succeeded Dr. Field in the pastorate of this church from 1865 to the time of his death in 1876.

This was a period of great importance for the town and its inhabitants. The Civil War had not ended when Dr. Sears succeeded Dr. Field, and the trying time of reconstruction came within his ministry. Questions of internal improvement became prominent. In all these matters he gave wise and practical counsel, and served the town in many and varied ways. He revised the covenant of the church and increased its membership. At his initiative and urgency the parish in 1874 built a new vestry with Sunday-school rooms. It was during his ministry that he wrote his greatest literary work, entitled, "The Fourth Gospel—The Heart of Christ," a book of ripe scholarship and research and pure diction, which made a profound impression upon the religious public. In many hymnals are included his well-known Christmas lyrics, "It came upon the Midnight Clear" and "Calm on the Listening Ear of Night." But most of all, by his devout and conscientious ministry, by his lovely and refining personality, by his eloquent preaching and his inspired pen, he gave impetus and sanction and power to the best in the community, and, dying, added to the list of the town's worthy ministers a most illustrious name.

Rev. Francis B. Hornbrooke succeeded Mr. Sears, and was installed October 18, 1876, and resigned in October, 1879, to take charge of a larger congregation at Newton.

Rev. Hobart Clark succeeded Mr. Hornbrooke in March, 1880, and resigned in February, 1882, and removed to England.

Rev. Charles F. Russell followed Mr. Clark in November, 1882, the interval being filled by Rev. Chandler Robbins, who

ECCLESIASTICAL ORIGIN OF THE TOWN

became a resident of Weston after resigning from the Second Church in Boston.

From the settlement of Mr. Mors in 1702 to the death of Dr. Sears in 1876, a period of one hundred and seventy-four years, there had been but six ministers over this church. They are buried in the town within a short distance of each other, with the exception of Mr. Mors, who, after leaving Weston, was settled in what is now Canton, where he died.

It has been necessary to dwell at unusual length on the history of the church in Weston, as its history is that of the early settlement and the Farmers' Precinct. In those early days there was but one church, but one congregation, around which the settlers gathered, and paid their tithes for the support of the gospel. All things pertaining to the church were voted at town meeting, and that down to a very late period,—as solid a union of Church and State, while it lasted, as ever existed in the old country. As the town and precinct records are all lost, the history of the Weston church is the history of the town down to 1746 and 1754.

II.

GENERAL DESCRIPTION AND MILITARY ORGANIZATION.

In 1711/12 the Precinct of Weston, called the Farmers' District, assembled and drew up a petition to the Great and General Court, praying that the precinct be incorporated as a town, and chose a committee of three to carry their petition to the legislature. This petition was presented by Captain Francis Fulham, Lieutenant Josiah Jones, and Mr. Daniel Eastabroke. A petition was also presented to the town of Watertown, that the Farmers' Precinct be allowed to form a separate town. "The Town of Watertown by a free vote manifested their willingness that the said precinct should be a township, according to their former bounds," with proviso and conditions, viz.:—

1. That the Farmers continue to pay a due share of the expense of maintaining the great bridge over Charles River.

2. That they pay their full and due share of the debts now due by the town. (This second proviso does not seem to have been insisted upon.)

3. That they do not in any way infringe the rights of proprietors having land, but not residing among the Farmers. (The petition of the precinct to the legislature cannot be found.)

The following Act of Incorporation of the Town of Weston is copied from the Court Record of Acts and Resolves, vol. ix. p. 216, in the State Library:—

THURSDAY
January 1st, 1712/13.

Present in Council.

His Excellency Joseph Dudley, Esqr Governor.
The Hon. William Tayler Esq., Lieut. Governor.

Elisha Hutchinson	Joseph Lynde	Edward Bromfield
Samuel Sewall	Eliakim Hutchinson	Ephraim Hunt
John Phillips Esqr	Penn Townsend Esqr	Isaac Winslow Esqr
Peter Sergeant	Andrew Belcher	Daniel Epes.

Upon reading a Petition of Francis Fulham, Josiah Jones, and Daniel Eastabroke, a Committee of the West Precinct in Watertown, commonly called the Farms, Praying that (Having the Consent of the Town therefor) They be granted to be a distinct Township, to enjoy the Privileges and Immunities which other Towns do and may by Law enjoy—Ordered, that the Prayer of the Petition be granted, and that the West Precinct in Watertown, commonly called the Farms, be erected and made into a Township, to contain all the Lands and Farms within the boundaries following: That is to say, To extend from Charles River to Stony Brook Bridge, and from the said Bridge up the Brook Northerly to Robert Harrington's Farm; and the brook to be the Boundary; Including the said Farm, and comprehending all the Farms and Farm Lands to the lines of Cambridge and Concord; and from thence all Watertown lands to their utmost Southward and Westward Bounds, The town to be named Weston, subject nevertheless to the Reservations and Savings made by the Town of Watertown in their setting off the said Lands—And further granted that the Inhabitants of Weston have use and exercise all such Powers, Privileges and Immunities as other Towns have and do by Law use and enjoy, as to the Choice of Town officers, allotting out Lands, Raising of Taxes and for ordering of other Town affairs.

Concur'd by the Representatives.
Consented to, J. DUDLEY.

The Precinct of Lexington was made a township in March, 1712/13, over two months after the town of Weston. In the article of its incorporation a proviso was inserted that Lexington should bear a part of the two-thirds of the charge of the great bridge over Charles River in Cambridge annually. This bridge was built in 1662 (destroyed in 1685). The expense of its maintenance was apportioned two-sixths upon Cambridge, one-sixth upon Newton, and three-sixths upon Middlesex. In 1733 the second bridge was destroyed by ice, and rebuilt by the sale of town lands belonging to Cambridge. It was again rebuilt in 1862, at the expense of Cambridge and Brighton.

The importance of these bridges and the early mode of reaching the town of Boston by carriages and teams will be treated of later on. Weston continued to pay its share toward the maintenance of the great bridge at Watertown down to the year 1803.

The town of Weston lies twelve miles west of Boston. It measures about five and a half miles north and south and three and a half miles east and west, and contains about eleven thousand acres of land. It originally formed a part of Watertown, settlements from which made up what are now Waltham, Weston, and Lincoln. The population of Weston, according to the 1910 census, is 2,259 souls. The town is bounded on the north by Lincoln; on the east by Waltham and Newton, Stony Brook and Charles River being the dividing line (Charles River divides it from Newton); southerly by Wellesley; westerly by Wayland (formerly East Sudbury) and Natick.

The old post-road from Boston to New York passes through the centre of the town, and for many years was one of the most important and best travelled roads of the Union. Over this road, in the mail-coach, travelled John Adams when on his way to Washington to take the oath as President of the United States, as did Daniel Webster and Samuel Dexter when they first went to Congress. They breakfasted in the old tavern on Ball's Hill, in its day one of the most important taverns in Massachusetts, but now gone to decay and condemned. Could the history of this house be told, it would make very interesting reading. Down to very nearly our own day it was famous among the lovers of good cheer, frequented by the Strattons, Rutters, Smiths, and others, who were its constant guests, particularly at night, in the times when card-playing was not looked upon as a vice. The Lancaster turnpike, or, as we call it to-day, the Concord road, passes through the northern part of the town, and in former years was the great thoroughfare between Boston and New Hampshire, and into the Canadas. The Framingham turnpike runs through the southern part of the town, but was of less importance in point of travel. It was over the post-road, so called, in the centre of the town, and over the south (or Framingham) road, that the prisoners, after the surrender at Saratoga, passed on their way to Winter Hill, Somerville, and there still exists in West Newton the bar-room at which the British and American officers stopped on their way, to take a drink. This tap-room is still in very much the same condition as at that period.

Weston is a generally uneven and broken tract of land. High cliffs and rocks are found within its limits. There are still grounds for believing that Mount Feake and the other very high rock, mentioned by Governor Winthrop, lie within the Weston boun-

rant was issued to the militia of Watertown for impr
"twenty soldiers, with provisions, arms, amunition and
ing," for the defence of the colony. In Captain Mason's
thereto (Mass. Archives, vol. 68, fol. 74) may be seen
names of the inhabitants of Weston, or what was then styl
"Farmers' District." The list follows:—

Names of those who responded.	*Those most fit to goe upon the Ser*
Daniel Warren Sr.	Daniel Warren Sr.
John Bigulah Sr.	John Bigulah Sr.
Nathaniel Hely	Nathaniel Hely
Joseph Tayntor Jr.	Joseph Tayntor
John Whitney Sr.	John Whitney Sr.
George Harrington	George Harrington
James Cutting	William Hager Jr.
Wm. Hager Jr.	John Parkhurst
John Parkhurst	Michael Flagg
Michael Flagg	Jacob Bullard
Jacob Bullard	Isaac Learned
Isaac Learned	Joseph Waight
Joseph Waight	George Dill
George Dill	William Prior, Jr.
Jonathan Smith	Nathaniel Sanger
Wm. Prior Jr.	Moses Whitney
Nathaniel Sanger	John Windham
Moses Whitney	Math Bamsham
Enoch Sawtelle	Joseph Smith
John Bright	John Barnard
John Hastings	
John Bacon	
John Chadwick	
John Windham	
John Barnard	
Ephraim Gearfield	
Joseph Smith	

Sd   HUGH MASON, Water

Jacob Fullam, of Weston, son of Squire Fullam, joined tl
pedition, commanded by Captain Lovewell, against the "Pe
ket" tribe of Indians in 1725. Fullam held the rank of ser
This tribe of Indians, with Paugus, their chief, had its ho
the White Mountains, on the Saco River in New Hamp

The town is elevated above the adjacent country, and the
from its heights are unsurpassed by any within twenty
of Boston. The soil is rich, though in parts rocky. Per-
one reason of the undeniable salubrity of the town, over
every other section of our State, arises from the fact that
ubstratum of the soil is blue gravel. The hills are full of
gs. A number of brooks and rivulets run into streams which
y into Stony Brook and Charles River. These brooks,
ie greater part, rise within the town, and are fed by springs.
rt of None-such Pond is within the southern limits of the
The meadows in former days were much used for the ex-
on of peat of excellent quality,—an article now gone out of
al use. Snake Rock at Stony Brook, more generally styled
il's Den," is a cave which, tradition says, was formerly a
of refuge and deposit for thieves and their plunder.
e inhabitants of Weston are mostly farmers, and perhaps
are few other towns in the Commonwealth where the land
escended from the early settlers to their descendants in such
ken succession as in the case of Weston. It is pleasant
s of to-day to look back through the lists of the soldiers of
arly French and Indian Wars, the patriots of the Revolution,
he men of the sectional war of 1861, and find among them
, very many, of the descendants of the pioneers of the
ers' District, which came out from Watertown in 1650. Wes-
an count among its inhabitants many who have distinguished
selves in every walk of life, as soldiers, lawyers, judges, mer-
s. An account of some of these will be found as we go on.
ere were no Indian settlements within the bounds of Weston.
country hereabouts was probably used as their hunting-
ids. They had their settlements higher up on the banks
e Charles and Sudbury Rivers. The only tradition of a
tened incursion into the limits of the town relates to the time
attack on Sudbury in 1676, when the Indians planned the
iction of Watertown and the other settlements. They then
rated to the western part of the town, and burnt a barn
ing on the farm now of Mr. Nahum Smith. It does not
ir that any one was killed by them at that time. A few
hs before the attack on Sudbury, December, 1675, a war-

They were very troublesome, and this expedition was undertaken to capture and destroy them, and also to gain the large bounty offered by the province, of £100 for every Indian scalp. The expedition consisted of about forty men. They were led into an ambush by the savages, and the greater part were killed, including Captain Lovewell and Sergeant Fullam. Sergeant Fullam is reported to have distinguished himself in this fight. He killed one savage in a hand-to-hand encounter, and, when a second savage came to the rescue of his friend, Fullam and the second savage both fell at the same instant, killed by each other's shot. There was an old song about this fight, one verse of which runs as follows:—

"Young Fullam, too, I'll mention
Because he fought so well;
Trying to save another man,
A sacrifice he fell."

The first steps taken toward a military organization were in September, 1630, induced probably by the danger which was threatening the charter of the province. This charter King Charles was said to be about to withdraw, and the withdrawal, had it been undertaken, would in all probability, in the then temper of the colony, have brought matters to an early crisis. The complications in which the British king found himself engaged on the Continent of Europe about this time led to the American colonies being for a time forgotten.

In 1636, at the time of the Pequot War, a more general organization of the militia took place. In this year all able-bodied men in the colony were ranked into three regiments, the Middlesex regiment being under command of John Haines. In 1637 lieutenants and ensigns were appointed for the train-bands in the towns. Information concerning these train-bands is difficult to obtain. Neither town nor county records give any very satisfactory information of them at this early date. All persons above the age of sixteen were required to take the oath of fidelity, and that was probably the age when they became subject to military duty. It was not uncommon for men to hold office in the military service to a very advanced age. In fact, they were never too old for duty.

In 1643 the danger from the Indians and the scattered population of the township led to the league of the four colonies of Massachusetts, Plymouth, Connecticut, and New Haven, under the title of "the United Colonies of New England." These four States, or colonies, contained thirty-nine townships, with a population of about 24,000 inhabitants. In 1648 the Narragansett settlers asked leave to join the confederacy; but they were refused, as not having any stable government. Of the 24,000 people in the confederacy, 15,000 belonged to Massachusetts, while the three other colonies had a population of only about 3,000 each. In 1643 the thirty towns of Massachusetts were divided into four counties,—Middlesex, Essex, Norfolk, and Suffolk,—each county, as before said, containing a regiment, the chief commander of which held the rank of lieutenant, and the second in command was styled sergeant-major. The history of the Middlesex regiment, which more particularly interests Weston, will be found in its place. The train-bands organized at this time in every part of the colony were intended for any public service in which they could be utilized. But, out of the total number in the train-band, one-third were set apart under the title of "Alarm Men." These men were to be ready at a moment's notice to repel any Indian invasion of the town or settlement. They were the home guard, and never went on expeditions calling the train-band away from home. They were reported separately on the "return lists" which the commander of the train-band was required to send to his colonel or superior officer. Some of these lists will be found later on in this volume. The "Alarm Men" took their arms to the fields when they worked at a distance from home. They took their guns to meeting on Sunday, and stacked them in the church during divine service. After meeting they were formed in front of the church and inspected by the captain of the train-band (under whose orders they were, as forming part of his company), and in his absence by one of the deacons of the church. Every man was provided with a certain amount of powder and ball, furnished by the precinct, and, if any of the precinct ammunition had been used in hunting or otherwise, the delinquent was made to pay for such ammunition. All the early settlers were famous marksmen. The rifle was their usual weapon. One of the most frequent sources of complaint against the "Alarm Men," as well as the men of the train-band, was the illegitimate use of powder and ball in hunting and turkey matches. Turkey shootings in the fall of the year formed a favorite amusement, and continued all over New England down to 1840. The matches would now be considered as against law, and come under the head of cruelty to animals, but in their day they served an excellent purpose and made good marksmen, as many a bloodthirsty Indian could (if alive) attest. Even boys at twelve and thirteen years of age were familiar with gun and rifle, and were excellent shots. The change from this school of the soldier, as it certainly was in early days, was very perceptible in the War of 1861. It was then found that a large percentage of the agricultural contingents were utterly ignorant of the first principles of loading and firing a gun, and in this respect were very much inferior to the rank and file of the enemy. At a later period, when the danger from Indian incursions had passed, the "alarm list," taken from companies, still continued, and, as we approach the Revolutionary period, they were styled "Minute Men," and were held in readiness against the British, as were their fathers against the savages. The company returns still contained the "alarm list and minute men" down to about 1800.

John Speen and his Indian kindred, who owned 16,000 acres of land, described as the Indian plantation of "Naticke," were induced by the General Court to give up their title freely in 1650, and their consideration was the "bettering of their souls" (!), reserving the right to take up lots after the English fashion, and also in the turbary, piscary, and staveries.

From 1700 until 1715 there were continual petitions from the towns about Natick for a division of this Indian commonage at Natick; and finally Adam Winthrop, Governor John Leverett, Judge Sewall, and the overseers of Harvard College formed the scheme of settling an English missionary at Natick. The heirs of the Speens were found, and those of the chief praying Indians of Eliot's day,—in all about nineteen families. The Indian missionary, Rev. Oliver Peabody, was made a "co-heir" with them, making twenty proprietors of John Speen's 19,000 acres. Hon. Francis Fullam, of Weston, a justice of the Middlesex

Court, was intrusted with the business of forming the proprietorship; and he selected Samuel Jones, of Weston, to survey the land, a task he had completed by 1716. By 1719 the proprietorship had got into working order, and it was announced that the minister should receive his portion, the chiefs 60 acres apiece, all others 30 acres, and 100 acres should be set apart for the ministry. Elijah Goodnow was proprietors' clerk. In 1799 the town took possession of the ministerial lot, and erected a meeting-house upon it, the first meeting-house belonging to the town, all former meeting-houses being missionary affairs.

III.

CIVIL AND ECCLESIASTICAL ORGANIZATION AND FRENCH AND INDIAN WARS.

We have seen, in the preceding chapter, that the Farmers' District, or what is now Weston, was made into a legal precinct in 1698, with all the rights, privileges, and duties which go with a precinct organization. It has been shown that, after some delays and difficulties which arose concerning the settlement of a minister over the Farmers' church, Rev. William Williams was chosen pastor in 1709, and that soon after, in 1710, the Weston church was fully organized by the choice of deacons and the signing of the covenant by the eighteen members who then formed the church. The church records are full and complete in all that pertains to organization and matters purely ecclesiastical, by which is meant the record of births, baptisms, marriages, and deaths. They are of great value to us of the present day. The careful entry of all things pertaining to church matters is in perfect keeping with the exalted character of its eminent pastors,—Williams, Woodward, and Kendal. With all the above, and valuable as the church records are to-day, we have no precinct records down to the separation of Lincoln from Weston in 1746, a period of forty-eight years. We shall find in the next chapter that the town after its incorporation in 1712 performed all the functions which may have belonged to a precinct down to the year 1746, when a precinct record was begun, but continued only for the period of eight years, when its records again are merged into the town records, and entirely cease to exist. Whatever precinct records may have existed, and probably did exist, previous to the year 1746, are entirely lost, along with the records of the town.

The Lincoln petition to be set off from Weston was made in 1742, but was not granted until 1746. The petition of the people of what is now Lincoln to be set off into a separate precinct grew, as we have seen, out of the great difficulties they labored under of reaching the place of public worship in Weston, in consequence of the bad condition of the roads leading thereto, and the great distance from their homes they were obliged to travel, which in winter particularly rendered the proper observance of the Lord's Day impossible to them. Although the petition of these people was presented to the General Court in 1742, it was not until 1744, August 16, that the order granting their prayer was issued in the shape of the following document:—

Read and ordered that the Petitioners serve the Towns of Concord, Lexington and Weston with copies of this petition, that so they show cause if any they have, on the first Tuesday of the next sitting of this Court, why the prayer thereof should not be granted.

Sd   J. Cushing, Speaker.

The town of Weston made no objections to the separation or to the bounds regulating that precinct. At the time of the above separation the inhabitants of Weston addressed a petition to Edward Trowbridge, Esq., justice of the peace, for a precinct warrant. In the warrant that he issues he states that the inhabitants had "never yet assembled." It must be borne in mind that this was forty-eight years after Weston had been made a precinct and thirty-four years after the incorporation of the town.

Middlesex, ss.

Weston, November 19th, 1746.

To Edward Trowbridge, Esq., one of His Majesty's Justices of the Peace of the County of Middlesex.

Whereas by an order of the Great and General Court of the Province of the Massachusetts Bay, passed the 26th day of April last, a number of the Inhabitants of Weston with others, inhabitants of Concord and Lexington, are set off to be a precinct and thereby the remaining part of the said town of Weston is an entire parish. Therefore we are to request that your honor would issue a warrant for calling the first precinct meeting in the first precinct of Weston to choose precinct officers as the law directs.

James Mirick	Nathaniel Allen
Jonathan Bullard	Abijah Upham
John Walker	John Hastings
Daniel Livermore	Elisha Jones

MIDDLESEX, SS.

To JOHN WALKER of Weston in said County, yeoman, Greeting.

Whereas application has been made to me the subscriber by more than five of the Freeholders of the First Precinct in Weston in writing, under their hands, for calling a meeting of the inhabitants of said precinct, *never yet assembled.*

You are hereby in his Majesty's name required to notify ye free holders and other inhabitants of said precinct qualified to vote in town affairs, that they assemble at ye public meeting house in Weston aforesaid, on Thursday ye eleventh day of December next at 2 o'clock afternoon. Then and there, first, to choose a Moderator of ye said meeting and then to choose a clerk to enter and record all such votes and orders as from time to time shall be made and passed in said precinct, and also a Committee for ye calling meetings of the said precinct in the future.

Sd   EDWARD TROWBRIDGE, J. P.

MIDDLESEX, SS.   WESTON, December 11th, 1746.

In obedience to this warrant I have notified the Inhabitants within mentioned to meet at ye within mentioned time and place for ye ends within mentioned.

Sd   JOHN WALKER.

At the meeting, as above warned, which assembled on the twenty-fifth day of December, 1746, Mr. John Walker was chosen moderator, and Elisha Jones, Nathan Fisk, and John Walker assessors. At this meeting no treasurer was elected, but in the March meeting the following year Elisha Jones was made clerk and treasurer, and Ensign Joseph Woolson was chosen to take care of the meeting-house.

An interesting precinct meeting took place on the 25th of March, 1751. Francis Fullam presided, and after solemn prayer to God for his direction and assistance in so weighty a matter as the choice of a minister of the gospel to settle with them it was voted to invite Mr. Samuel Woodward to settle in the ministry of the church, the vote standing sixty-eight in favor, and not a vote for any other person. Deacon "Perkhurst," Deacon Allen, and Deacon Upham were made a committee to desire Mr. Williams, the former pastor, to deliver to the committee the church covenant, records, and papers which belonged to the church and which were in his keeping. It was also voted at the April meeting to give Mr. Woodward, as an encouragement to settle with them, the sum of £133 6s. 8d. At the fall meeting of 1752, in concurrence with the church, it was again voted to give a call to Mr. Woodward, and the vote stood eighty in favor and none for any other person. His yearly salary was fixed at £66 13s. 4d. for such time as he should remain in the work of the gospel ministry. Colonel Fullam, Deacon Parkhurst, Deacon Allen, Deacon Upham, and Captain Jones had been previously chosen a committee to wait upon Mr. Woodward and acquaint him with the votes of the precinct. His letter is dated Newton, June 4, 1751.

To the Church and Congregation in Weston:

Gentlemen,—It is some considerable time since you were pleased to honour me with an Invitation to settle with you in the Ministry, which was backed with a desire that my resolution of the matter might be as speedy as was consistant with prudence. Wherefore, gentlemen, after my hearty thanks for the favourable opinion you have conceived of my labours, I would inform you that although your circumstances seemed to call for a sudden answer, yet the work you call me to engage in (as it appears to me) is of such moment, that the most mature consideration can't be more than it deserves. I have therefore been asking that wisdom from above that is profitable to direct: and I have kept you in suspense the longer because in the multitude of counsellors there is safety: and am now ready to inform you that the unanimity of your call appears matter of great encouragement to me, and affords a happy prospect of the good success of my ministry: and notwithstanding your circumstances are something peculiar, yet I hope the consideration of duty would be more than a counterbalance for all the difficulties which at present appear. But, gentlemen, you are all, I presume, sensible of the great inconvenience and danger there is in a minister's being dependent upon the favour of his people. He must needs then have a great temptation to unfaithfulness: lest otherwise he hurt his private interests. Wherefore as I propose to devote myself (by the grace of heaven) to the service of that people's souls whose minister I am: so I desire that if I sow unto them spiritual things, it may not be thought a great thing (by them) if I so far reap of their carnal things as to render my life comfortable. And now, gentlemen, notwithstanding your proposals as to the nominal sums seem to be considerable: yet who is there among yourselves, were he to estimate what he spends in his family, that would not find that were he to purchase all by the penny, it would cost him more than sixty six pounds, thirteen shillings and four pence per annum? Gentlemen, upon consideration that you propose this without any privileges or perquisites which are common in other towns (I mean with

THE OLD JONES TAVERN, CENTRAL AVENUE.

It was formerly owned by Ephraim Bigelow, and later by William Smith and his descendants. His grandson, Joel Smith, occupied the tavern before the Revolution, and it is here that Howe, the British spy, was traced by the Liberty Men of Weston (see page 77). Later the property was purchased by Colonel John Jones, whose descendants still own and occupy it.

THE ARTEMAS WARD HOUSE, CENTRAL AVENUE.

Built about 1785 by two brothers named Eaton, and purchased about 1789 by Artemas Ward, son of General Artemas Ward, of Revolutionary fame. Through various purchases it became in 1836 the property of Mr. Benjamin Pierce, Sr., and is still owned and occupied by his descendants.

respect to a parsonage or any donations in lands or buildings or with regard to wood), and upon consideration that yours must needs be a place of great expense because near a great road, my best friends in, as well as out of, the ministry assure me from their own experience that I can by no means live with your offers. And now upon the whole, gentlemen, I think that nothing short of the addition of thirty cords of wood and in some other way a valuable consideration more to my yearly salary can be sufficient encouragement for my acceptance of your call. . . .

            Sd Samuel Woodward.

Mr. Woodward ended by accepting the call in a letter dated June 17, 1751, and was granted thirty cords of wood. He was also granted £26 13s. 4d. for his ordination expenses. In 1773 his salary was increased by £13 6s. 8d. The precinct meetings continue down to March, 1754, when they cease entirely, and the town records commence in the same book, under date March, 1754. No mention is made of the transfer of church matters to the town; but from that date the town, in town meeting assembled, assumes all the duties toward church affairs (as we have seen by old town-meeting records) that they performed after the incorporation of the town. As the record books now stand, it would appear to any stranger that the precinct was set off in 1746 and the town incorporated in 1754. Bond gives the names and the year of each and every representative to the General Court from the town of Weston from 1712 to 1754, and it stands to reason that there always had been regular and legal town meetings throughout the interval of the lost records. From 1754 on the inhabitants in town meeting assume all charge of the church, pay the minister's salary, provide his firewood, make all the repairs the church requires, seat the congregation, and from time to time build and let the pews. In 1755 it would appear that the first pews were built upon petition of individuals who were willing to pay (in consideration of the use of them), the money to be expended in building a porch on the foreside of the house and also stairs in the porch to go into the galleries. A life interest in these pews was granted upon payment of certain rates and the pews were to be built at the cost of the applicants. It may prove interesting in our day to be made acquainted with the manner of the disposal of these pews and the names of those who were the first owners. (Up to this period the congregation was seated on benches, and the places on these benches were redistributed by order in town meeting every few years.)

To Elisha Jones, the second pew east from the pulpit.
To John Warren, the second pew in the north-west corner.
To Theophilus Mansfield, the pew next to the south door on the east.
To Nathaniel Felch, the pew between the men's stairs and the west door.
To Braddyll U. Smith, that next the middle alley on the women's side.
To John Walker, that next the middle alley on the men's side.
To Nathan Fisk, the middle pew on the women's side.
To Abraham Gale, the middle pew on the men's side.
To James Stimpson, the pew next the women's stairs.
To Joseph Steadman, the pew next the men's stairs.

The town was extremely watchful that no persons should be permitted within town limits who would be likely to become a charge and burden upon the town, and any inhabitant of the town who harbored any such person and failed to give notice to the Selectmen was prosecuted to the extent of the law, and was responsible personally for all charges the town incurred. Accordingly, we find that in the year 1755/6 Bathsheba Moulton, widow Mary Flagg (and her infant child), Jane Thomas and Hannah Hagar, and Thomas Partridge and his wife were ordered out of town.

In 1764 the town ordered that the church be newly shingled, and that a workhouse should be built, and an acre and a half of land should be purchased of Josiah Smith adjoining the land he gave to the town for a workhouse. This workhouse cost the sum of £208 19s. 10d., and was situated on what is now land of Mrs. James B. Case, nearly opposite Mr. Pennock's house. After 1781 it was let from year to year as a dwelling and finally taken down.

In 1767 the gallery pews were made in the church, although previously there had been opposition to this being done. The people this year were reseated in the church. The towns of Watertown, Waltham, and Weston owned jointly a farm near Wachusett Hill. It is probable that this was a poor-farm, where the people at the charge of these towns were sent, and either supported or made to work out their board. A committee appointed by the town of Weston sold the town's interest in this farm for £267 6s. 8d., and it was after the sale of this farm that the town voted to build in Weston the workhouse above mentioned.

CIVIL AND ECCLESIASTICAL ORGANIZATION 33

An act was passed in the General Court of Massachusetts Bay in the reign of George II., held at Boston in 1760, for assessing the sum of £97,345 13s. The assessment of the following towns in Middlesex County is interesting as showing the relative value of property in these towns, viz.: Waltham, £339 16s. 3d.; Weston, £302 4s.; Watertown, £374 14s. 4d.; Lincoln, £261 19s. 1d.; Lexington, £447 12s. 8d.; Newton, £638 6s. 8d.

Weston seems to have gained in importance, as shown in the relative enumeration for beef, as seen by an order of the legislature requiring the following amount of beef for the supplies for the army in the year 1780, viz.: Waltham, 7,200 cwt.; Weston, 7,930 cwt.; Watertown, 8,340 cwt.; Lincoln, 5,640 cwt.; Lexington, 7,770 cwt.; Newton, 10,980 cwt.

An order was passed in the legislature, June 30, 1781, to raise 2,700 men for the army at West Point, at the earnest request of General Washington. The Weston quota was eleven men, the same number as Watertown and one more than Waltham.

In 1755 Massachusetts held 3,000 slaves. Of this number Boston had 1,000, and Weston 10. In 1773 there were 16 slaves in Weston, and 218 voters.*

Although we have no detailed records of the part the Weston contingent took in the French and Indian Wars from 1753 to 1759, what little we have will not fail of interest to the descendants of the men whose names are upon our muster-rolls, the more so as many of the names on these lists are still on the voting lists of our own time, the latter representing direct descendants of the former. While our ancestors of a century and a half ago were fighting for the crown, and most frequently at their own expense, they were being instructed in the school of the soldier, and were veterans when the War of the Revolution broke out. Many of our most distinguished generals and officers of the Revolution served in the ranks as soldiers of the crown. During the French and Indian Wars, from 1735 to 1760, it became necessary to keep open direct ways of communication between eastern Massachusetts and the frontiers of Canada. Massachusetts, until

* In July, 1771, Nathan Patch, of Worcester, for the sum of £40, sells to Isaac Jones, of Weston, a negro female slave, about twenty years old, together with her wearing apparel. She was then called by the name of "Lucy," but the said Jones proposed to call her "Venice." The sale was made by regular deed as of real estate.

1740, claimed all the territory that now constitutes the States of Maine, New Hampshire, and Vermont, and manned and supported the forts at Keene, N.H., and on the Connecticut River at Westmoreland, Charlestown, N.H., Fort Dummer, and Brattleboro, Vt. To make the transportation of ammunition of war possible to these frontier forts, roads had to be and were constructed. Massachusetts constructed the road through New Hampshire to Crown Point on Lake Champlain. To hold Crown Point was of first importance, as it was through this route that the French and Indians made their incursions upon the eastern settlements. The Indians had trails through northern Massachusetts and New Hampshire on which they travelled with their booty and captives, but these were useless for the transportation of guns and heavy material of war.

Weston men served in the expedition of 1755 in the Massachusetts regiment commanded by Colonel Moses Titcomb. The major of this regiment was Ephraim Williams, of Newton. The same year Major Williams was made colonel of a Massachusetts regiment. There seems to have been no little difficulty in placing Colonel Williams where he belongs, but, judging from the pages of the Jones genealogy, there can be no further question. Ephraim Williams's father married for his second wife Abigail Jones, daughter of Josiah Jones, of Weston. After his marriage he came to Weston to live, moving from Newton in 1753. Mr. Williams lived in the house which at one time stood facing the Baptist parsonage. Mr. Williams's son, Major Ephraim Williams, came to Weston with his father, but soon after the father moved to Stockbridge. Both father and son had received from the crown large tracts of land in Berkshire County, as had also Colonel Josiah Jones. These lands were granted them for services in the earlier wars and in payment for dues. Below is a bill * made out

```
*1753.              Major EPHRAIM WILLIAMS, Dr.
        Feb: 20th To Saddle . . . . . . . . . . . . . . . . . . . .  £2 : 10 : 8
                 " a pair saddle bags . . . . . . . . . . . . . .     17 : 4
                 " ye change of hats . . . . . . . . . . . . . .      2 : 8
                 " one Dollar . . . . . . . . . . . . . . . . . .     6 : 0
                 " a bridle . . . . . . . . . . . . . . . . . . .    16 : 0
                 " pair brass stirups . . . . . . . . . . . . . .    16 : 0
                 " a fringe housen . . . . . . . . . . . . . . .    1 : 9 : 4
                 " cash for mending watch . . . . . . . . . . .       12 : 0
        1754
        Jan. 20  " a quilted saddle . . . . . . . . . . . . . . .   2 : 12 : 0
                                                                   £10 : 2 : 0
```

to Major Ephraim Williams (dated February, 1753) for his military equipment for the expedition of that year,—the material purchased of the Joneses in Weston. The Joneses kept a store at that time in a building east of the present house.

Colonel Williams was never married. The night before the battle in defence of Fort William Henry, at Lake George, in 1755, Colonel Williams made his will, bequeathing his lands in Berkshire County to found a school. The school was founded under the title of Williams College. The bequest at the time of his death was valued at $10,000.

Colonel Williams was killed with Colonel Titcomb and old Henrick, the Indian sachem, on the morning of the fight. In this battle Israel Putnam was a private, and John Stark, the victor of Bennington, was a lieutenant. I cannot find that there was any family relationship between Colonel Williams's family and that of Rev. Mr. Williams of the parish in Weston. It has been claimed that Rev. Mr. Williams was his uncle, but of this there is doubt. Mr. Williams was connected with the Connecticut Williams family.

In 1758 we have the list of the men from Weston who enlisted or who were impressed for His Majesty's service within the Province of Massachusetts Bay to serve under Jeffrey Amherst. This list is interesting as giving the ages of the men enlisted and the number of years they served.

Return of the Men Enlisted or Impressed for His Majesty's Service within the Province of Massachusetts Bay under Jeffrey Amherst, Esq., General and Commander-in-Chief for the Invasion of Canada, 1758.

Names.	Place of residence.	Age.	In a former expedition, etc.
Noah Norcross	Weston	23	1755, 6, 7, 8.
Joseph Norcross	"	21	1758.
Isaac Norcross	"	20	1755, 6, 7.
Asa Smith	"	17	Owned his own gun.
Ichabod Stanley	"	23	1758.
Stephen Harrington	"	19	1758.
David Allen	"	50	Owned his own gun.
Daniel Coolidge	"	17	
Wm. Norcross	"	35	1755, 6, 7, 8.
John Bemis	"	46	1757, 8.

Names.	Place of residence.	Age.	In a former expedition, etc.
Samuel Cory Jr.	Weston	32	Owned his own gun.
Elijah Spring	"	22	
Thaddeus Spring	"	19	
Abijah Livermore	"	21	
Nathaniel Livermore	"	20	
Joseph Livermore	"	19	
James Martin	"	23	1757.
William Bond	"	20	Owned his own gun.

N.B.—Cuffee Peacock, slave of Jonathan Bullard of Weston, was in Captain Jonathan Brown's company of Colonel Williams's regiment in the attack on Canada from May 2 to November 9, 1758.

List of the Train Band in Weston in 1757.

Ichabod Stanley.
Jonathan Fiske.
James Mansfield.
Jonathan Walker.
Joseph Jones.
Samuel Stimson.
Stephen Harrington.
Thaddeus Spring.
Nathaniel Dewing.
Jonathan Jones.
Solomon Wheeler.
Oliver Robinson.
Jacob Adams.
William Bond.
Elijah Gregory.
Thomas Fuller.
Israel Jones.
Henry Bond.
Henry Smith.
Benjamin Dolbear.
Jonas Bowman.
Samuel Gooding.
Christopher Capen.
John Binney.
Moses Harrington.
Samuel Jones.
Asa Woolson.
Abijah Livermore.
John Abbott.
Joseph Norcross.
Simeon Hagar.
Increase Leadbetter.
William Norcross.
Isaac Whittemore.
Jonathan Sheppherd.
Nathan Parkhurst.
Woodis Lee.
Jonathan Stedman.
Abijah Steadman.
Elisha Jones.
Isaac Allen.
Henry Spring.
John Warren.
Jonas Harrington.
Jonathan Stratton.
Benjamin Bond.
Abraham Jones.
Samuel Child.
Aaron Jones.
John Mirick.
William Lawrance.
David Allen.
Daniel Smith.
John Allen.

CIVIL AND ECCLESIASTICAL ORGANIZATION

Samuel Cary.
John Lamson.
Nathan Woolson.
Isaac Hobbs.
Joseph Lovewell.
Elisha Gale.
Jonathan Stimson.
Joseph Stimson.
Edward Hastings.
Jonathan Benjamin.
Isaac Gregory.
Timothy Bemis.
Jeremiah Fuller.
William Whitney.
Samuel Lawrance.
Nathaniel Felch.
Josiah Parkhurst.
Samuel Lamson.
Francis Jones.
Daniel Gearfield.
John Walker.
Samuel Gearfield.
Abijah Wheeler.
Elisha Fullum.
Elisha Gregory.

John Bemis.
Andrew Stimson.
Abraham Whitney.
Thomas Russell.
William Smith.
Thomas Upham.
David Stearns.
Joseph Whitney.
Joseph Garfield.
Thomas Rand.
James Livermore.
Jabez Harrington.
Benjamin Jones.
Ebenezer Phillips.
Isaac Jones.
Nathan Jones.
Henry Gale.
Joseph Bigelow.
Jonathan Hagar.
Elisha Cox.
Benjamin Hagar.
Benjamin Peirce.
Isaac Cory.
James Smith.
Thomas Hodgkins.

The foregoing is a true list of the Train Band in the town of Weston.

[Signed] ALBERT BRADDYLL SMITH, *Clerk*.

MIDDLESEX, SS.   WESTON, April 18, 1757.

Mr. Braddyell Smith, clerk of the Military Company in said town, made oath that this is a true list of the Train Band in Weston.

[Signed] Col: ELISHA JONES, *Justice Peace*.

[Copied from State Records, vol. 95, fol. 277.]

Alarm Men in Town of Weston, 1757.

Josiah Livermore.
Isaac Hager.
Nathan Fisk.
John Walker.
Theophilus Mansfield.

Abraham Bigelow.
Nathaniel Jennison.
Nathaniel Felch.
Joseph Weelson.
Nathaniel Bigelow.

Jonathan Binny.
Ebenezer Hobbs.
Samuel Baldwin.
Josiah Allen.
James Mirick.
David Flagg.
Nathaniel Williams.
Jeremiah Whittemore.
James Stimson.
Thomas Flagg.

Samuel Train.
Joseph Norcross.
Josiah Smith.
Nathaniel Stimson.
Henry Leadbetter.
Thomas Benny.
William Whitney.
Josiah Parkhurst.
Benjamin Brown.
Samuel Woodward (Rev.).

This is a true Alarm List made by Capt. Elisha Jones.

[Signed]   Att. BRADDYLL SMITH.

MIDDLESEX, SS.   APRIL 18, 1757.

Mr. Braddyll Smith, Clerk of the Military Company in Weston, made oath that according to the best of his Knowledge The foregoing is a True List of the "Alarm" men Belonging to said Company.

Col. ELISHA JONES, *Jus. Peace.*

Roll of Captain Henry Spring's Company of Weston in Colonel William Williams's Regiment, December, 1758.*

Elisha Flagg,	49 Days.	Samuel Jones,	49 Days.
Elisha Spring,	54 "	Increase Leadbetter,	47 "
Noah Norcross,	49 "	Joseph Stimpson,	47 "
Benjamin Dolbear,	23 "	Joseph Jones,	47 "
John Bemis,	23 "	John Abbot,	47 "
Elisha Cox,	31 "	Samuel Stimson,	47 "
Ichabod Stanley,	23 "	Samuel Cory,	47 "
William Bond,	27 "	Henry Smith,	47 "
James Bigelow,	50 "	Christopher Capen,	41 "
James Mansfield,	47 "	Joseph Allen,	58 "
Abijah Livermore,	45 "	William Cory,	51 "
Jonathan Walker,	47 "	Josiah Mirick,	30 "
Thaddeus Spring,	50 "	Stephen Harrington,	46 "
Solomon Wheeler,	47 "	Joseph Norcross,	47 "
Oliver Robinson,	47 "		

* The men were paid "6d. per day."   State Records, vol. 97, p. 5.

IV.

The Old Town Records.

The records of the town of Weston, as has already been stated, are lost from the date of its incorporation in 1712 to the opening of the second volume of records in 1754, a period of forty-two years, the more to be regretted as these years cover its first records as a town, which would be of great interest to-day, besides which we are deprived of all knowledge of the part the inhabitants took in the French and Indian Wars of that period. What would seem strange, if these records were lost previous to the opening of the second volume, is that no mention should have been made of their loss at the date of 1754. The labor and research of the writer in seeking out these documents cover some four or five years. By the kindness of those who have taken an interest in the hunt for any part of the records scattered about among family papers, the search has been, to a moderate degree, successful. The portions recovered will be given here, for they will prove of interest as filling the gap in some small measure of what has been lost. A curious fact in relation to the recovery of what documents have been unearthed is that they have been sent to the writer by persons no longer belonging to the town of Weston.

Mr. Kendal in his centennial sermon mentions that in the year 1718 a motion was brought forward in town meeting to build a new meeting-house, but the subject was deferred. However, in 1721 the subject was considered, as follows:—

At a Town Meeting of the Inhabitants of Weston orderly warned and met together on Monday ye 5th day of March 1721 to hear ye towns Treasurers accounts; to elect and choose Select Men and all other town officers as ye Law directs, to know ye towns minds whether they expect ye Committee to lay ye foundations of ye New meeting house and also to know the towns mind relating to their giving.

Lieut: **Josiah Jones**, *Chosen Moderator.*

The town treasurer's accounts read:—

Voted by said town at said meeting that they do expect ye towns treasurers accounts.

The town then proceeded to ye choice of Selectmen.

Selectmen, 1st Lieut: Josiah Jones. 2d Benoni Garfield. 3d James Jones. 4th Dea: Benjamin Brown. 5th Sergt. Joseph Allen.

Town Clerk, Deacon Benjamin Brown.

Town Treasurer, James Jones.

Constables, 1st Jonathan Bigalo. 2d Joseph Brooks.

Assessors, 1st Joseph Woolson. 2d Benoni Garfield. Dea: Brown.

Surveyors, 1st John Madab. 2d John Jones. 3d John Parks. 4th John Lamson.

Tythingmen, 1st Thomas Upham. 2d John Warren.

Fence Vewers, 1st Jacob Pierce. 2d Josiah Coolidge.

Hogrives, 1st Jacob Fullam. 2d Abijah Upham. John Whitney and Samuel Allen.

Sealer of Weights, John Fitch.

Voted that ye assessors take the Invoice.

Sexton, Richard Norcross.

Voted by ye Town that their Service go at large for ye year.

Voted by said Town that the Committee prepare ye foundations for ye New Meeting house & to appropriate their proportion of the bills of credit to this object.

All the above sworn in March 12th 1721.

In 1720/21 the General Court, to meet public charges, authorized the province treasurer to issue bills of credit, which were to be distributed by loan at five per cent. per annum to the different towns, in a specified proportion according to each town's proportion to the last province tax, one-fifth part of which sum loaned was to be refunded each year. The first emission of these bills, under this act, was to the amount of £50,000. There is no record of the part of Weston in these bills. We have also the following record:—

The select men of Watertown met on December 26th 1718 and adjourned to meet on the first Wednesday of January next, to consider what may be most proper or further to be done in the affair about the Bridge over Charles River, and the select men of Weston have present notice of the same, who are desired to be present at the same meeting, to hear what proposals are made by Jonathan Groom of Newton as to the building of a Bridge over said river.

The town of Weston entered with Watertown into a contract for the building of this bridge. By the wording of this notice to the Selectmen of Weston, it would seem at first blush that this was the first bridge over Charles River at Watertown. But this must not be understood as stating that there never had been any kind of a bridge at Watertown before this date. The bridge above alluded to was evidently the first bridge for the passage of carriages and teams. The Watertown foot-bridge, later adapted for horses, was probably the first bridge of its kind built in Massachusetts. At the time of the early settlements, and even down to the time of the Revolution, all travelling was done on horseback, and teams were transported to Boston at different points by ferriage. For many years Boston could only be reached by land through Roxbury. In 1722 Thomas Prentice and Thomas Learnard, the men who built the Watertown bridge in 1719, appealed to the towns of Watertown and Weston for additional remuneration, as they find they have been very great losers, and state that other towns are backward in paying their share for the building. The town voted to dismiss the petition.

Here follow certain fragments of the town records from 1722 to 1746:—

At a General Town Meeting of ye freeholders and other Inhabitants of Weston qualified according to Law to vote In town affairs: orderly warned and met together, on ye third day of August 1722.

1. In order to hear the accounts of ye Committee, who were chosen to procure a frame for a new meeting house, &c.

2. To know ye Towns mind what they will do with respect to the Covering and Closing or finishing the new Meeting house.

BENJAMIN BROWN *chosen Moderator*.

1st, *Voted* by said town at ye above said meeting, that the Committees accounts be referred to some other Town meeting when it may be convenient: and if they be then offered to the Town.

2d, *Voted* by said Town at said meeting: that they will forthwith proceed to cover and close ye new meeting house with the materials that are provided by ye Committee.

3d, *Voted* by said town at said meeting that Benjamin Brown, Benoni Garfield: Ebenezer Allen: Joseph Allen: and James Jones be a Committee for the town to manage the affairs of Covering and closing the new meeting house.

At a General Town Meeting of the freeholders and other inhabitants of ye Town of Weston qualified as ye Law directs to vote in Town Affairs: orderly warned and mett together: on Monday ye 5th day of November 1722.

1st, To grant the Reverend Mr. William Williams his sallary for his Labour in ye Gospel Ministry amongs us ye present year, begining the 10th day of September 1722 and to take care of cutting and carting his firewood this year.

2d, to hear the Committees accounts how they have improved the Public money that was appropriated to the building a new meeting house.

3d, To hear the account of what hath been done in hand labour and carting for said house.

4th, To see if ye town will grant a rate of so much as upon Computation shall be thought convenient: so ye labour that hath been done at said house may be proportioned: and that there may be money for ye further carrying out work on said house.

5th, To see what the Town will do about schooling.

BENJAMIN BROWN *chosen Moderator.*

1. *Voted* by said town at said meeting that they do grant to the Reverend Mr. William Williams ye sum of Seventy and four pounds for his sallary: for his labour in ye Gospel ministry amongst us in this present year beginning the 10th day of September 1722.

2. And Six Pounds for cutting and carting his fire wood ye present year. *Voted* by said town at said meeting: that they would accept the committe accounts of laying out the sum of 181:16:5 of ye publick money towards the new meeting house.

3. *Voted* by said town at said meeting: that they accept ye credit offered by the Committee in said meeting: of the hand labor: carting of boards: and Cedar for the enclosing and also stone for ye foundations of the new meeting house amounting to the sum of 36:18.

4. *Voted* by said town at said meeting that they do grant the sum of one hundred and fifty pounds money, that so ye labor that hath been done may be proportioned and that there may be money for ye further

carrying on of the work of said meeting house: and that the said 150 Pounds be paid in by the last day of May 1723.

5. [The remainder of this report of the above town meeting is torn off.]

Here is an extract or close of a vote passed in a town meeting in Weston on Monday, the first day of March, 1730/1, relating to

a Town way leading from Lexinton through ye lands of Dea^n Benjamin Brown and Liut: Thomas Garfield and others, &c., viz. The above said way to be Two rods wide saving at ye Causeways above mentioned and to be opened at ye expiration of three years from the date above mentioned in ye meantime hang convenient Gates. The above said way Confirmed by the Town on the 1st day of March 1730.

JAMES MIRICK, *Town Clerk.*

The road from Lexington to Weston would seem to have been laid out as early as 1730, as will be seen in the following:—

An extract for a particular and private way marked out by the Selectmen of Weston in the Northerly part of Said Town from Lexington line to the Town road by Josiah Brewer's. The Selectmen judging it necessary. Beginning at Lexington line, so running Southerly over John Headley's land and through Joseph Brooks' land the said Brooks to have liberty to hang a gate on the said way at his Southerly bounds, till such time as there is a way laid out in Lexington to accomodate the said Joseph Brooks, so through other land of said Headley, so through the land of Joseph Peirce, through a piece of Judah Clark's land and through the land of Jonathan Jackson to Deacon Benjamin Brown's and Thomas Garfield's corner, so entering at the corner on said Garfield's side of said corner and running on the Devission line Southerly to the next Squadron Strait and coming out at said squadron half on the one side and half on the other side of the said Division line, so along still Southerly one rod on each side of said line to the causid and over said causid but one rod wide, so unto the Drawbara one rod in each then turns South easterly on and through said Brown's land as marked, viz., a gray oak tree on the east side thence to a walnut tree on the West side, thence to a pine on the West, then bowing about to another pine on the east side, then to another pine on the east side, through to another pine on the east side. The turning about toward the east under the hill side to a gray oak tree on the north, then turning Southerly to a white oak tree on ye east side, thence to the end of the two rods reserved by Deacon Brown between Josiah Brewer & Daniel Carter. So along Southerly on said

Two rods to the squadron line to a heap of stones on a rock on the said squadron line. (So over Brewer's land and Jackson's land to the Town road first mentioned.) The way upon record out of which this is extracted was brought to the Town for confirmation at their annual meeting on the 1st day of March 1730/1 and voted in the affirmative.

Extract from the Weston Book of Records, pages 130, 131.

Examined per NATHANIEL GODDARD, *Town Clerk*.

It would seem at this period, when a road was made through land of owners, such as that of the above-mentioned Brown and Garfield, instead of the town paying damages, the owners were allowed to erect gates and charge toll. There seems to have grown out of the above privilege granted to Brown and Garfield a complaint made to the Selectmen in 1734/5 by both Brown and Garfield. As is probable (there being no paper to show by whom), a petition had been made to the town to have the gates removed, etc. Both Brown and Garfield protest against any action being taken by the town.

This matter of the Brown and Garfield gates seems to have come up continuously until 1735, when, at a town meeting held May 13 of that year, the town voted to reconsider the privilege granted to Brown and Garfield, but that the road should not be laid open till after the first day of December next ensuing. The action of this meeting is attested by Ebenezer Allen, town clerk.

The road of which mention is made in the following presentment before the Court of Sessions was probably a part of the Lexington road before mentioned. This road over Lamson's Hill has no longer any existence. It was a narrow rod-wide road, running from the meeting-house past Richardson's farmhouse, formerly the dwelling of John Lamson, along the wall north-east through the meadow, over the hill now heavily wooded, still belonging in part to the Lamson estate, and coming out on the old road near house of Jesse Viles. It was over this road, still traceable, that Captain Samuel Lamson marched his company to Concord on April 19, 1775. A part of this old road still has a wall on each side.

At a meeting of the Selectmen of Weston with Justice Fullam, held in May, 1734, they addressed John Jones, one of the Surveyors of Highways, the following warrant, viz.:—

At a meeting of the Selectmen of the town, in order to appoint to the Surveyor of said town, their respective divisions or Districts of highways to amend and repair for this succeeding year, have appointed to you the Division and district as follows, viz, Begining at Needham line, near Nathaniel Dewing's, and along by John Hastings and Thomas Peirce into ye great country road near Mr. Williams. 2dly from Thomas Peirce to Needam line near the house of Josiah Upham and ye way from Thomas Peirce to ye run of water east of Colonel Fullam's barn, and from thence by Jonas Harrington's out into the way near Bullard's: and from Abel Allen's house out into ye Town way near Adam Smith's.

The persons named with those of their families upward of sixteen years old are in proportion enjoined by law to work at high way belonging to your Division or District:

Deacon John Parkhurst.	Jonas Livermore.
George Parkhurst.	Thomas Peirce.
Adam Smith.	Joseph Lovel.
Abel Allen.	John Train.
John Felch.	Samuel Train.
Nathaniel Felch.	Nathaniel Dewing.
Ebenezer Allen.	Nathaniel Jennison.
Benjamin Bullard.	John Jennison.
John Barnard.	Jonas Harrington.

Joseph Livermore.

WESTON, May 22, 1734.

BENJAMIN BROWN,
EBENEZER ALLEN, } Selectmen.
JOHN JONES,

FRANCIS FULLAM, *Justice of Peace.*

This is the only allotment of surveyors to be found, and the above list remained in force until 1737, when a new one was drawn, but the names are not given.

In 1738 the town was presented at the Court of Sessions for obstructions on the king's highway "leading from the Meeting House to what is called the Concord road, and near a place called

Lamson's hill in Weston." Below will be found the statement of the case as appeared in the petition or presentment:—

To the Sheriff of the County of Middlesex, his under sheriff or Deputy, Greeting,—

Whereas before the Justices of His Majesty's Court of General Sessions of the Peace, begun and held at Charlestown in and for the County of Middlesex, aforesaid, on the second Tuesday of March last, the Grand Inquest for the body of the said County, did present that the King's Highway leading from Weston Meeting house to what is called Concord road in the County of Middlesex, aforesaid, then was and for the space of three months last past hath been, and still continues to be very much obstructed for the length of almost a quarter of a mile at and near a place called Lamson's hill in Weston, in the County aforesaid. It being there very steep, dangerous and full of great rocks so as renders it almost impassable for teams, and carts loaded, so that the same is and hath been for the time aforesaid a common nuisance, and yet like to continue so, and the said Grand Inquest further presents that it belongs to the Inhabitants of the town of Weston, to repair, amend, and render the same passable for loaded teams, carts and horses &c, all which is in evil example to others and contrary to law as also to the Peace, Crown and dignity of our Lord the King.

These are therefore in his Majesty's name to will and require you to summon the selectmen of the Town of Weston, aforesaid, to appear at the next Court of General Sessions of the peace to be holden at Cambridge within and for the County of Middlesex on the third Tuesday of May next, then and there to make answer to the said presentment and to abide and perform the judgment of the said Court that shall be given thereon: and you are likewise required to summon as witnesses for the King, John Walker, Deacon John Warren, Samuel Miller and Josiah Hobbs: hereof fail not and make return hereof under your hand, with your doings therein before the sitting of said Court. Dated at Charlestown the 14th day of April In the eleventh year of His Majesty's reign Anno Domini 1738.

By order of Court.

THADDIUS MASON, *Clerk.*

MIDDLESEX, ss., April 29th, 1738.

A true copy examined

per RICHARD FOSTER, Jr., *Sheriff.*

At a general town meeting of the freeholders and other inhabitants of Weston, qualified according to law to vote in town affairs, on the twelfth day of May, 1738, it was—

THE REV. DR. FIELD MANSION, CENTRAL AVENUE.

Built by Isaac Fiske in 1805, and became the property of Rev. Dr. Field in 1815, whose descendants still own and occupy it.

THE GOLDEN BALL TAVERN, CENTRAL AVENUE.

Built in 1768 by Colonel Isaac Jones. The old sign of the Golden Ball still exists. Its fame as a tavern lasted eighty years. It was the headquarters of the local Tory element during the Revolution. The house is still owned and occupied by the descendants of Colonel Jones.

Voted by said Town at said Meeting that they desire Francis Fullam, Esq., and Deacon Benjamin Brown to make answer to the presentment of the way over Lamson's hill, so called, at the next Court of General Sessions of the Peace to be holden at Cambridge on the 3d day of May current.

A true copy taken off from Weston book of Records

examined per EBENEZER ALLEN, *Town Clerk.*

MAY 19th, 1738.

In August, 1744, the inhabitants or proprietors of tenements in the easterly part of Concord and the northerly part of Weston and the westerly part of Lexington petitioned

His Excellency William Shirley, Captain General and Governor-in-chief in and over his Majesty's Province of the Massachusetts Bay in New England, to the Honourable his Majesty's Council, and the honourable House of Representatives in General Court assembled at Boston August 10, 1744, That your Petitioners labour under great difficulties and inconveniences by reason of their distance from their respective places of publick Worship in said town; their families being many of them numerous, in the winter season more especially they have been obliged for many years past to promote and maintain the preaching of the word of God amongst them in a private House, or otherwise many of them must have been deprived of the great benefit thereof; your Petitioners have applied themselves to the said towns to consent that they should be set off from their respective Towns or otherwise to relieve them, both which they refused your Petitioners. Difficulties yet remaining, whereas your Petitioners have not where to go but to your Excellency and Honours for relief in the premises, We humbly pray this honourable Court will be pleased to take their case into your wise and serious Consideration and make them a precinct, and invest them with such priviledges as this honourable Court shall see fit, the bounds of the lands for which your Petitioners pray may be made a precinct, begins where the line between Sudbury and Concord goes over the Great river, so called, and so to run down said river to a brook running out of Well meadow, so called, from thence to the South easterly side of Walden Pond, so called, from thence to the South Westerly Corner of Daniel Brooks' land lying upon the South side of the County road and then across the said road to the South West Corner of said Brooks' land upon the North side of said road from thence in a straight line to the North west Corner of said Brooks' meadow by a way leading to Brick Kiln Island, so called, and by said way to a small White oak tree at the North West Corner of said Brooks' field, upon said Island, from thence in a straight line to a small black oak tree at Bedford line in Timothy Wheeler's land near the end of a ditch, and by Bedford line to Concord corner, adjoining to Lexington, and from thence in a strait line to the Bridge in Concord road, Westerly of Thomas Nelson's house; thence to the top of a little hill eastward of Nehemiah Abbott's house, from thence to Waltham North west Corner including Ebenezer Cuttler's land, from thence to the South west Corner of John Bemis' land, from thence to the South east Corner of Concord, and from thence by Concord line to the place first mentioned, or by any other such bounds as the Court shall see meet, &c., &c.

Ebenezer Hunt.	John Wright.	Jeremiah Clark.
Thomas Baker.	Ambrose Tower.	Thomas Garfield, Jr.
Samuel Dakin.	David Reed.	Benjamin Brown, Jr.
Joseph Parks.	Mary Conant.	Hannah Corey.
John Headley.	Nathan Brown.	Zebediah Smith.
Timothy Wesson.	Edward Flint.	John White.
Benjamin Monroe.	Stephen Wesson.	Ebenezer Lamson.
Jonathan Gore.	John Adams.	Joshua Brooks.
Samuel Bond.	Jon: Wellington.	Thomas Garfield.
Thomas Wheeler.	John Gore	Benjamin Brown.
Ephraim Flint.	George Peirce.	James Brooks.
Joseph Peirce, Jr.	Joseph Brooks.	Robert Gage.
Joseph Brooks, Jr.	Judah Clark.	Ephraim Sagard.
John Garfield.	Amos Merriam.	John Whitney.
Ebenezer Cutler.	Joseph Peirce.	Benjamin Allen.
Jonas Peirce.		

The inhabitants of the south side of Weston seem to have had equal trouble with those of the north side in their travelling to and from the house of public worship. The petition for a new road leading to the meeting-house is preserved, but the names of the petitioners, with the exception of those of Jonathan Stimson and Ebenezer Allen, are torn off the existing copy. The following is the petition:—

WESTON, February 15, 1742.

To THE SELECT MEN OF WESTON, &C.

The petition of us the subscribers humbly show that we labor under very great difficulty in travelling to and from the place of public worship in said town by reason of the badness of some parts of the way, which we apprehend can never be made much better, as also by reason of the many great crooks and turns which are therein: which makes the way so much the longer for our petitioners to travel every Lord's day: Therefore your petitioners humbly pray the said selectmen would please to take our circumstances into your consideration and lay out a way through the land of Daniel Modub and James Stimson Jr. along under the westerly side of the great hill, and also through the lands belonging to the heirs of George Parkhurst, deceased, and through the lands of the Reverend Mr. Williams and others across the meadow land to the meeting house: which will very much redress our difficulties in travelling morning and evening: and sundry of us which now cannot with any comfort do it may then go to their respective houses in the intervening season on the Lord's days: and your humble petitioners as in duty bound shall ever pray.

The petition to the General Court, as seen above, was signed by fifty-six heads of families. It will be seen by these petitions of the inhabitants of what is now Lincoln that they were laboring under the same difficulties in their distance from meeting-house that caused the inhabitants of the Farmers' district to apply for separation from the Watertown precinct in 1695, and which was finally accomplished in 1698. As we have seen, the refusal of the Weston town officials to repair their roads communicating with Lincoln led to the petition to the Governor and General Court to be made into a separate precinct in 1744, which being granted in August, 1746, with the injunction that they serve the towns of Concord, Lexington, and Weston with copies of their petition, so that they may show cause, if any, why their prayer should not be granted, Weston made no objection to their being so set off. However, when the precinct of Lincoln applied to the General Court to be incorporated as a town, in 1754,—

at a Town Meeting held in Weston April 11, 1754, it was *voted:*
1. That the prayer of the Petitioners ought not to be granted because it included four families that have never belonged to said precinct of Lincoln, viz., Theophilus Mansfield, Benjamin Hager, John Binney, and Thomas Russell.
2. Because the parties above named are unwilling to be set off, but choose rather to remain with the town of Weston.
3. *Voted* that they consent that the other inhabitants of Weston included in said petition be set off as a Township with the following bounds.

The bounds referred to are those before given.

The discovery of an old document, the existence of which does not seem to be known in our day, is of great interest in the history of the difficulties which seem to have beset both the north and south sections of the town upon the question of reaching the meeting-house on the Lord's Day, owing to the bad condition of the roads at all times, but particularly in winter. A scheme was set on foot on the north side of the town to have the meeting-house removed to the North Road, or Lancaster Turnpike. This petition was signed by forty-eight heads of families, and is sufficiently curious to warrant the whole story being inserted here. It certainly forms an episode known to few, if any, persons of the town at the present day. Here follow the names of those signing the petition on the north side of the town:—

Ensign Joseph Livermore. John Warren. Isaac Gregory.
Lieut: Josiah Livermore. John Whitney. Moses Jones.
Capt. Joseph Harrington. Joseph Whitney. William Bond.
James Mirick. Abijah Wheeler. Benjamin Bond.
John Mirick. Wid: Sarah Warren. John Walker.
Joseph Woolson. Isaac Cory. John Hager.
Abraham Whitney. William Whitney. Nathaniel Walker.
Nathaniel Goddard. Thomas Russell. Nathaniel Allen.
William Smith. Samuel Philips. Edward Gearfield.
Ebenezer Hammond. Nathan Fiske. Jonathan Stratton.
Nathan Upham. Braddyll Smith. John Lamson.
Jeremiah Whittemore. Daniel Carter. Isaac Allen.
Ebenezer Hobbs. Josh. Wellington. Henry Spring.
Josiah Hobbs. Isaac Hager. Jonas Allen.
Elisha Warren. Shubal Childs. William Lawrance.
Nathaniel Livermore. John Train. John Bemis.
Deacon Warren.

It would seem that, to checkmate this movement for the removal of the church to the north side, a counter-movement was made on the south side. This south-side movement would seem to have been rather to serve the purpose of a check to the north rather than any desire that the church should be moved south. The list is signed by fifty-five heads of families. Rev. William Williams heads the south-side list:—

Rev. William Williams. Jonas Harrington. Elisha Jones.
Col: Fullam. Josiah Colledge. Capt. Jones.
John Jones. Isaac Harrington. Joseph Woolson.
Widow Train. Nathaniel Jameson. Thomas Flagg.
Benjamin Harrington. Joseph Bigloe. Samuel Severns.

Jonas Harrington.	Jonathan Stimpson.	William Upham.
Daniel Livermore.	Abraham Gale.	Abijah Upham.
Nathaniel Felch.	James Stimson.	Thomas Upham.
Ebenezer Allen.	William Smith, Jr.	Abraham Gregory.
Abel Allen.	Jonathan Bigloe.	Abraham Bigloe.
John Allen.	Benjamin Bigloe.	Samuel Hunt.
Ebenezer Allen.	Nathaniel Bigloe.	Francis Fullam.
Adam Smith.	Joseph Norcross.	John Felch.
Noah Shephard.	Deacon Parkhurst.	David Allen.
Jonathan Bullard.	Joseph Parkhurst.	Benoni Flagg.
Thomas Peirce.	Daniel Smith.	Daniel Medub.
Joseph Lovell.	Nathaniel Stimpson.	George Harrington.
John Hastings.	Thomas Spring.	William Buxten.
Nathaniel Dewing.		

Deacon Benjamin Brown writes the petitioners of the north side, where his lands lay, an able, well-reasoned letter, in which he gives his reasons for not signing their petition. (They had evidently been annoyed at his refusal to do so.) The letter is here inserted, since it explains the whole business fully, and is withal very interesting:—

Dear and Honored Sirs,—I being yesterday closely questioned whether I had done justice to my opposing neighbours in joining with the petitioners, I freely acknowledge that as I profess to be a Christian I am under obligation to render a reason of my conduct to every man that does soberly ask it of me: and soever I was not joyned with you formerly: what was then my reluctance was 1, I thought that in as much as the meeting house was sot near the middle of the town that if we on the north should get off the meeting house must be removed. 2d, That in as much as I had helped to build one meeting house and settle one minister &c., and had now my own family to take care of I might be excused as having done the work of my day. But what gave a turn to my mind was as to the first, it was told to me by a person over in the town: said he, if you do get off the meeting house will never be moved, for said he, those that remain on the North won't vote it away from them: and the Warrens corner and the Allens corner, so called, will still remain at a considerable distance: and all they that are upon the great road can't be better on't and all that are at a convenient distance on the South they won't give a penny to move it: and then you will find but a very few that will vote for moving it, and then besides if any should petition the General Court to move it they will find that if it should be moved it must go over on ye southerly side of a Great meadow that lyeth in the way: and would said house be removed it would encommode more of the remaining inhabitants than where it now standeth.

3ly. My neighbours used these arguments with me: viz., that although I might possibly travel so far myself: yet there were ten or eleven families of my neighbours that the nearest of them had near a mile farther to travel to meeting than I had: and some of them had no way at all to go to meeting and some of those that had: the way was so untollarable that at some times in the winter it was altogether impossible for a man to ride along either double or even single: the bushes and trees hanging down, being loaded with snow: besides the way being very rocky and mountainous: and that the town, although being often requested, had done nothing effectual for their help—and further they told me that when any thing of this nature was done it was necessary that some persons must do it themselves for the sake of others or else there could be no relief in such cases, which seemed to me were reasons that I was not able to gainsay: and which I hope will not be unseasonable for me at this time to offer.

Your much obliged and humble servant,

BENJA. BROWN.

WESTON, April 23, 1746.

It may prove interesting to see the invoice, as it was then called, or the tax list of the inhabitants of Weston in the year of its incorporation as a town. While many of the names are those of persons who were then residents of Weston, but are no longer on our tax lists, and many more are those of persons now belonging to the town of Lincoln, still there remain on the list the names of many families now with us.

The Tax Rate in Weston in 1712.

	£	s.	pce.
Captain Jones	1	6	3
Captain Fullam	1	6	3
Mr. Woollson	1	0	0
Corporal Benjamin Harrington	1	7	9
Joseph Livermore		15	9
Lieutenant John Livermore	1	14	0
Joseph Wollson	1	0	0
Ebenezer Hunt		10	6
Nathaniel Whitney		10	6
William Whitney		16	8
Samuel Whitney		10	6

THE OLD TOWN RECORDS 53

Richard Robins		18	3
Daniel Warren	1	16	6
Joshua Biglo		17	9
Joseph Abbott	1	11	6
Joseph Allen	1	16	10
Simon Tozer		12	7
Joseph Dunn		17	9
Abbot Allen	1	14	8
Samuel Jones	1	11	5
Corporal Benjamin Allen	1	14	9
Nathaniel Jones	1	10	6
Michael Falshaw		18	2
Samuel Philips		10	0
James Biglo		10	0
James Jones	1	16	4
Benjamin Bullard		19	3
Daniel Livermore		19	8
Thomas Fladge [Flagg]	1	17	4
Joseph Whitney		17	0
Jonathan Stimpson	1	11	0
Isaack Madob [Modock]		12	3
Ensign Josiah Jones	2	3	3
John Smith	1	2	10
Thomas Spring	1	11	5
John Parkhurst	1	16	10
Nathaniel Coolidge	1	11	10
Abolm. Allen	1	1	6
Samuel Jones		15	9
Corporal Benjamin Allen	1	1	0
Nathaniel Jones		15	9
Michael Falshaw		7	3
Samuel Philips		10	0
James Biglo		9	6
James Jones		12	5
Benjamin Bullard		10	6
Daniel Livermore		10	6
Thomas Fladg [Flagg]	1	1	0
Joseph Whitney		10	6
Jonathan Stimson		4	0
Isaac Madoc		10	6
Samuel Robins		10	6
Ensign Josiah Jones	1	1	0
John Smith		12	7
Thomas Spring	1	1	5
John Parkhurst	1	1	0

Nathaniel Coolidge		13	0
Richard Norcross	1	4	0
John Wellington	1	11	5
Benjamin Brown	1	3	7
Thomas Gearfield	1	2	2
Benoni Gearfield	1	12	3
Benjamin Gearfield	1	8	0
John Warren Jr.	1	14	5
Charles Chadwick		19	7
John Wright		16	8
Joseph Wright	1	14	6
Jacob Piori	1	0	4
Thomas Waight	1	16	2
William Fisk		17	5
Lieutenant John Brown	2	14	9
Jonathan Bullard	1	7	9
Jonathan Bullard Jr.	1	17	4
Joseph Bullard	1	4	0
Joseph Lovewell [Lovell]	1	3	0
Richard Norcross		10	6
John Wellington	1	1	0
Benjamin Brown			
Thomas Gearfield		5	9
Benoni Gearfield	1	1	0
Benjamin Gearfield	1	8	0
John Warren Jr.		17	3
Charles Chadwick		12	0
John Waight		16	8
Joseph Waight		10	6
Jacob Piori		10	6
Thomas Waight	1	1	0
William Fisk		5	5
Lieutenant John Brown	1	8	3
Jonathan Bullard	1	7	9
Jonathan Bullard Jr.	1	1	0
Joseph Bullard		15	9
Joseph Lovwell		11	6
Francis Pirrico	1	2	7
Daniel Madob Jr.		12	3
James Stimpson	1	17	11
Samuel Gonorans	1	2	10
George Robinson	1	13	11
John Jones		11	6
Daniel Estabrook	1	13	3
Caleb Grant	1	1	4

THE OLD TOWN RECORDS 55

Joseph Pierce		6	8
Samuel Lov	1	8	6
Jonathan Biglo	1	2	7
John Mixor	1	10	0
John Sawin	1	14	9
Ebenezer Allen		19	7
Daniel Madob		9	7
Richard Parks		13	4
Thomas Woolson Jr.		12	7
Corporal John Warren	1	4	1
Benjamin Harrington	1	2	7
George Robinson	1	1	0
Capt. John Warren	1	4	0
Benjamin Harrington		14	3
Thomas Wollson		6	4
Richard Parks		13	0
John Sawin	1	1	0
Samuel Love		15	9
Caleb Grant		10	8

V.

THRIFTY FINANCE OF YE FATHERS (RATES, TAXES, BOUNTIES, ETC.).

The Narragansett townships were grants by the General Court to each county of the State, divided among the several towns by lot. These grants of land were by way of payment and gratuities to the soldiers of the crown in previous Indian wars. The Middlesex grants and several divisions were made about 1734. There were six townships, or allotments. Weston and Sudbury drew Township No. 2. The loss of records of the town prevent any full or interesting account of the part Weston had in this township (now Westminster). In 1737 John Sawin, of Natick, drew his father's, Francis Sawin's, lot in No. 2. John, Thomas, and Manning Sawin owned a part of the Livermore farm in Weston, afterwards sold to John Train. The only documentary evidence of the part Weston took in Township No. 2 bears date of June, 1736, when Mr. Abijah Upham is appointed collector of the Narragansett grantors, originally of Weston, with orders to collect the sum of five pounds on each lot or right in said township for the encouragement of settlers. The following names are those of proprietors belonging to Weston:—

Ebenezer Boynton, Lot No. 51. Drawn by Deacon Brown, £5.
Onesiphorus Pike, Lot No. 81. Drawn by Benj: Robbins, £5.
Thomas Cory, Lot No. 44. Drawn by Ebenezer Cory, £5.
Nathaniel Norcross, Lot No. 37. Drawn by Nathaniel Norcross, £5.
Daniel Warren, Lot No. 34. Drawn by Daniel Warren, £5.

A total of £25. This is signed by Joseph Bowman, Richard Foster, Jr., and Benjamin Brown as assessors.

Newton would seem to have also been included in Township No. 2, as a list was addressed to Edward Jackson, as collector of that town.

The following letter from Rev. Elisha Marsh, settled over Township No. 2, has a pathos about it that makes it worthy of being entered here. Judging from his statement of his condition for want of his salary, unpaid for years back, it would appear that the settlers or the grantors were deficient in religious zeal, or perhaps the distance which separated them rendered them somewhat careless in their treatment of him. The letter, however, speaks for itself:—

NARRAGANSETT, No. 2: Decr. 30th, 1737 (?).

Mr. BROWN,

When I was down last I desired Mr. Cooke to acquaint the Committee of my request, which was that there might be a Proprietors' meeting called as soon as possible, and see whether they would make my sallary good, according to contract, that I might know what to depend upon. Sir, you can't but know that since my settlement, everything of the neccessaries of life is almost if not quite doubled and I can't possibly live unless I have my sallary: and have it paid when it is due to me, but instead of that I am greatly injured and abused either by the Committee or the Clerk or Proprietors or all of them. Dear, how do you and the rest of the Committee think I can live without my just dues from the Proprietors, when by reason of the war I have not been able to raise my provisions but must buy all, this present year, but pay which way without money? I have not received all of my fourth year's salary yet by considerable, and not one penny of the fifth, and you know how far the sixth year is advanced. This is in my opinion, and I think must in all honest people be looked upon wrong and oppressive, the wise man tells us the ringing of the nose brings forth blood, and opression will make a wise man mad. If there is not a meeting called immediately and I am paid of what is my due, and I have my full sallary I must be obliged to take some other measures. Pray don't oblige me to it, by the Committee neglecting their duty. Let a meeting be called directly and you will oblige your sincere and abused friend and servant.

ELISHA MARSH.

In 1738 appears the following bill for building the meeting-house at Township No. 2, now Westminster:—

Dr.	The Proprietors for Building the Meeting House.		Cr.
1738.		1738.	
To Building the House	£365:0:0	July 5. By Cash	£54:0:0
" Sundry Articles Do	1:10:0	Sept. 8. By Cash	50:0:0
		Dec. 20. " "	30:0:0
	£366:10:0	1739	
		June 6. " "	45:0:0
		Oct. 31. " "	15:0:0
		Nov. 9. " "	15:0:0
		By Paid John Wood Glazier by Mr. Joseph Lynd	6:0:0
		1740	
		May 17. By Cash	35:0:0
		July 2. " "	30:0:0
		Sept. 24. " "	60:0:0
		1741	
		June 10. " "	26:10:0
			£366:10:0

It is to be hoped this is only a copy, although it has all the character of an original bill. It is not, however, receipted, which perhaps was not necessary. In 1744 appears the following account of the Proprietors' Standing Committee, by which we see they began to pay up some part of poor Mr. Marsh's salary:—

The Standing Committee for the Proprietors of the Narraganset Township No. 2 who were appointed to inspect their Treasurer's accounts (viz. Mr. Daniel Cook), and to lay them before the Proprietors, as also to call to account such as had before neglected to account with the former Committee, do now report thereon, as followeth, viz., that the Balance of the former acct. due the Proprietors September
    17th 1744 was the sum of £359:13:10
and that upon Sept. 19, 1744 the proprietors at their General
    Meeting granted a Tax of one pound, new Tenor to be
    laid upon each rate, which amounts to the sum of—in
    old Tenor— 472:0:0
also on said day granted the Revd. Mr. Marsh his second
    year's sallery, viz., forty-five pounds, Current money:
    which in old Tenor amounts to. 180:0:0
Also on said day they granted the Revd. Mr. Marsh his third
    year's sallary, viz., £45: Current money, which in old
    Tenor amounts to 180:0:0
        Total £1191:13:10

THRIFTY FINANCE OF YE FATHERS

Mr. Benjamin Brown, of Weston, seems to have been the principal manager of the township. His bills and accounts run from 1736 to 1750, when he makes a general settlement with Mr. Cook, the treasurer of the proprietors. There exists a map of this township, with a list of all the grantees. Should it be found, it will appear in an appendix.

Before leaving the period of the earliest history of Weston, it will be interesting to give a tax rate previous to the incorporation of the town,—that of 1708,—by which we shall notice who were the inhabitants at that early period and the then rate of taxation. The province tax for the west precinct of Watertown, by assessment made September 17, 1708, by Benjamin Gearfield, Palsgrave Wellington, and John Warren, assessors, was £101 12s. of which sum £80 15s. 6d. was collected. It will be noticed that on all very old tax rates, or invoices, as they were called, there is a column set apart and styled "Faculty." This denotes that any person in the town having a "knack" at anything, or a faculty of trade wherewith he earned his livelihood, was supposed to be taxed thereon, probably very much in the sense of our present license. But, as it will be noticed that all under this head, even Captain Jones and Squire Fullam, confessed to no "Faculty," it is to be presumed that it was not insisted upon by the assessors. In all the rates that have been examined none have been found where a person has confessed to possessing any faculty for anything, and yet these old settlers had certainly one great faculty,—that, at least, of getting on in the world with a multitude of circumstances of those early times which, to say the least, would be considered difficult to surpass in the present day. The habit of passing over or ignoring the disagreeable questions which assessors are apt to indulge in has been successfully handed down to our own day, with more or less success. Assessors of those early times were probably as disagreeable companions in the spring of the year as are those of the present epoch.

HISTORY OF WESTON

The Provincial Tax Rates or Assessment made September 17, 1708, for the West Precinct.

Heads.	Yearly		Income. Multiplied by six.		Quick		Stock.		Trade or Faculty.			£	s.	d.
h.	£	s.	£	s.	£	s.	£	s.				£	s.	d.
1	1	00	6	00	7	00	00	00			Charles Chadwick.	–	19	7
1	–	–	–	–	9	–	–	–			John Waight.	–	16	8
1	2	–	12	–	7	14	–	–			Joseph Waight.	1	4	6
1	1	10	9	–	5	–	–	–			Jacob Pierce.	1	–	4
–	5	10	33	–	16	4	–	–			Thomas Waight.	1	16	2
1	–	10	3	–	7	10	–	–			William Fisk.	–	17	5
1	7	–	42	–	18	14	–	–			Lt. John Bruer.	2	14	9
–	4	–	24	–	13	12	–	–			Jonathan Bullard.	1	7	9
1	4	–	24	–	13	–	–	–			Jonathan Bullard Jr.	1	17	4
1	2	10	15	–	3	18	–	–			Joseph Bullard.	1	4	–
1	1	10	9	–	8	10	–	–			Joseph Lovewell.	1	3	0
1	2	–	12	–	5	–	–	–			Francis Pierce.	1	2	7
1	–	–	–	–	3	–	–	–			Daniel Modup Jr.	–	12	3
1	4	–	24	–	13	16	–	–			James Stimpson.	1	17	11
1	2	–	12	–	5	8	–	–			Samuel Souverans.	1	2	10
1	3	10	21	–	3	–	–	–			Geo. Robinson.	1	13	11
1	–	–	–	–	5	10	–	–			Geo. Robinson Jr.	–	14	–
1	–	–	–	–	2	–	–	–			John Jones.	–	11	6
1	3	10	21	–	10	10	–	–			Daniel Easterbrook.	1	13	3
1	1	–	6	–	–	8	–	–			Caleb Grant.	1	1	4
–	1	10	9	–	–	–	–	–			Joseph Pierce.	–	6	8
1	2	10	15	–	10	–	–	–			Samuel Lov.	1	8	6
1	1	10	9	–	7	18	–	–			Jonathan Biglo.	1	2	7
1	3	–	18	–	8	18	–	–			John Mixor.	1	10	–
1	3	10	21	–	12	10	–	–			John Sawin.	1	14	9
1	1	–	6	–	7	6	–	–			Ebenezer Allen.	–	19	7
–	2	–	12	–	1	10	–	–			Daniel Modup.	–	9	7
–	3	–	18	–	–	–	–	–			Richard Parks.	–	13	4
1	–	–	–	–	3	10	–	–			Thomas Woolson Jr.	–	12	7
1	1	10	9	–	10	10	–	–			Corp. J. Warren.	1	4	1
1	2	10	15	–	2	–	–	–			Ben: Harrington.	1	2	7
1	–	–	–	–	–	–	–	–			Nathl. Brown.	–	10	–
1	–	–	–	–	–	–	–	–			James Bassford.	–	10	–
1	4	–	24	–	12	18	–	–			Capt. Jones.	1	17	4
1	5	10	33	–	17	16	–	–			Capt. F. Fullam.	2	7	6
–	4	10	27	–	17	14	4	–			Thomas Woolson.	1	15	11
–	4	–	24	–	13	12	–	–			Corp. B. Harrington.	1	7	9
–	3	10	21	–	9	16	–	–			Jos: Livermore.	1	2	8
1	10	–	60	–	16	–	4	–			Lt. J. Livermore.	3	9	3
–	4	–	24	–	12	2	–	–			Jos: Woolson.	1	6	8
1	3	–	18	–	–	–	–	–			Ebenr Hunt.	–	13	4
1	4	–	24	–	9	2	–	–			Wm. Whiting.	1	14	6
1	–	–	–	–	9	–	–	–			Wm. Whiting.	–	16	8
1	–	–	–	–	2	–	–	–			Saml. Whiting.	–	11	6
1	1	–	6	–	5	–	–	–			Richd. Robbins.	–	18	2
2	4	10	27	–	20	12	–	–			Daniel Warren.	2	15	2
1	3	10	21	–	10	18	–	–			Joshua Biglo.	1	13	8

THRIFTY FINANCE OF YE FATHERS

Heads.	Yearly		Income.		Multiplied by six		Quick Stock.		Trade or Faculty.			£	s.	d.
h.	£	s.	£	s.	£	s.	£	s.	£	s.		£	s.	d.
2	3	–	18	–	12	8	–	–			J. Allen Senr.	2	2	6
1	4	–	24	–	12	8	–	–			Joseph Allen.	1	16	10
1	2	–	12	–	7	18	–	–			Simon Tozer.	1	4	9
1	1	–	6	–	4	10	–	–			Joseph Doan.	–	17	9
1	3	10	21	–	12	8	–	–			Abel Allen.	1	14	8
1	3	–	18	–	10	18	–	–			Saml. Jones.	1	11	5
1	3	10	21	–	12	16	–	–			Corp. B. Allen.	1	14	9
1	2	10	15	–	12	16	–	–			Nathl. Jones.	1	10	6
1	1	–	6	–	5	–	–	–			Michael Falghaw.	–	13	2
1	–	–	–	–	–	–	–	–			Saml. Philipps.	–	10	–
1	–	–	–	–	–	–	–	–			James Biglo.	–	10	–
1	4	–	24	–	11	14	–	–			James Jones.	1	16	4
1	1	10	9	–	3	10	–	–			Benj: Bullard.	–	19	3
1	1	10	9	–	5	–	–	–			Daniel Liensmouth.	–	19	8
1	4	–	24	–	12	18	–	–			Thomas Flagg.	1	17	4
1	1	–	6	–	3	10	–	–			Joseph Whiting.	–	17	–
1	3	–	18	–	10	10	–	–			Jonathan Stimpson.	1	11	1
1	–	–	–	–	3	–	–	–			Isaac Modup.	–	12	3
1	1	–	6	–	5	8	–	–			Saml. Robbins.	–	18	5
1	5	–	30	–	14	18	–	–			En: Josiah Jones.	2	3	3
1	2	–	12	–	5	8	–	–			John Smith.	1	2	10
1	3	–	18	–	11	10	–	–			Thomas Spring.	1	11	9
1	4	–	24	–	12	8	–	–			John Parkhurst.	1	16	10
1	3	–	18	–	11	14	–	–			Nathl. Coolidge.	1	11	11
1	2	–	12	–	6	18	–	–			Richd. Norcross.	1	4	1
2	3	–	18	–	10	18	–	–			John Wellington.	1	11	5
1	1	10	9	–	9	8	–	–			Benj: Brown.	1	3	7
1	1	10	9	–	7	10	–	–			Thomas Garfield.	1	2	2
1	3	–	18	–	12	8	–	–			Benoni Gearfield.	1	12	3
1	2	10	15	–	9	8	–	–			Benj: Gearfield.	1	8	–
1	3	10	21	–	12	16	–	–			John Warren Jr.	1	14	5

To Benjamin Brown, Constable of Watertown, this is your part of the Province Tax, for you to collect and pay, according to your Directions in the Treasurer's Warrant and amounting to the Sum of £101 12s.

BENJ: GEARFIELD,   ⎫ *Assessors*
PALSGRAVE WELLINGTON, ⎬   *for*
JOHN WARREN,   ⎭ *Watertown.*

The country hereabouts must have been infested at an early period with noxious animals, among these squirrels and blackbirds, probably to the great injury of the crops. A record exists covering several years, beginning in 1731 (but probably earlier records existed), where bounties were paid by the town for the killing of all such animals. In 1731 £7 19s. 4d. was paid; another year, £14 4s. 8d.; and again £11 11s. 10d. The statutes provided that towns might pay a bounty for the killing of wolves, crows, squirrels, and other wild animals, and all birds that were destructive of crops. The bounty for killing crows in the months of April, May, and June varied in different years. Twenty-five cents was paid for old crows, and half that for young ones, and half a cent for red-winged blackbirds. Swine and cattle were allowed to go at large in this and most towns of this State from a very early period and down to our own day. The nuisance was not abated here until late in the '40's. The law regulating the going at large of swine was never enforced in Weston, so far as the records show. The law stated that they should be properly yoked and ringed, and further set forth "that no yoke shall be accounted sufficient which is not the full depth of the swine's neck above the neck, and half as much below the neck: and the sole or bottom of the yoke to be three times so long as the breadth or thickness of the swine's neck." The standing complaint in Weston regarding animals going at large was the damage done by horses, which in early days got their principal feed in the roads and in the gardens of the inhabitants.

Following is one of the old accounts of the town relating to aforesaid bounties:—

THE OLD FLAGG TAVERN, CENTRAL AVENUE.

Here General Washington, when President, passed a night on his way to Boston. Here, too, President John Adams stopped. This tavern was for many years the principal stopping-place for the New York mail-coaches. It was destroyed by fire November 6, 1902.

THE OLD MARSHALL HOUSE, CHURCH STREET.

Confiscated by the government after the War of the Revolution, and later bought by Colonel Thomas Marshall, great-uncle of General James F. B. Marshall, who, after service in the Revolutionary War, came here to live. It was later owned by William M. Roberts, who in 1867 sold it to General Charles J. Paine. In 1882 it was moved from its former location on Highland Street to its present site on Church Street by Charles H. Fiske, who now owns and occupies it.

THRIFTY FINANCE OF YE FATHERS 63

Payment made in 1742 Old and Young £11: 11: 10.

	Squirrels.	Old Black Birds.	Young Black Birds.	Other Animals.
Jonas Cutter	8	2	–	
Enoch Garfield	7/3	5	–	1 Grey Squirrel
Timothy Brown	5/3	1	4/3	4 " "
John Gore	2	3	–	
Joseph Brown	4	3/3	–	
Thomas Cory	13	6	–	
James Brown	–	5	1	
B. Munnimont	9/12	2/8	7	
John Jackson	3	–	–	3 young greys
Jonathan Corey	6	2	2/4	
Benjamin Corey	1/5	4	–	
D. Fletcher	38/7	10	1	10 young squirrels
J. Hoadley	43/42	1/4	–	
B. Monroe	20/4	5	–	
Joseph Brooks	15	5	4	
Elisha Cutter	5/48	5	–	
J. Wellington	4	16/6	–	
E. Corey	1	–	–	
Jonas Cutter	6/15	–	4	1 Jay
J. Brooks	8/14	6/13	–	
Timothy Brown	32	13	3	
Benjamin Monroe	42	10	8	
Joseph Brooks	55	34	18	

The military company of Weston was in active duty in 1710. In the diary of the clerk of the company at that time he makes charges on the several training-days of two shillings for the drummers' dinners, and enters the following fines of the rank and file for non-attendance at drills and training-days, viz.:—

July 12, 1710. Received of Thomas Flagg a fine of 3s.
July 15, 1710. Received of Joseph Whitney a fine of 3s.
August 9, 1710. Received of Isaac Modob a fine of 10s.
August 9, 1710. Received of Saml. Severance a fine of 5s.
August 9, 1710. Received of Thomas Flagg a fine of 5s.
October 16, 1710. Received of James Jones a fine of 5s.
October 16, 1710. Received of Benj: Bullard a fine of 5s.

These accounts run from 1710 to 1718, when he resigns and passes all funds in his possession into the hands of Captain Fullam. In the same book is a charge for making town rates for the year 1707,—six days' labor, twelve shillings. This assessor should have lived in our days, and charged one hundred dollars.

His duties were more arduous, probably, considering the times in which he lived, much more so than at the present time, at least judging from the labors of the committee chosen in town meeting to collect the minister's salary. This committee undoubtedly found it very hard work, for we find on Amos Lamson's ledger sundry charges to this committee for rum, brandy, crackers, and cheese, which attest the difficulty they labored under in performing their task.

As has been stated in a previous chapter, great precautions were taken by the town officials, from a very early date, that no persons should be allowed to remain within the town limits who were likely to become a town charge. All persons harboring such persons were liable to a fine, besides which they became responsible for the costs attending their future care. Heads of families were obliged to give notice to the Selectmen of all these unfortunates in their employ, giving their place of birth and the period of their stay. Our records are full under this head from 1756 to the period of the Revolution. And even in our own day great precautions are still taken that strangers from other towns shall not come on the town for support. The following were warned and cautioned out of town:—

1756. Bathsheba Moulton, Jonathan Knight, Christopher Capen, and Mary Priest.
1757. Jonas Bowman, Mary Chubb, Silence Chubb, and Samuel Gooding and wife, from Waltham.
1771. Nathaniel and Lois Parkhurst, wife and daughter, from Waltham.
Jacob Bull, wife and six children, from Cambridge.
Susannah Gage and daughter from Lincoln.
Lucy Jones from Worcester.
Percival Clark, Abijah Hurd and M. Willard from Newton.
Jedediah White, wife and six children, from Watertown.
Reuben Shed from Billerica.
Jeremiah Goodnow, wife and four children, from Marlboro.

And so on. The record book of these warnings is quite full. It is said that such poor folk were sent out from certain towns to other localities to be rid of them, and in the hope that they might gain a foothold somewhere.

Here is another item from the old records which may prove interesting; namely, a table showing date of the erection of some of the early houses in Weston. It is taken from the Natick Historical Records by Horace Mann, Esq., and concerns the houses of:—

Nemiah Williams, 1749
Adam Betty, 1757
Danl. Parks, 1750
William Keny, 1754
William Tenny (?), 1750
Timothy Bemis, 1765
Joseph Underwood, 1748
   (later of Nicholas Boylston)
Saml. Child, 1749
John and Saml. Train, 1738
Joshua Train, 1740
William Train, 1747
James Stimpson, 1756
Samuel Stimpson, 1761
Saml. Jenison, 1754
Nathan Fiske, 1760

Thaddeus Spring, 1760
Jonathan Spring, 1764
Tho: and Epm. Peirce, 1766
Danl. Wyman, 1740
Saml. Severence, 1741
Josiah Coolidge, 1758
   (this is the Schwartz house)
Josiah Smith, 1757
James Livermore, 1750
Saml. Livermore, 1757
   (this is the Albert Hobbs house)
Abraham Gale, 1751
Abraham Jones, 1765
Isaac Jones, 1752
   (Golden Ball Tavern)
William Upham, 1760

The old house which stood where now is located the Richardson farm-house was erected by John Lamson, who came from Reading to Weston in the early years of the eighteenth century. It was probably one of the oldest houses near the centre of the town. The barn, built probably at the same time as the house, was in perfect preservation when taken down by Mr. Cutter, and the oak timbers of it were used in the new house now occupied by Mr. Richardson.

As the custom existed for so many years throughout our country of binding out to apprenticeship (for the purpose of learning a trade) boys averaging the age of twelve or fourteen, usually until they reached the age of twenty-one, it will not be amiss to give here the indenture made between Benjamin Brown, Jr., and Isaac Hobbs, of Weston, in 1762. It is perhaps useless to add in this our day of progress that the boys of this early period started out to make their way well equipped in the knowledge of some trade which rendered them independent in a great measure of the vicissitudes of life. It is a question whether higher education has in every respect placed the rising generation in as favorable a position (taking our young people as a whole) to win their pathway upward and prevail.

This Indenture Witnesseth that I Benjamin Brown Jr. of Lincoln in the County of Middlesex, a minor, Hath put himself, and by these presents doth voluntarily, and of his own free will and accord, and with the consent of his father Benjamin Brown aforesaid, put and bind himself Apprentice to Isaac Hobbs and Mary his wife of Weston in the County aforesaid, to learn tanning and curreing Art, Trade or Mystery, and with the said Isaac & Mary Hobbs after the Manner of an Apprentice, to serve from the 16th day of January A.D. 1762 for and during the term of five years and two months, to be complete and ended: During all which term the said Apprentice the said Isaac Hobbs faithfully shall serve, his secrets keep, his lawful commands gladly everywhere obey; he shall do no damage to the said Isaac Hobbs nor see it to be done of others, without letting or giving Notice thereof to the said Isaac Hobbs, he shall not waste the said Isaac Hobbs' goods, nor lend them unlawfully to any: he shall not commit Fornication, nor contract matrimony within the said term: At Cards, Dice, or any other unlawful game he shall not play, whereby his said master may have damage, with his own goods nor the goods of others: he shall not absent himself by day or by night from his said master's service without his leave; nor haunt alehouses, Taverns, or Play houses, but in all things behave himself as a faithful Apprentice ought to do towards his said master and mistress during the said term of five years and two months. And the said Isaac Hobbs doth hereby covenant and promise to teach and instruct, or cause to be taught and instructed in the Art, Trade, or calling of tanning and curreing by the best ways or means he may or can be taught, (if the said Apprentice be capable to learn) finding unto the said Apprentice suitable meat, drink, washing and lodging (and also to be well instructed in reading, writing and cyphering, during the said term): And at the expiration thereof to give unto the said Apprentice two good suits of apparel for all parts of his body, one for Lord's days the other for common use—suitable for such an apprentice. In Testimony whereof the parties to these presents have hereunto interchangeably set their hands and seals the 16th day of January in the 2d year of the reign of our Sovereign Lord, George the 3d King of Great Britain, A.D. 1762.

VI.

WESTON IN THE REVOLUTION.

1763–1775.

The contest of the colonies with the English Parliament may be said to have begun soon after the peace of 1763, at which period the Indians were generally subdued. We have seen that the French and Indian Wars preceding this date had been excellent training-schools for our inhabitants. The ability of the colonies to defend themselves had been demonstrated,—and that, for the greater part, at their own expense, as whatever recompense they received from the British crown was rarely in money, but mostly in land grants, the Massachusetts troops being allotted lands in the remote sections of the State, then a wilderness.

One thing had been thoroughly shown in these wars, and that was the incompetency of the British generals sent over to command the troops in the subtle warfare of the Indian tribes. The American system of "bushwhacking" (a word that has become historical since the War of the Rebellion), at which the colonists had become adepts in their Indian experiences, was incomprehensible to these foreign soldiers. Our colonists soon discovered that their own officers were better able to conduct military operations and lead them to victory than the titled aristocrats of England. From all this it was but a step for them to discover their ability to maintain their independence of all foreign control. The wars that England had been called upon to sustain on the Continent for a quarter of a century had impoverished its treasury, and Parliament undertook to tax the colonies, and thereby in a short space of time succeeded in utterly alienating the people from the mother country.

The Stamp Act of the year 1765 may be regarded as the beginning of our Revolution. Whatever previous Acts had been attempted in the way of taxation had not materially touched the distant sections away from tide-water. The effect of the Stamp Act upon the agricultural population was necessarily insignificant, and the country towns were slow in responding to the stirring appeals of Samuel Adams and James Otis. A great gloom had settled over Massachusetts. The courts were closed and business was at a standstill. There is no record by which we can judge of the effect of the Stamp Act on Weston. Perhaps its influence may have been modified by the fact that a similar Act had been passed by the province of Massachusetts in the January session of the General Court in 1755, and possibly the English Act may not have had the influence with the people of the country towns it otherwise would have had but for this previous tax. This Act of Massachusetts of 1755 may be found in Volume XIV. of the State Register of that year, together with a description of the stamps used at that period. To give an idea of the magnitude and importance of the Act of 1765: blank bail-bonds had been sold before the Act for £15 the ream; stamped bonds cost £100; a ream of insurance bonds or policies that formerly cost £20 were under the Act to cost £190. The effect of this law was to cause the settlement of lawsuits and disputes by arbitration rather than through the medium of the courts.

The only mention in the Weston town records of the Boston riots, which grew out of the Stamp Act, is found in the account of the November meeting of that year, when the town voted that Samuel Phillips Savage, Elisha Jones, and Captain John Brown should be a committee to draw up instructions to their representative Abraham Bigelow in relation to these riots, and the committee reported as follows:—

The Town directs you to give your vote in the General Assembly to make full compensation to the late sufferers in the Town of Boston, by the rioters on the 27 day of August 1765, that they be paid out of the public Treasury: and that you also do your best endeavour that the same be replaced in the Treasury by action against the said rioters.

The custom prevailed before the Revolution, and during a period somewhat later, for the inhabitants in town meeting, throughout New England, to draw up instructions for their representatives to follow at the General Court, regulating their action and their votes on particular subjects of general interest. These instructions were always obeyed, and it was not infrequently that the representatives were called upon to explain their action in certain cases before a town meeting. Such action on the part of towns has now become obsolete, and, in fact, would be universally resented to-day on the part of public servants. The town meetings are of purely New England origin, at least so far as this continent is concerned, and they have had more to do with the foundation of our institutions and government, both State and Federal, than has been sufficiently considered or credited to them.* With us here they were the outgrowth of the church assemblies and conferences. Our earliest records are those of the precincts, presided over by elders and governed by church regulations. No man could vote in precinct or town affairs, or be made a freeman, unless a member of the church in good standing. Town meetings originated here, at our own doors. They are the best examples of pure democracy that are left to us throughout New England. Nor do they vary essentially from what they were a century ago. All tax-payers had an equal voice in matters pertaining to public affairs. They voted their own taxes and all money for public purposes, and kept a keen eye on appropriations and expenditures. They held all town officers to a strict accountability in the performance of their respective duties. Massachusetts has never lost her attachment to this system of self-government, and it would be well if all the people could act upon its principles to-day as strictly as was formerly the case. The large increase in population has interfered in too many cases with the direct action of the people at large in public affairs. Political machinery has now intervened between the people and their purposes and responsibilities. The power once emanating

* To the town meetings of New England more than to anything else are due the supremacy of the English in America and the failure of the French to hold their own during the long struggle for the possession of Canada. In the next and harder struggle, that for independence of Great Britain itself, the towns again had a decisive part. When Governor Bernard, the royal governor, obedient to his instructions from home, prorogued the Assembly, and left the province of Massachusetts without a legislature, the king and his ministers thought by this course they had deprived the patriots of their opportunity for concentrated action and that they could nip in the bud the incipient rebellion. And so it would have proved, had it not been for the town meetings, which were the real fountain of power, so that in place of one General Assembly the royal governor found he had to deal with two hundred or more local assemblies, small, indeed, for the most part, but self-reliant, aggressive, trained to the consideration of public affairs, and ready for action.

directly from the people has become a delegated power, and the party caucus now usurps the place once held by them. The rage for municipal government has become the fashion, and, in so far as this delegated power gains foothold, in that ratio the people lose their hold and their interest in town meetings. Without these town meetings and the direct action which they had upon public affairs, it is doubtful if the Revolution would have been successful. The public spirit and love of freedom, together with the jealousy with which the charter rights of the colony were held and maintained, were the means by which men and money were provided to carry out the war, and which no action of the weak Provincial Congress could have accomplished. Middlesex County took the lead in all the preliminary acts that led up to the Revolution. To Samuel Adams and James Otis is due in great part the inspiration which gave nerve to the actions of the town meetings of that period. In this again we see the conservative influences of these town meetings. While the Boston leaders of the advocates of rebellion against the Acts of the British Parliament were sending out letters and broadsides calling upon the towns to back them up in their daring attacks upon the existing royal government, the towns were backward in taking any hasty action. They calmly calculated the chances and costs. The Stamp Act, the Tea Party, and the Boston Massacre (or the mobs as some old heads, who should know better, now call the defensive acts of our forefathers) do not seem to have created any very marked ruffle on the calm surface of the Weston town meetings. In fact, they are nowhere mentioned on the records. It required the march of the British regulars on Lexington and Concord to arouse the sleeping lion, who, when once thoroughly aroused, as was the case on the ever memorable 19th of April, never again drew in his claws until every shred of British and royal dominion had been torn to pieces, —to the regret, it would seem, of some of our latter-day historical oracles. In speaking of the famous Tea Party, we must not overlook two of our townsmen who figured on that occasion. Samuel Phillips Savage, of Weston, was made moderator of an adjourned meeting held in the Old South Church in Boston on December 14, 1773, called to consider the question of the introduction of the tea into Boston. Mr. Savage continued as moderator of the meetings until the evening of the 16th, when the tea was steeped in the salt water of Boston Harbor. Samuel Hobbs, also of Weston, at work in Roxbury as a journeyman in Simeon Pratt's tannery, took part in throwing the tea overboard.

The most important steps taken to arouse the dormant sense of the country towns to the coming storm was the action of Samuel Adams at Faneuil Hall in Boston on the 20th of November, 1772, at which meeting was organized the famous Committee of Correspondence, the influence of which was to play so great a part in the plan of resistance. A letter was forwarded to the selectmen of the various towns, expressing a belief that the wisdom of the people would not "suffer them to doze or sit supinely indifferent, on the brink of destruction." In a few days many towns sent in their adhesion to the plan proposed. This Committee of Correspondence was a sharp thorn in the side of the officers of the crown, and was particularly obnoxious to the Tory element. They looked upon it "as the foulest, subtilest, and most venomous serpent ever issued from the egg of sedition." This secret correspondence was not confined to Massachusetts or to New England, but spread throughout the neighboring and distant colonies, and became the means of uniting all the people of the continent.

At a town meeting held in the month of March, 1773, Colonel Elisha Jones was elected to represent the town in the General Court for the following year. The Liberty Men of the town took umbrage at his election, as Colonel Jones was a strong and bitter Tory, and some of the most prominent among them drew up the following protest, which was sent to the House of Representatives:—

To THE HONORABLE HOUSE OF REPRESENTATIVES SITTING AT BOSTON
June 8th, 1773.

Humbly shews the Subscribers, Inhabitants of Weston; That Hon[ble] House after Declaring the late choice of a Representative in Weston to be illegable, ordered a Precept to issue to the Selectmen of said Town Directing them forthwith to assemble the Inhabitants thereof, in order to elect some person to Represent them, in the Present Session of the General Court, as well as the Remaining Sessions of the year, and the said Selectmen were possessed of said Precept on the last day of May last, but have taken no other notice thereof than to propose a meeting of their own, some time about the middle of this month of June: Then to determine whether they will give the Town an opportunity to chose a member or not; which conduct of the Selectmen gives great uneasiness to the Inhabitants of Weston, as we are thereby deprived of the Priviledge of a Representative in the General Court, which other towns enjoy, and we esteem a priviledge which we desire to share in. Therefore we humbly pray that the Honble House would take our circumstances into their wise consideration and releive us from such arbitrary proceedings, by directing the said Selectmen to appoint a meeting for the purpose aforesaid. And also appoint some suitable, impartial gentleman to preside at said Meeting as in duty Bound will ever pray.

    [Sd]   JONATHAN BULLARD   JACOB MIRRICK
           ISAAC JONES   JOSEPH HARRINGTON Jr.
           ELISHA HARRINGTON   PHINEHAS UPHAM
           JOHN FLAGG   SAMUEL TRAIN
           JONATHAN STRATTON   ASA SMITH
           WILLIAM LAWRANCE   JOHN MIRICK
           JONAS SANDERSON   SAMUEL CHILD
           DANIEL LIVERMORE

Weston did not appoint a Committee of Correspondence until the town meeting of September 29, 1774, when Benjamin Peirce, Thomas Upham, and Samuel Baldwin were chosen such a committee. Somewhat later a Committee of Public Safety was added to that of Correspondence. There is no record of the doings of the Weston Committee of Correspondence, if we except an entry in Force's Archives, vol. iii., 4th Series, where mention is made of a letter addressed by Benjamin Peirce to Rev. Asa Dunbar under date of September 8, 1775, in which exceptions are taken to remarks made by him in a sermon delivered on Fast Day. These remarks were distasteful to the Liberty Men, and against them they entered complaint.* As there is

---

* An occurrence took place in April, 1774, which displayed the courage and open avowal of resistance to the royal government. In 1722 the government, in order to render the judges of the Supreme Court independent of the people of the province, made provision for their being in future paid out of the royal exchequer. The power and dignity of this court as then conducted was very imposing, and raised it above the ordinary criticism with which the other branches of the government were discussed. In view of the unlimited power of this court to fine and imprison such as presumed to disturb the course of its proceedings, it is difficult to imagine the gravity of a measure which had for its purpose to assail one of its members, and that in the person of its chief justice. Chief Justice Oliver alone had accepted his salary

no record of any Mr. Dunbar among the clergy of this section, he was probably a stranger to the town.* At the town meeting of September 29 Captain Elisha Jones, being a Tory, was recalled as the representative of the town at the General Court, and Captain Braddyll Smith was appointed in his place.

At this meeting Josiah Smith and Samuel Phillips were appointed to attend the Provincial Congress at Concord to be held October 2, and Captain Braddyll Smith was added to go with them. No instructions were given to their representatives at Concord. The session was, for a great part of the time, held in secret, and adjourned after three days to meet at Cambridge, October 17. The Congress at Cambridge lasted eleven days, and was presided over by John Hancock. It undertook to frame a form of government for the people, but to this Weston refused its consent. The Congress appointed a Committee of Public Safety, composed of nine persons, with power to call out the militia, if necessary; also a committee of five persons with power to procure cannon, muskets, and ammunition, and to provide stores for the troops that the Committee of Safety might call into service. They appointed five commanders of regiments, viz.: Jedediah Preble, of Falmouth; Artemas Ward, of Shrewsbury; Seth Pomeroy, of Northampton; John Thomas, of Marshfield; and William Heath, of Roxbury.

The question has often been asked, By whom and by what authority were issued the commissions of general officers at the beginning of the Revolution? Previous to that period, commissions were issued by the secretary or deputy secretary and countersigned by the royal governor. The last commission under the crown to the Third Middlesex Regiment, appointing Nathan Barrett, of Concord, senior major of the regiment,

from the crown, and in consequence had made himself the object of general odium. The term of the court was to be held in April, 1774, at Worcester. A panel of fifteen jurors attended. Instead of offering themselves, as usual, to be sworn as jurors, they handed the court a written protest, signed by them all, in which they refused to act as jurors if Chief Justice Oliver was to act as one of the judges, and they declare that "by his own confession he stands convicted, in the minds of the people, of a crime more heinous than any that might come before him." Fortunately, for some unknown reason, he did not attend the term of the court.

* The editor of this posthumous history of Weston finds on a slip of paper in the manuscript the following note, presumably intended by Colonel Lamson to be inserted here: It is, however, known that a Rev. Asa Dunbar, of Salem, married Mary, a daughter of Colonel Elisha Jones, of Weston, October 22, 1772.

and dated February 14, 1776, is signed by Perez Morton, deputy secretary, and countersigned on the margin by the members of the council, beginning at the top of the commission. On the 3d of May, 1776, Major Barrett is made lieutenant-colonel of the same regiment, but there is no mention of King George in this commission. It is issued by a majority of the council, and signed by J. Avery, deputy secretary. This council was composed of the following persons: Joseph Powell, Artemas Ward, William Spooner, H. Gordon, Benjamin Austin, A. Fuller, T. W. Dana, Samuel Niles, Jos. Stimpson, John Pitts, Eleazer Brooks, Oliver Wendell, Oliver Prescott.

The commission of 1781, making Francis Faulkner colonel of the Third Regiment, is dated July 1, 1781, and is issued by John Hancock, governor and commander-in-chief, countersigned by him and signed by the Secretary of State.

The Congress of Cambridge elected Henry Gardner, of Stow, as treasurer and receiver-general, in place of Harrison Gray, who was treasurer under the crown. Orders were issued that all funds and taxes in the hands of collectors, throughout the province, should be paid over to Henry Gardner instead of being paid into the royal treasury.

At a town meeting held January 2, 1775, John Allen, Israel Whittemore, and William Whitney were chosen a Committee of Inspection to enforce the non-importation agreement of 1770, and they were ordered to report the names of any or all persons who may have disobeyed the injunction. Tar and feathers were sure to follow any Tory disobedience of town-meeting ordinances.

At this meeting it was ordered that £45 6s. 6d., which was Weston's proportion of the province tax for 1774, be paid by the town treasurer into the hands of Henry Gardner, Esq., and that he take his receipt in full for the same. The town also voted to hold their treasurer free from all personal liability in the matter.

Colonel Braddyll Smith was again delegated to represent the town at the Provincial Congress to be held at Cambridge on February 1. The Middlesex County was represented by forty members. Congress adjourned to meet at Concord, March 22,

WESTON IN THE REVOLUTION 75

and continued its sessions in that town until April 15, four days before the British attack on the town.*

As we approach the period of the battle of Concord, we find that the "Liberty Men" were wide-awake and watchful of all the movements of the British troops in Boston. A thorough system of information had been established by means of beacon lights and other effective means. This organization does not appear to have been established upon any given rules or by any body of leaders, either in Boston or elsewhere, but rather to have been the spontaneous action of the Liberty Men generally, and in each town, who passed the word of warning one to another. In fact, the acts of all suspicious persons were made known far and wide with a promptness which is surprising. Each Tory household was as carefully watched in the country towns as were the British in Boston, and to this is due the little aid the British general received from them. The Tories considered their lives and property at the mercy of the Liberty Men. This rendered them apprehensive and timid, discouraging them from taking part in the defence of the crown, which they otherwise would have been inclined to do. The Journal of John Howe, who was a sergeant in the British army, relates the adventures of only one of three parties sent out over different routes by General Gage early in April, 1775, to discover what arms, ammunition, and provisions were in the hands of the rebels. Howe's Journal is particularly interesting to us of Weston, as the town played a conspicuous part in defeating the original plan of the British general. This was, namely, a movement of troops to secure the stores of the Continentals at Worcester. The spy's report was very unfavorable as to the possibility of reaching Worcester, the roads being unfit for transportation of artillery and, above all, dangerous in consequence of the general preparation of the people to repel an invasion. Howe's report was instrumental in changing General Gage's original plan to attack Worcester, and at the

* The records of the Secretary of State give the following account of the different congresses. The first congress was held at Salem, October 7, 1774; then at Concord, October 11, 1774, adjourned to October 15; at Cambridge, October 17, 1774, adjourned to December 10; at Cambridge, February 1, 1775, adjourned to February 16; at Concord, March 22, 1775, adjourned to April 15; at Concord, April 22, 1775, adjourned to the same day; at Watertown, April 24, 1775, adjourned to May 29; at Watertown, May 31, 1775, adjourned to July 19.

last moment Concord was made the objective point. So much of Howe's Journal (printed by Luther Roby, Concord, N.H., 1827), which is somewhat long, as has connection with Weston, is here given in condensed abstract:—

On April 5, Howe was selected to accompany Colonel Smith who was to examine the road, bridges, and fording places and discover the best route to Worcester for an armed force to march and destroy the stores and ammunition deposited there. Howe goes on to state: We dressed ourselves as Countrymen, with grey coats [probably frocks], leather breeches, and blue mixed stockings, with flag handkerchiefs round our necks, a small bundle tied up in a homespun handkerchief in one hand and a walking stick in the other. Thus equipped we set out like Countrymen to find work. At Watertown where we stopped at the tavern for breakfast, a negro woman recognized Colonel Smith, and when he asked her if she could tell him where he could find work, she looked him in the face, and said, "Smith, you will find employment enough for you and all General Gage's men in a few months." Smith was thunder-struck, my own feelings were not much better; the black woman had been living in Boston and had acted as washerwoman for the British officers, and thus recognized Smith. We travelled about one mile and found the road good: here we got over a wall out of sight to consult what was best to be done. It was not safe for Smith to continue on, he gave me his book, pencil and ten guineas and returned to Boston, leaving me to pursue the route. Smith said if he came out with his regiment over that road he would kill that black wench. He also told me if I got through all right he would insure me a Commission. The last I saw of him, he was running through the barbary bushes to keep out of sight. I found the road good to Waltham Plain. Here I pretended to be a gunsmith and was told to go to Springfield, where they wanted guns, as they expected the regulars out of Boston, and they meant to be ready for them. I took some rum and molasses, knowing it to be a Yankee drink. From the plain I found the roads hilly, stony and crooked for about three miles, when I came to a hollow with a narrow causeway over it [Stony Brook]; here I left the road and went below to see if there was any place where our artillery could cross, but found none. I examined above and found it bad. Here I saw a negro setting traps: about ten feet from this narrow road stood the largest buttonwood tree I ever saw. The negro said that the people were going to cut it down to stop the regulars from crossing with their cannon. [This tree stood on the edge of the little pond near the house of Mr. Turner.] I asked him how they would know when the regulars were coming in time to cut the tree down. He said they had men all the time at Cambridge and Charlestown watching them. This tree would completely blockade the road. I asked the negro how far it was to a tavern; he said a mile, by Weston Meeting house, and another half a mile above, the first kept by Joel Smith [now house of Mrs. John Jones], a good tavern and a good liberty man; the other was kept by Captain Isaac Jones, a wicked Tory, and said a good many British officers go there from Boston. I found the road to Smith's hilly, stony and crooked. Came to Smith's tavern, where two teamsters were tackling their teams. I asked them if they knew of any one who wanted to hire; one of them answered, he did not know of any body who wanted to hire an Englishman, for they believed I was one: they said I looked like them rascals they see in Boston. I went into the house and asked for a drink of rum and molasses, one of the men followed me and told Smith he guessed I was a British spy. Smith questioned me very closely, where I was from and where I was going. He sent me to Captain Jones who kept a tavern at the sign of the Golden Ball. I handed Captain Jones a letter from General Gage. He took me by the hand and invited me up stairs. I informed him of all that had taken place since I left Boston: it being fourteen miles. He told me it would not do for me to stay at his house over night, for his house would be mobbed and I would be taken a prisoner. He gave me some dinner and sent me by his hired man to the house of one Wheaton in a remote part of the town, where I must remain, until he sent for me [the Dr. Wheaton house is now that of Mr. Ripley]. The man told Dr. Wheaton I was a British spy. I was conducted into a chamber, where I found a bottle of Brandy, candles and paper. I went to work to write up my journal. The next day Captain Jones' man came and told me that the news of what had occurred at Watertown between Col. Smith and the black woman had reached Captain Jones's in the night, by the same teamsters that had seen me at the Smith tavern. By eleven o'clock that night some thirty men had collected at the Jones tavern [with tar and feathers.] Capt. Jones gave them permission to search the house. The black girl told them some persons had been sent into Jericho swamp. After dinner Dr. Wheaton introduced me to his two daughters as a British officer in disguise and we played cards until tea time. That night Captain Jones's man came to take me to Marlboro'. We came out on the road about a mile above Jones's on the Worcester road. I found the roads good to the Sudbury river, twenty-five miles from Boston. I examined the river for a fording place, should the bridge be destroyed, and found a fordable place in Framingham. We went to the house of Squire Barnes [Barnes had married Jones' daughter]. I gave him a letter from General Gage. He had already heard of the Watertown affair. I had also been seen examining the bridge over Sudbury river. Squire Barnes gave me an account of the militia and ammunition from Worcester to Weston. While we were talking, a knock came at the door. He told me if he did not return at once to make my escape out of the window and make for the swamp and go to Concord. When I leaped upon the shed, snow

having fallen, I fell to the ground on my back. Picking up my bundle
and hat, I ran for the swamp. When I got away some distance, I looked
back and could see lights dodging at every window. [The people were
searching the house for him. Having got to Concord, he falls in with
Major Buttrick and Major Parmenter, who invite him to dinner and then
take him to the storehouses to see the guns, as he pretends to be a gunsmith. He examines closely the doors and locks of the storehouses, and
sets off for Lexington on pretence of getting his tools. He reaches Boston
on the 12th, and makes his report to General Gage, who takes his papers
and gives him fifty guineas.] The General asked me how large an army
it would take to get to Worcester and return safe. I told him if he should
send 10,000 men and a train of artillery to Worcester, which is 48 miles,
the inhabitants generally determined to be free or die, that not one of
them would get back alive. Here Smith exclaimed, "Howe has been
scared by the old women." Major Pitcairn said not by a negro wench
anyway, which turned the laugh on Smith. The General asked what I
thought of destroying the stores at Concord, only eighteen miles. I told
him a force of 500 mounted men might go in the night and return safe,
but to go with 1,000 foot, the greater part would be killed or taken. He
asked me what I thought of the Tories. I told him they were generally
cowards and no dependence was to be placed on them.—Howe was engaged on the 18th of April to carry letters to the Tories in Malden,
Lynn, and Marblehead. He arrived at Concord in the midst of the fight
on the 19th, and was sent back to Boston for reinforcements.*

Regardless of Howe's admonitions, General Gage sent out
to Concord infantry instead of cavalry, and the result was not
far different from that predicted by the spy.

The news that the "British are coming!" passes from town to
town with the speed of a modern telegram. Parson Woodward,
of Weston, sends his family into the woods for safety, and they
drive their cow with them. Mrs. Woodward seizes a skillet as
she leaves the house, telling the children they may need it. The
Weston company gathers at the house of Captain Samuel Lamson, then situated where now stands the farm-house on the
Richardson place, and Parson Woodward after a prayer takes
his gun and falls into the ranks with the men. Numbering one
hundred men and three officers, they strike for Concord over
Lamson's Hill. On their way they meet a man on horseback,
probably Howe, the spy, who tells them the British are driven

* Mrs. E. T. Lamson, of Weston, mother of D. S. Lamson, remembered seeing Mr. Howe
when she was a young girl in Boston.—Ed.

THE COBURN HOMESTEAD, CHURCH STREET.

This estate came into the possession of Mr. Jonas Coburn in 1801. It was formerly owned by Mr. Aaron Whittemore. For many years and until his death it was the home of Mr. Isaac Coburn, and is still owned by his descendants.

THE OLD NATHAN HAGAR HOUSE, NORTH AVENUE, CORNER OF CHURCH STREET.

Built in 1786 by Deacon Isaac Hobbs, Jr., whose daughter married Nathan Hagar. Their descendants still own and occupy the house. The land has been in the possession of the same family for one hundred and eighty-three years.

out of Concord, and directs them to go through the woods to the Lexington road, where the company strike the retreating British and follow them to Charlestown.

The Muster-roll of Captain Samuel Lamson's Militia Company.*

	Length of Service in Days.		Length of Service in Days.
Captain		David Sanderson	3
Samuel Lamson	3	Abraham Harrington	"
		John Walker Jr	"
Lieutenants.		Saml. Underwood	"
Jonathan Fiske	"	Eben Brackett	"
Mathew Hobbs	"	Oliver Curtis	"
		Josiah Corey	"
Sergeants.		Reuben Hobbs	"
Josiah Steadman	"	Thomas Rand	"
Josiah Seaverns	"	Thomas Rand Jr	"
John Wright	"	Benjamin Rand	"
Abraham Hews	"	Benjamin Peirce	"
		David Fuller	"
Corporals.		Saml. Child	"
Abijah Steadman	"	David Livermore	"
Simeon Smith	"	Jonas Harrington 3d	"
		Jacob Parmenter	"
Drummer.		Thomas Corey	"
Samuel Nutting	"	Roger Bigelow	"
Privates.		Elijah Kingsberry	"
Nathan Hager	"	Jonas Underwood	"
Jonathan Stratton	"	Convers Bigelow	"
Isaiah Bullard	"	William Bigelow	"
John Allen Jr	"	John Stimpson	"
John Warren Jr	"	Thomas Williams	"
Jonathan Warren	"	Increase Leadbetter	"
Wm. Hobart	"	Elisha Stratton	"
Micah Warren	"	Isaac Hobbs	"
John Frost	"	Benjamin Bancroft	"
Abijah Warren	"	Samuel Twitchell	"
Isaac Flagg	"	William Bond Jr	"
Isaac Walker	"	John Flint	"
Isaac Cory	"	John Norcross	"
James Jones	"	William Cary	"
Amos Jones	"	John Bemis	"

* The company marched from Weston under Lamson's command on the 19th of April, 1775. See Lexington Alarm List, vol. xii. p. 170.

	Length of Service in Days.		Length of Service in Days.
Daniel Lawrence	3	John Gould	7
Jedediah Bemis	"	John Lamson	"
Lemuel Stimpson	"	Solomon Jones	"
Benjamin Dudley	"	Phineas Hager	"
William Lawrance	"	Paul Coolidge	"
Nathaniel Parkhurst	"	Samuel Taylor	"
Samuel Fiske	"	Jos. Lovewell	"
Elias Bigelow	4	Peter Cary	"
William Whitney	7	Thaddeus Fuller	"
Abraham Sanderson	"	Joseph Peirce	"
Samuel Train Jr	"	Samuel Woodward	"
Josiah Allen Jr	"	Elijah Allen	"
Daniel Benjamin	"	Hezekiah Wyman	"
Joseph Whitney	"	Ebenezer Steadman	"
Jos. Steadman	"	William Bond	"
Jonas Peirce	"	Joel Smith	"
Nathaniel Boynton	"	Joseph Jennison	"
Eben Phillips	"	Moses Peirce	"
Jedediah Wheeler	"	Daniel Bemis	"
Benjamin Peirce	"	Daniel Stratton	"
John Peirce	"	Amos Parkhurst	"
William Jones	"		

Muster-roll of Captain Israel Whittemore's Militia Company of Artillery.*

Names.	Residence.	Rank.	March.	One Penny a Mile.	Services.	Travel.
Israel Whittemore.	Weston	Captain	Apl. 19	2:10	4 days	34 miles
Josiah Bigelow.	"	Lieutenant	"	2:10	4 "	"
John George.	"	2d Lieut.	"	2:10	3 "	"
John Whitehead.	"	Private	"	2:10	4 "	"
John Pownall.	"	"	"	2:10	3 "	"
Nathan Weston.	"	"	"	2:10	3 "	"
Joseph Russell.	"	"	"	2:10	—	"
Nathan Smith.	"	"	"	2:10	3 "	"
John Flagg.	"	"	"	2:10	3 "	"
Jonathan Lawrance.	"	"	"	2:10	2 "	"
James Smith Jr.	"	"	"	2:10	2 "	"
Thaddeus Garfield.	"	"	"	2:10	4 "	"
Alpheus Bigelow.	"	"	"	2:10	3 "	"
Thomas Russell.	"	"	"	2:10	4 "	"

Sd Israel Whittemore,
Captain.

* This company also marched from Weston to Concord on the 19th of April, 1775. The total amount paid for their services was £5 17s. 2d. See State Records, vol. 13, fol. 20. Examined and compared by Josiah Johnson and Jonas Dix, Committee.

WESTON IN THE REVOLUTION

A new organization of the militia was made in February, 1776. The Third Middlesex Regiment was composed of three companies in Concord, Weston, Lexington, Acton, and Lincoln. Eleazer Brooks of Lincoln was colonel, Francis Faulkner lieutenant-colonel, Nathan Barrett of Concord first major, and Samuel Lamson of Weston second major, Joseph Adams surgeon. On Monday, March 13, 1775, there was a review of all the militia held at Concord, and a week later at Acton. Congress ordered that provisions and military stores sufficient for 15,000 men should be collected at Concord and Worcester.

Charlestown sent 20 loads, containing 20,000 pounds of musket-balls and cartridges, 206 tents, 113 spades, 51 axes, 201 bill-hooks, 19 sets of harness, 14 chests of medicine, 27 hogsheads of wooden ware, 1 hogshead matches, and 20 bushels of oatmeal. Boston sent 11 loads, containing 150 tents, axes, hatchets, spades, wooden spoons and dishes, 47 firkins and 2 barrels butter, and 80 barrels of beef. Marblehead sent 14 hogsheads, containing 35 half-barrels of powder, 318 barrels of flour (a part of this flour was destroyed on April 19), 7 loads of salt fish (17,000 pounds), 18 casks of wine, 47 hogsheads and 50 barrels of salt, 4 loads of tents, 1 bundle of sheet lead, several hogsheads of molasses, and a quantity of linen. Salem sent 35,000 pounds of rice. Nor is this all the stores that were collected. On April 18 these stores were ordered to be divided in nine different towns. One-third was kept in Concord, one-third in Sudbury, and one-third in Stowe. 1,000 iron pots were sent to Worcester.

At the battle of Concord and during the retreat of the British to Charlestown, of the provincials 49 men were killed, 36 wounded, and 5 missing. Captains Charles Mills, Nathan Barrett, Jonas Brown, and Abel Prescott, Jr., were wounded. Captains Isaac Davis, Abner Hosmer, and James Hayward, of Acton, were killed. Luther Blanchard was wounded, Captain Wilson, of Bedford, killed, and Job Lane wounded.

Of the British 73 were killed, 172 wounded, and 26 missing. Among these were 18 officers, 10 sergeants, 2 drummers, and 240 of the rank and file. It is stated that none of those taken prisoners returned to the British army.

The files of the Provincial Congress give the loss at Lexington of property destroyed by the British on the 19th of April as £2,576 2s.,—real estate £615 10s., and personal £1,960 12s. But as this estimate was made in 1782, or seven years after the fight, the Selectmen state that the loss and damage could not be ascertained at that date.

The battle of Bunker Hill on June 17, following the fight at Concord, closed all political connection of the colonies with the British government. While that battle was a virtual defeat of the Continental forces, the victory, if so it can be called, of the ministerial party, was of the kind that in their results overturn empires, as was proved in this case. The news of this battle was taken to England by Captain Derby, of Salem. He reached England in advance of General Gage's official report. The news created a great sensation throughout the country. A strong sympathy was manifested for the Americans, and a London paper of that date states that a subscription of £100 had been raised for the benefit of the widows and orphans of the brave Americans who had been inhumanly murdered by the king's soldiers. The records of the town of Weston make no mention of there having been any of its inhabitants in the battle of Bunker Hill. Mr. Abraham Hews, our former postmaster, once told the writer that he remembered, when a boy, sitting on his father's doorstep and hearing the report of the guns that were being fired on that day.

At a town meeting held on the 25th of May, 1775, Colonel Braddyll Smith was chosen to represent the town at a Provincial Congress to be held in Watertown on the 31st of May, and to continue as their representative for six months and no longer; "to consult, deliberate, and resolve upon such further measures as under God shall be effectual to save this people from ruin." It was also voted later that Colonel Smith should use his influence to raise more men "to defend our lines against our enemies."

It may be well here to consider the drift of the country at this time. Our grandfathers looked upon themselves as Englishmen, and were proud of England. Their determination to resist unjust measures and laws which were infringements on their charter rights (which charter they had received at the hands of the king alone) was not associated in their minds with the idea of a separation or disaffection towards England and the king. The possibility of contending against the mother country by force of arms was thought impracticable, and not until after Concord fight and the battle of Bunker Hill did the Liberty Men of the country feel confident of success. Throughout the Revolution such facts as that the Tory element openly sympathized with the enemy; that the timid among our own people feared the country had been led too far on the road to a contest which would ultimately lead to destruction; that there existed a state of depression over defeat and want; and that universal uncertainty prevailed, the friends of freedom being goaded by the satire and ridicule of the Loyalists everywhere,—such things as these, I say, can be little understood at the present day. From the commencement two men, above all others, seem to have had a clear purpose and unfailing confidence in the result, and to have inspired others both with energy and courage in the fight for freedom. They were George Washington and Samuel Adams. At the beginning of the Revolution, Massachusetts was entitled to have one of its officers appointed to the command of the army, the more so as the contest was within her territory; but she relinquished her claim to Virginia, and Washington was made commander-in-chief. The appointment of Washington to supreme command was a great disappointment to John Hancock, who felt he was entitled to that position; but that he was not qualified for so exalted a position was best exemplified by his display of wounded self-esteem and his want of courtesy towards Washington. Washington arrived in Cambridge on July 2, 1775, and, while his headquarters were being prepared for him in the Vassal house, he was entertained at the expense of the Congress sitting in Watertown. Congress provided him with a steward and cooks. The following bill paid by Congress (Journal of Congress, pp. 493-495) goes to show that not all the spirits and old Madeira, not all the lemons and loaf sugar, were in control of the British in Boston. Washington could not have depended on the Prohibition vote, had he lived in our day. Temperance, as now understood, had little to do with the making or unmaking of our great men a century ago. President Lincoln was about right. When told of General Grant's intemperate habits, he inquired what liquor he drank, as he would like to send some of it to other generals he could name. The bill above alluded to is sufficiently curious to be given here:—

GENERAL WASHINGTON & CO.   TO SOLOMON LOTHROP.   Dr.

To 6 Bottles of Madeira	£1:10:0
" 5 Dozen Lemons	1:3:10¼
" 6¾ lbs. Loaf Sugar	0:11:3
" 7 Quarts Brandy	14:0
" 24 Dinners	2:8:0
" 7 Ditto for Servants	10:6
" 1 Bowl of Punch	1:4
" 1 Gallon Spirits	8:0
" 13 Suppers	16:9
" 2 Quarts Spirits	4:0
" 13 Breakfasts	16:9
" 1 man to make Liquor	3:0
" 6 Bottles of Madeira	1:10:0
" 1 Dozen Lemons	4:9½
" 5 Do. Do.	1:5:0
" 3 Bottles Jamaica Rum	6:0
" 1 Bottle West India Rum	1:4
" 12 Bottles Madeira	3:0:0

and so on, a long list, amounting to £24 6s. 9d. Congress cannot be accused of overlooking the spiritual condition of the staff.*

Washington took command of the forces before Boston on July 3. He found an army destitute of every munition of war,— of powder, in particular. The powder-house at Mystic was for the greater part stored with barrels which, instead of containing powder, were filled with sand, the better to deceive the enemy, should a spy by chance look in. Watson, in his reminiscences, tells some amusing stories of the motley gathering of inexperienced men, assembled to defend their country, animated with zeal and patriotism, but entirely ignorant of military discipline. While passing through the camp, he overheard a dialogue between a captain of the militia and one of his privates, which well illustrates the character of the army. "Bill," said the captain,

---

* When General Washington was on his way to take command of the army at Cambridge, he passed over our Weston road with his staff, and stopped for dinner at the Baldwin tavern in Wayland. Mrs. Baldwin made great preparations for the dinner, but, much to her disgust, Washington went into her kitchen and asked for a bowl of bread and milk [or corn mush and milk?] which he ate there, leaving his staff to eat the formal dinner. This tavern was burned, but the property is yet in the Baldwin family.

"go and bring a pail of water for the mess." "I shan't do it," was Bill's reply. "It is your turn now, captain: I got the last one." Even the elements of subordination had then scarcely been introduced. Officers and men had rushed to the field under the ardent impulse of a common patriotism, and the selection of the officers by the troops (or their appointment) was rather accidental and temporary than controlled by any regard to superior qualifications. All the warlike stores in Massachusetts on April 14, 1775, according to a return made by the several towns, were little more than half a pound of powder to a man, as shown herewith:—

Fire Arms	21,549
Pounds of Powder	17,441
Pounds of Ball	22,191
No. of Flints	144,699
" " Bayonets	10,108
" " Pouches	11,979

In a Weston town meeting held June 18, 1776, it was voted by the citizens to instruct their representative to use his influence for independence from Great Britain, "if the Honorable Congress thinks it best for the interests of the Colony." The town also voted that their representative should not be paid out of the public chest, which was still in the hands of the royal governor. At the May meeting it had been voted that he should be allowed four shillings a day out of the town rates for one hundred and thirty-seven days' services in the Congress. At this meeting Major Lamson receipts for the use of two guns belonging to the town 12s., and also for powder, ball, and flints from Selectmen amounting to £23 10s. 2d.* General Washington having decided to fortify Dorchester Heights, and thus command the city of Boston and force Lord Howe to evacuate that city, which he had held for

---

* Mr. Shattuck, in his valuable and now exceedingly rare book giving the history of Concord, says (p. 353): "A new organization of the militia was made in February, 1776, and Concord, Lexington, Weston, Acton, and Lincoln were assigned to the Third Middlesex Regiment in Oliver Prescott's brigade, Eleazer Brooks, colonel, Francis Faulkner, lieutenant-colonel, Nathan Barrett, first major, and Samuel Lamson, second major, Joseph Adams, surgeon. The captain of the Weston company was Jonathan Fiske; Matthew Hobbs, first lieutenant; Josiah Seavers, second lieutenant. In March, 1780, the Weston company was commanded by Matthew Hobbs; Josiah Livermore, first lieutenant; and Daniel Livermore, second lieutenant."

a year and a half, the Third Middlesex Regiment was ordered on the 4th of March to occupy the Heights, and the Weston company, which was a part of this regiment, proceeded to the appointed position under Captain Jonathan Fisk. The officers of the Third Regiment at this time were Colonel Eleazer Brooks, of Lincoln, Lieutenant-colonel Nathan Barrett, of Concord, and Major Samuel Lamson, of Weston. The names of the Weston company are as follows (Mass. Reg. Rolls, vol. 19, p. 88):—

Captain Jonathan Fisk.	Isaac Flagg.
Sergeant Samuel Fisk.	Ebenezer Steadman.
Sergeant Isaiah Seaverns.	Nathaniel Howard.
Corporal Abijah Stedman.	Joshua Peirce.
Corporal Simeon Smith.	Thaddeus Fuller.
Fifer Abijah Seaverns.	Abraham Harrington.
Privates Isaac Corey.	James Cogswell.
William Bond.	Joshua Jennison.
Benjamin Dudley.	Elijah Kingsbury.
Isaac Walker.	Benjamin Upham.
Uriah Gregory.	Samuel Pratt.
Solomon Jones.	John Allen Jr.
Edward Peirce.	James Hastings.
Nathan Hager.	Joseph Steadman.
Michael Warren.	John Warren Jr.
Jonathan Warren.	John Wright.
Thomas Russell Jr.	John Stimpson.
Benjamin Stimpson.	Lemuel Stimpson.
David Steadman.	John Peirce.
Benjamin Peirce Jr.	Thomas Williams.
Reuben Hobbs.	Abel Flint.
Silas Livermore.	John Hager.
Samuel Underwood.	Wm. Hobbs.
Benjamin Rand.	Thomas Rand Jr.
Jonathan Stratton Jr.	Jonas Underwood.
Joseph Russell.	

The company travelled twenty-eight miles, and served five days.

At the town meeting held in June it was voted to appoint one of the Selectmen to take a census of the town as directed by Congress. There is no record of the result of this census. It is to be regretted that the records of the town do not give the organizations, companies, and regiments to which the Weston men who fought in the Revolution were assigned. We have the payments made to all who served in the war and some of the campaigns in which they took part, but nothing more definite. A more detailed account would have added interest to the descendants of all the old soldiers. The little that has been accomplished in identifying our soldiers in the several commands of that period has been done in searching through the rolls at the State House, and in some instances these are not complete. Returns of companies and regiments were not attended to with the promptness and regularity of our own days. There are extant records which show sharp and frequent reminders from the headquarters of the army about the delinquency and carelessness of officers in this respect.

In town meeting held July 1, 1776, it was voted to give £6 6s. 8d. to each man (in addition to the bounty granted by the General Court); *i.e.*, to those men that were to go to Canada. Major Lamson, Ensign Isaac Hobbs, and Captain John Warren were appointed a committee to hire the money, and the town treasurer was ordered to give his security on behalf of the town at 6 per cent. interest.

The Weston men who went to Canada at this time are Converse Bigelow, John Warren, Jr., Samuel Train, Matthew Hobbs, John Hager, Lemuel Stimpson, James Cogswell, Benjamin Rand, Samuel Danforth, William Helms, Paul Cooledge, John Baldwin, Benjamin Bancroft, Daniel Sanderson, Reuben Hobbs, Elias Bigelow, Thomas Russell, Jr., John Stimpson.

Nearly all of the above men were of the Weston company. The Weston men who were in Captain Asabet Wheeler's company (of Colonel John Robinson's regiment) in 1776 at the siege of Boston and stationed at Cambridge were Josiah Cary, Roger Bigelow, Paul Cooledge, Converse Bigelow, Nathaniel Bemis, Elias Bigelow, Daniel Benjamin, Nathaniel Parkhurst, Oliver Curtis, Phineas Hager, Lemuel Jones, Daniel Livermore, Thomas Bigelow, A. Faulkner.

The three months' and ten-day men at Cambridge were as follows, and they received £346 11s. 2d.: Edward Cabott, Joseph Coburn, Isaac Gregory, Isaac Peirce, Artemas Cox (Wyman), Daniel Bemis, John Bemis, Joseph Mastick, Peter Cary, Simeon Pike, Keen Robinson, Daniel Rand, Thomas Harrington.

The five months' men at Cambridge were paid £200 18s. They were Philemon Warren, Joseph Stone, John Hager, George Farrar, Jedediah Warren, Nathan Fisk, Henry Bond, Josiah Jennison, Nathan Hager.

The Weston men to guard the beacon on Sanderson Hill in Weston were as follows (they were paid £127 8s.): Jonas Sanderson, Nathaniel Felch, Joel Harrington, Nathaniel Parmenter, Thaddeus Peirce, Daniel Rand.

This beacon is spoken of in General Sullivan's Memoirs, and was the connecting link of signals between the army at Cambridge and Sullivan's command in Rhode Island.

The nine months' men for the Continental army were as follows, and they were paid £900 bounty money: Keen Robinson, Jeduthun Bemis, Joseph Mastick, James Bemis, Samuel Bailey, Daniel Davis, Peter Cary.

On July 4, 1776, Congress issued to the country the Declaration of Independence by the representatives of the United States of America in General Congress assembled, and in council at Boston, July 7, it was ordered to be printed and a copy sent to the minister of each parish, and that the ministers be required to read the same on the first Lord's Day after they shall have received it, and that it should then be copied into the town records as a perpetual memorial. The Declaration of Independence was read in Weston by Rev. Samuel Woodward on the eighth day of September, 1776.

At a special town meeting held January 27 the petition of Josiah Smith and others, inhabitants of Weston, was read:—

To the Selectmen of Weston, Gentlemen:

Whereas it is difficult coming to justice in drafting men to go to the service of the United States by a common draft, we think it more just and equitable to come to justice for the town to choose a Committee to hire men whenever there shall be a call for men, and to have them paid by an assessment on ye inhabitants and estates by the same rule that common town rates are made and collected and in the same way, and ye money when collected to be delivered to said Committee in order to pay ye men: And also to make an estimate of what every person has done in the service since ye 19th of April 1775.

It was voted to choose five as such committee; namely, John Warren, Thomas Rand, Abraham Jones, Isaac Hobbs, and Samuel Livermore. This committee continued throughout the war, and did valuable service. At the same meeting it was

Voted to allow £3 to each man that was in service at Cambridge for eight months.

Voted that £10 be allowed each man in service 12 months and marched to New York.

Voted that £18 be allowed each man in service twelve months and marched to Canada.

Voted that twelve shillings be allowed each man in service two months at Cambridge, February and March.

Voted that £5 be allowed to each man in service five months at Ticonderoga.

Voted that £2 be allowed each man in service four months in Boston.

Voted that £5 be allowed each man in service two months at Horseneck.

Voted that £7:10 be allowed each man in the Jersies.

Voted that £1:10 to men in service 5 months in Boston.

Voted that 18 shillings be allowed for service 3 months in Boston.

At a town meeting held February 17, 1777, it was voted to add four more to the committee on the war; and Colonel Smith, John Lamson, Deacon Russell, and Deacon Upham were chosen to be of that committee.

The close watch which the friends of liberty held over the unfriendly, or Tory, element among them, is well exemplified in an occurrence which took place in Lincoln in August of 1777. The account is taken probably from a diary, as no name is signed to the statement: "This very day a mob came, it being on Sunday morning: the mob consisted of sixteen persons, by violence drove me away and kept me under guard for twenty six hours, insulting me to the highest degree." He then gives a list of the names of the persons who composed the mob: Colonel Abijah Peirce, Lieutenant Samuel Hoar, Lieutenant James Parks, Sergeant Ephraim Flint, Sergeant Daniel Harrington, and eleven others. This person, whoever he was, had probably ventilated his Tory proclivities, and been arrested by a company of soldiers.

The Third Middlesex Regiment served on the Hudson River and the Canada border, and it is probable the Weston company was with the regiment at White Plains in October; but there is no record on the town books of their services, beyond the payment made to Weston soldiers. The eight months' men on North River, New York, are as follows, and were probably drafted: Oliver Curtis, Ebenezer Philips, Joseph Stone, John Hager, John Richardson. There were eight Weston men in Captain Jesse Wyman's company, of Colonel Josiah Whiting's regiment serving in Rhode Island, discharged at Point Judith: Oliver Curtis, Joseph Mastick, George Farrer, Amos Hosmer, Buckley Adams, Joseph Stone, Josiah Parks, Eleazer Parks.

A draft was ordered by Colonel Brooks of one-sixth of Captain Fisk's Weston company (Records, vol. 53, p. 192), dated August 18, 1777, as follows: William Hobbs, Samuel Nutting, Silas Livermore, Alpheus Bigelow, Nathan Warren, Daniel Benjamin, Joel Harrington, Isaac Jones, Jr., Phineas Hager, Phineas Upham, Isaac Flagg, Thomas Hill, William Bond, Amos Harrington, Isaac Harrington, Jr., John Allen, Jr., Jeduthun Bemis, Daniel Weston.

Captain Fisk reports that Isaac Jones, Jr., could not be found. The six months' men who served in Rhode Island were as follows: Abel Peirce, Phineas Stimpson, Jonas Parmenter, David Livermore, John Roberts, Solomon Parmenter, William Richardson, Samuel Bond, Alpheus Bigelow, Panamuel Pratt, Daniel Bemis, Abner Mathias, Nathan Fisk, Amos Peirce, Phineas Hager, Silas Livermore, Jonas Underwood, James Peacock, James Coggswell, Joseph Storrs, John Bemis, Joseph Walker.

When Washington was defeated at Brooklyn, the army came near being broken up by the discharge of short-term enlisted men, and Washington appealed to the Continental Congress to organize an efficient army. As an inducement to enlist for the term of the war, Congress offered a bounty of £20 at the time of muster and the following grants of land: to a colonel, 500 acres; to a major, 400 acres; to a captain, 300 acres; to a lieutenant, 200 acres; and 100 acres to privates and non-commissioned officers. Massachusetts passed a resolve requiring each town to furnish every seventh man of sixteen years of age, excepting Quakers. By this order Weston's quota was eighteen men.

The town borrowed money of the townspeople to pay for the men ordered, in sums as follows:—

Samuel Fisk	£145:12:0	Anna Bigelow	£31:4:0
Jonathan Fisk	113:3:0	Elisha Warren	15:7:6
Jacob Bigelow	61:16:0	Joseph Russell	4:16:0
John Sanderson	61:4:0	Abijah Warren	15:14:0
William Hosmer	154:10:0	Sarah Cox	27:3:0

Amounting in all to £633:5:6

The full amount of money borrowed of sundry persons for the use of the town from May, 1778, to 1779 was £4,281:5:0
Town Debt 3,965:9:11

It is possible that the records of the campaign of Ticonderoga and Crown Point are defective for the reason that at the surrender of Ticonderoga by General St. Clair, on the 5th of July, the American army lost their effects. We have a record of the application made by Colonel Thomas Marshall to the General Court, to be reimbursed for his outlay in providing clothing for his command after the surrender. General Burgoyne surrendered his army at Saratoga on the 17th of October, and General Brickett escorted one wing of the British prisoners over the Framingham turnpike, or our south road, through Newton to Winter Hill in Somerville. General Glover escorted the other wing of prisoners over our Main Street to the same destination. General Glover's troops passed a night on our Main Street.* Over one hundred men enlisted in the army from Weston in 1777. In the year 1778 four men from Captain Fisk's company enlisted in the Continental army, viz.: John Norman, Isaac Green, Peter Cotton, John Tibbetts.

* On August 29, 1777, Lieutenant-colonel Paul Revere, in command of Fort Independence, was ordered to march with five drummers and five fifers, one hundred and twenty sergeants, corporals, bombardiers, gunners, and matrosses, with their commissioned officers, to Worcester, there to meet and take charge of the prisoners captured at Bennington by General Stark. They left Watertown at six o'clock, breakfasted at the Golden Ball Tavern in Weston, and dined at Sudbury. While there, Colonel Revere received a letter from Mrs. Jones, of Weston, complaining that her store had been broken open and twelve loaves of sugar stolen. She suspected the soldiers of doing the deed. Colonel Revere had all the packs searched, but found nothing. He says in his report that he suspects they stole the sugar themselves, and out of pretence charged our people. The sugar, he says, belonged to the government, and they are Tories. When he was at the Jones tavern, the pocket of Captain Todd's servant was picked and two dollars taken therefrom while the coat was hanging in the kitchen.

From Worcester several hundred prisoners—Highlanders, Germans, Canadians, etc.— were marched to Boston.

These four men not being on the muster-roll of the company, were undoubtedly hired (or substitute) men.

In July Major Lamson, by order of Colonel Brooks, drafted three men from the Weston company to serve as guards to the prisoners at Winter Hill, viz.: John Bemis, Isaac Gregory, and Nathaniel Wyman. Major Lamson in his return states that John Walker, Jr., a Continental soldier of Weston, has not returned to his duty as he promised to do, and the major suggests that Colonel Brooks should issue an order for his return at once (Records, vol. 53 [23 ?], p. 192).

The nine months' men drafted from Weston to serve at Fishkill, N.Y., were as follows (vol. 28, p. 160): Samuel Bayley, Keen Robinson, James Beaman, Peter Cary, Jeduthun Bemis.

On October 15, 1778, Colonel Brooks, of the Third Middlesex Regiment, was made brigadier-general, and was succeeded in command of the regiment by Nathan Barrett, of Concord (vol. 28, p. 120).

At a town meeting held the 18th of May, 1778, it was

Voted to choose a committee of nine to report upon the proposed plan of government.

Voted that Elisha Warren be dismissed as treasurer, and that Isaac Hobbs be appointed in his place.

Voted that £433 : 6 : 8 be granted Rev. Samuel Woodward as a gratuity for the present year.

At an adjourned town meeting held June 8, 1778, it was voted to act upon the constitution and form of government sent to the town for its consideration. The vote stood:—

For the approbation of the constitution, 6.

Against it or in disapprobation, 57.

At an adjourned meeting held on the 22d of October, 1778, the town voted the following instructions to their representative at the General Court:—

Mr. JOSEPH ROBERTS:

Sir,—As you are chosen by the inhabitants of this town to represent them in the General Court, your constituents think they have a right to instruct their representative from time to time as they shall think needful. Therefore, the inhabitants of this town think it proper to give you the following.

1. That you use your best endeavours in the General Court to have such laws made as may prevent the return of any of those persons into this town or state who have sought and received protection from the British army.

2. That you also endeavour in said Court, that the Judge of Probate be lawfully authorised to appoint agents over the estates of all such persons as have died in the town of Boston or elsewhere while under the protection of the British army.

At a town meeting held the 24th of May, 1779, it was

Voted to send two delegates to the convention, for the sole purpose of forming a new constitution or form of government. [Joseph Roberts and John Allen were chosen.]

That the delegates transmit to the Selectmen a printed copy of the form of government they shall agree upon, in order that the same may be laid before the town.

Voted the sum of £3,000 to support the war.

At a town meeting held the 2d of August, 1779, it was

Voted to hear the proceedings of the convention, held at Concord on the 14th of July last, for the purpose of forming a constitution or form of government.

Voted unanimously that we approve of and will abide by the proceedings of said convention.

Voted to chose two delegates to attend the convention at Concord the first Wednesday in October next. [Samuel Fisk and Thomas Rand were so chosen.]

A subject brought before the Concord convention was that of domestic trade, the establishing of a system of prices at which the necessaries of life were to be sold. The scarcity of money, the high rates which towns were obliged to pay for money to support the war, and the unreasonable prices charged for all produce of daily consumption rendered action necessary. This convention fixed a scale of prices for goods and merchandise and for farm produce and wages. Weston chose a committee to see that the agreement was faithfully observed in this town, and to publish the names of those persons who did not comply with the regulation. The convention did thorough work and took in all kinds of business. The prices were in the depreciated currency of that time, which was about 20 shillings paper to 1 shilling in silver. This would bring the price of tea to $1.33 per pound, and wages per day in summer to 58 cents. West India rum, £6 9s. per gallon; New England rum, £4 16s. per gallon; coffee, 18 shillings per pound; molasses, £4 15s. per gallon; brown sugar, from 10 to 14 shillings per pound; tea, £5 16s. per pound; salt, £10 8s. per bushel; beef, 5 shillings per pound; butter, 12 shillings per pound; cheese, 6 shillings; hay, 30 shillings per cwt.; yard-wide tow cloth, 24 shillings per yard; cotton cloth, 36 shillings per yard; men's shoes, £6 per pair; women's, the same; carpenter, per day, 60 shillings; mason, per day, 60 shillings; common laborer, 48 shillings in summer; flip (West India), per mug, 15 shillings; flip, New England, 12 shillings; toddy in proportion. Extra good dinner, £1; common dinner, 12 shillings. Best supper and breakfast, 15 shillings; common supper and breakfast, 12 shillings. Horse-keeping, 24 hours at hay, 15 shillings; on grass, 10 shillings.

At a town meeting held the 15th of November, 1779, it was voted to choose a committee of five persons to ascertain the bounds of the meeting-house lot and the road adjoining thereto. Captain Estes How, Captain Whittemore, Lieutenant Stratton, Jonas Harrington, and John Allen were chosen such committee.

At a town meeting held May 29, 1780, it was voted to accept the committee's report relating to town lands, but the report is not entered on the records.

The two months' men for service in Rhode Island were Benjamin Peirce, Jr., Joseph Stone, Jonas Peirce, Nathaniel Billings, William Gill, Daniel Livermore.

The four months' men were Isaac Walker and John Bemis.

The nine months' men in the Continental army from Weston were Thomas Bemis, Jacob Bemis, Abel Peirce, Simeon Pike, Ephraim Capron, John Roberts. They were paid £2,216 7s.

For guarding the beacon: John Hager's son, Samuel Liver-

THE HOBBS HOUSE, NORTH AVENUE.

Built by Deacon Isaac Hobbs as a double house, one-half being occupied later by his grandson, Captain Samuel Hobbs, and the west end by Captain Henry Hobbs. Mrs. Samuel Hobbs was the daughter of Rev. Dr. Kendal, and resided here until her death in 1883. She was succeeded by her nephew, General James F. B. Marshall, who extensively remodelled the house and named it Kendal Green. It is now owned and occupied by George N. Abercrombie.

THE OLD WHITNEY TAVERN, NORTH AVENUE.

This ancient house, now owned by Thomas E. Coburn, has been a commonplace tenement house for seventy-five years or more, and its early history is almost forgotten by the few who ever knew it. Mr. Whitney, who owned and occupied it as a tavern, once kept the famous "Punch Bowl" tavern in Brookline.

more's son, Thomas Graves's son, Thomas Rand's son. They were paid £50.

There were seven three months' men sent to the army on the Hudson, besides those above mentioned; but they were all hired. The six months' men in the Continental army at Fishkill numbered 15, and were all hired by the town.

The three months' men from Weston were John Bigelow, Samuel Lamson, Jr., Thaddeus Peirce, Daniel Ward, Peter Cary, Jeduthun Bemis, John Clark, and two hired, or substitute, men. These men were paid in bills of the new emission at four for one.

At a town meeting held May 29, 1780, it was voted to accept the constitution or form of government as it now stands, "but it is our opinion that it should be revised within ten years." The vote stood: yeas, 54; nays, 20.

It was also voted to search for Mr. Goddard's deed of gift, to the town of Weston, of a piece of land near the meeting-house. No report is made by the committee appointed, which consisted of Captain Flagg, Israel Whittemore, and Thomas Spring. It is probable there is no such deed.

Sixteen men were raised for the Continental army. They were all hired men and strangers to the town. They were to serve six months. Two of these men deserted, and three were discharged.

A resolve of the legislature required the following amount of beef for Washington's army: Waltham, 7,200 cwt.; Weston, 7,930 cwt.; Lincoln, 5,640 cwt.

In 1780 the Weston company enlisted for three years, or for the war. The company was commanded by Matthew Hobbs, and the two Livermores were lieutenants. The company was employed in the western and northern parts of New York, and was discharged at Newburg on the Hudson. Captain Hobbs died in 1817.

At a town meeting held September 4, 1780, the vote for governor and lieutenant-governor was taken. His Excellency John Hancock had 38 votes; Hon. James Bowdoin had 29 votes. Lieutenant-governor Hon. Henry Gardner had 30 votes; Hon. James Bowdoin had 22 votes.

It will be interesting to follow the votes for governor and lieutenant-governor for the next few years, as indicative of the respective popularity of the leaders of the Revolution in this State. John Hancock was evidently the most popular of all, and it will be noticed that it required a long time for James Bowdoin to supersede him in the affection of the people. Bowdoin was one of the most efficient and public-spirited men who ever held the executive office of Massachusetts, and was free from many of the small traits of character which were prominent in Hancock. Samuel Adams was still the moving power in the background, giving force and animating the public mind to sacrifice and patriotism. Mr. Adams was secretary of the Provincial and State Council; but Jonathan Avery as deputy secretary signed public documents, and the military commissions of the day were countersigned by him.

At a town meeting held December 27, 1780, it was voted to grant money to purchase the Weston quota of 15,227 pounds of beef ordered by the General Court, and also voted to raise £20,000 for the purpose, and to procure the thirteen men called for by government and raise the money to pay them. It had now become difficult to find men willing to enlist, and equally difficult to hire men. The Continental currency had so far depreciated as to render it almost useless, and loans of money on any terms were extremely difficult to obtain. The times were very hard, and the necessaries of life exhausted all available means. The year ended in general gloom.

At a town meeting held January 8, 1781, it was voted to choose a committee of five to meet with Josiah Smith and his son Joel to set the bounds of the town lands near the meeting-house.

At a town meeting held March 5, 1781, it was voted to present Rev. Mr. Woodward the thanks of the town for relinquishing fifteen cords of his firewood.

At a town meeting held April 2, 1781, the votes for governor and lieutenant-governor were taken. His Excellency John Hancock had 30 votes; Hon. James Bowdoin had 28 votes. Lieutenant-governor Hon. Thomas Cushing had 23 votes; Hon. James Prescott had 16; Hon. Azor Orne had 14.

At the same meeting, "*Voted* to grant the Rev. Mr. Woodward

£33:6:8 for his salary for six months, in silver money at the rate of 6 shillings 8 pence per ounce, or the exchange in paper currency at 75 of the latter for one of the former."

The surrender of Lord Cornwallis and the British army at Yorktown, which occurred October 19, 1781, checked enlistments, and, although they continued on a small scale for a period, the war was felt to be virtually at an end.

At a town meeting held April 1, 1781, the votes for governor and lieutenant-governor were taken. His Excellency John Hancock had 49 votes; Hon. James Bowdoin had 21. Lieutenant-governor Hon. Thomas Cushing had 61.

At a town meeting held October 14, 1782, it was voted to hear the proposals of the proprietors of a bell, which was purchased with a view to the benefit of the town, and act thereon. It was voted to accept the offer of the bell, with the conditions thereunto annexed, which are as follows, namely: "The proprietors make a present of the bell to the Town, provided they will hang it decently for the use of the Town." It would be interesting to give the names of these proprietors; but the difficulty of obtaining an inspection of the papers in the town safe, which have not been examined for probably half a century, has been so great that it had to be abandoned by the writer. Documents belonging to the town are treated too much as private property, not to be examined or touched. At this town meeting it was voted to grant £66 13s. 4d. "for the relief of the distressed family" of the late Rev. Mr. Woodward, "our faithful and beloved pastor," also £15 for the funeral charges.

It is to be regretted that we have no record of the men from Weston who were killed or who died in the army of the Revolution. Mr. Woodward gives the names of only two,—Daniel and Elisha Whitehead. The company and regimental rolls contain no mention of casualties. We have no record of the pensions awarded to soldiers of that period. The wife of Colonel Samuel Lamson received from the government in lieu of yearly pension a life lease of a tavern which stood in the westerly part of Watertown, upon which site now stands a school-house.

Pursuant to the order of the honorable House of Representatives (May 1, 1781), the committee for the sale of the estates of conspirators and absentees lying in the county of Middlesex "ask leave to report that they have sold the Estates hereinafter mentioned and described at the time, to the persons and for the sums set against the same," namely:—

In Weston, March 9th, 1781.

Elisha Jones, Esq., House, two barns, 75 acres of land sold to Colonel Thomas Marshall for				£1,000
53 Acres of land sold to Thomas Rand				185
30 " "	"	John Coburn		155
43 " "	"	M. A. Townsend		152
20 " "		Natick sold to N. Jennison		75
25 " "		sold to J. Dammson		85
20 " "		sold to J. Roberts		40
Total amount received from sale of land of Elisha Jones, Esq.,				£1692

At a town meeting held February 24, 1783, the business was:—

1st, to know the minds of the Town whether they were ready to come to the choice of a Person to settle in the Gospel ministry, and it passed affirmatively by a vote of 43 to 19. *2d*, *Voted* to grant £200 settlement as an encouragement to Mr. Kendal to settle with us in the work of the ministry. *Voted* that the deacons of the church be a committee to inform Mr. Kendal of the proceedings of the town.

At an adjourned meeting of the town August 11, 1783,—

Voted, That Deacon Thomas Russell, Samuel P. Savage, Esq., Mr. Jonathan Stratton, Deacon Isaac Hobbs, and Deacon Samuel Fiske be a Committee to wait on Mr. Kendal and inform him that the town are now ready to receive his answer to their call to settle with them.

The meeting was adjourned for fifteen minutes, and Mr. Kendal came into meeting and exhibited his answer.

In town meeting held in March, 1783, it was voted that a committee be appointed to draft instructions to the representative of the town, who this year was Samuel Fiske, for his government in the General Assembly. The committee was composed of Samuel Phillips Savage, John Warren, Thomas Russell, Thomas Marshall, and Isaac Hobbs, and on May 26, 1783, submitted the following report, written by Mr. Savage:—

Mr. SAMUEL FISKE.

Sir,—The Freeholders and Inhabitants of this Town having elected you to represent them in general Assembly the ensuing year, and considering that some matters of the last importance to the happiness, if not to the being, of this Commonwealth, may very probably be laid before the house of Assembly for their Consideration, have thought proper to give you the following Instructions.

While conflicting with a powerful enemy, through a long and bloody war (though ever disposed for Peace that was safe and honorable), we flattered ourselves that when Peace returned, we should be quiet under our own Vine and Fig tree, and none would make us unhappy: but we were mistaken—for although we have sheathed the sword, yet, unhappy for us, a new scene of trouble opens by an article in the Treaty; for Congress are there bound earnestly to recommend to the different States, that they admit the Return of those men and restore to them their estates, who, at the beginning of the Contest, when their invaded Country called for their aid, fled to the Enemy, and many of them joined them in their endeavors to subjugate and ruin it. Is it possible the real friends of America can ever be happy if these men return, until the horrid scenes they have both devised and perpetrated be obliterated from our memories, or what is equally as impossible, they be so changed as to relish the pleasures which flow from real Liberty?

We cannot but approve the prudent conduct of the Commissioners of these States (ever we trust under the Guidance of unerring Providence) that the article though inserted, is but conditional, and not obligatory on the States: by which the happiness or misery of America, at present, seems to rest on the Virtue of the People and their Rulers. If ever a time called for the watchful eye, the wise head and the honest heart, it is now. We have waded through a sea of blood, and been at an immense expense of Treasure to support the glorious struggle; and we most sincerely hope we shall not now by *one weak act undo* what has cost us the blood of thousands to effect. Shall it ever be said those men participated of the first fruits of Liberty who for eight long years have strove to tear up the fair plant by the roots. The thought opens to the mind such scenes of distress, that it is painful to dwell upon it.

To you Sir, (next to Heaven) as one of Guardians of our Rights and Liberties, we look.—Our choice of you evidences how much we rely on your Wisdom and Integrity—yet we must instruct and enjoin it upon you, that when you know, or have reason to believe, this important matter is coming before the house of Assembly for their Consideration, that you be present, and to the utmost of ability, both by your vote and influence prevent, if possible, the return of these men, or either of them to this Commonwealth, or the Restoration of their justly forfeited Estates. There are other things which on this occasion, might have been mentioned, but as our principal Design is instructing you, as for your Government in the above mentioned matter, we shall only say, that every thing which to you appears of real Importance to your Country's peace, freedom, Sovereignty and Independence, you will be particularly attentive unto.

We are sure Sir the Goodness of your heart will keep you from a base act, and we trust your good sense and firmness will, in the hour of Danger, secure you against the poison of the smooth Tongue and the insinuating address of the Secret Enemies of your Country, who are lying in wait to deceive.

SAMUEL PHILIPPS SAVAGE
JOHN WARREN
THOMAS RUSSELL
THOMAS MARSHALL
ISAAC HOBBS

WESTON, May 26th, 1783.

At a town meeting held September 8, 1783,

Voted, That the 5th day of November next be the day for the ordination of Mr. Samuel Kendal.

Voted, That the method of procuring money to defray the expenses of said ordination be by way of collection, and that those who shall advance money for said purpose shall be allowed the same on the next tax assessment.

Voted, That Major Samuel Lamson, Enoch Greenleaf and Deacon Samuel Fiske be a Committee to Provide for the Venerable Council.

Protest. We the subscribers conceiving that the proceedings of this town of Weston in the meeting of this date, has been illegal and unconstitutional in calling, granting settlement money and salary to Mr. Samuel Kendal in settling among us in this place in the Gospel ministry—we hereby declare our protest against the said proceedings, and we advise that this our protest might be of public record in this town, and we plead the advantage of the Bill of Rights in that case provided.

JOSEPH HARRINGTON.	ISAAC JONES.
HEZEKIAH WYMAN.	SAMUEL TRAIN.
SAMUEL SEAVERNS, Jr.	JONAS HARRINGTON
MOSES HARRINGTON.	JOHN FLAGG.
ELISHA HARRINGTON.	WILLIAM CUTTER.
JOSEPH ROBERTS.	

No attention seems to have been paid to this curious protest. The names are probably of those who voted against the call of Mr. Kendal in the meeting of February 24 preceding.

As 1783 virtually closes the war period, it will not be amiss to give a brief account of the money expended and men provided by the following States:—

VII.

IN THE WAKE OF THE REVOLUTION.

1784–1800.

Having passed in review the period of the Revolution, from 1775 to the treaty of peace, we have seen that every available man of Weston had been in the army for a longer or shorter term of service, many re-enlisting several times and serving at remote points, the town straining every nerve to raise the means to carry on the war to a successful termination. We can form no adequate idea at the present day of the privations and sufferings our forefathers went through in the battle for freedom. These severe sufferings of body and soul were not alone felt by the soldiers in the field, but the women and children at home bore their full share of privation and want. All, then, were glad when they at last saw that their struggles were to have an end. There was no money, or what might be called money. The paper currency had depreciated to an extent which rendered it almost useless. Clothing was all home-made. Tea and coffee, sugar and salt, there was none. Flour had reached the price of $500 a barrel in currency, and at points where the army was stationed was not obtainable at any price. The flour mills had been destroyed both by friend and foe. It is a question whether our people, if they had had a forecast of what they would be forced to endure for seven long years, would have thought flesh and blood equal to the attempt of a war against the crown. Men's hearts had become heavy. Mothers in the absence of their husbands looked upon their children and trembled for their future. The inhabitants of the frontier towns were in constant dread of Indian incursions, and those at the seaboard dreaded British invasion and ravages.

But the war came to an end, and at once, on the cessation of hostilities, business of all kinds received a great impetus. The agricultural population soon felt the improved state of things.

Between the years 1775 and 1783 Massachusetts furnished 67,907 soldiers, while New York supplied only 17,781. In adjusting the war balance after the peace, Massachusetts had overpaid her share in the sum of $1,248,801 of silver money. New York was deficient in the large sum of $2,074,846.

New Hampshire, though almost a wilderness, furnished 12,496 troops for the Continental ranks, or quite three-quarters of the number enlisted in New York State.

New York was the Loyalist stronghold, and contained more Tories than any other colony in America (Sabine, vol. i. p. 29).

IN THE WAKE OF THE REVOLUTION 103

Abundance succeeded want and privations, which for so long a period had been the lot of all. Money was still scarce, and taxes very high in consequence of the debts incurred in prosecuting the war. This state of things continued for several years, and brought about the Shays Rebellion of 1787. Among farmers the system of exchange of work and barter took the place (in most instances) of hard money. Land was cheap and mostly wooded, and in the purchase of farms throughout New England the standing wood would pay for the land. Distances to market were little considered, if for no other reason than because at central points hard money was to be had for wood and all farm produce. Provisions became very cheap, even when compared with the prices of our own day: beef, 6 to 8 cents; veal, 4 cents; pork, 6 cents; butter, 12 and 14 cents; eggs, 8 to 10 cents; hay, $8 to $10 a ton. There being no coal, wood was in good demand, and Boston took all the wood at fair prices. The farmers even brought it from far Vermont and New Hampshire. Ox-teams were then the only motive power, and long journeys were but little regarded. In this work the boys came into play. Long lines of ox-teams—each load of from four to six cords of wood, piled high in the air—were driven by boys of fourteen and sixteen years of age. The trip to the market occupied several days and nights. Each division of eight or ten teams had one or two men along with the boys to sell the wood and help in case of accident. No money was to be spent on the road. Each boy had his allowance of crackers and cheese, which was to last until he got back home. Feed for the cattle was stowed away in bags on top of the loads. In the fall of the year the streets of Boston were a sight not seen nowadays. The official street-inspectors and anti-obstructionists live in pleasant times to-day; but in the early days of this century and down to 1840 lines of wood-teams with innumerable yokes of oxen filled the streets, the cattle feeding on the sidewalks.

A good story is told of old Solomon Rice, of Sudbury. After the Worcester Railroad bridge was built, crossing the road to Brighton, he noticed one day, when driving a load of wood, that the stakes of his wagon barely cleared the bridge. He went home and put in longer stakes and piled his wood to their top. When he reached the bridge, he whipped up his team, striking the bridge and scattering his wood all over the road. He sued the railroad for damages, and obtained a considerable sum of money, while the company were obliged to raise the grade of their bridge.

This wood-teaming continued profitable into the '40's, when the railroads bought the wood at their stations, to be used in their engines. Locomotives were not fitted for the use of coal until in the '50's.

There is probably no part in the lives of our honored ancestors so little understood by the young people of to-day as the principle of bondage, or apprenticeship, which was in general use down to about 1820. Let the well-dressed, comfortable, easy-going graduate of a high school put himself, for a moment only, in the place of a young boy of those days, of from fourteen to twenty years of age,—stout, ruddy, and full of health; dressed in a pair of leather breeches coming down to his knees; his legs covered with a pair of long blue woollen stockings reaching up to his knees; his feet encased in a thick pair of cowhide shoes, well greased; his shirt of blue homespun, and on a Sunday covered with a false bosom, which was taken off on his return from meeting and carefully folded away for the next Sabbath. Then think of him on a cold morning in winter, the thermometer below zero; snow blown through the cracks of his garret chamber, filling his breeches and freezing them stiff; the kitchen fireplace to be cleared of the snow which had fallen down the capacious chimney in the night; no matches, and lucky if the turf in the embers had not gone out, rendering the use of the tinder-box and flint a necessity.

Under the old system of apprenticeship, boys at about the age of fourteen were bound out by their parents for a specified term of years, usually until the age of twenty-one, when they were presumed to have become proficient in their trade and capable of establishing themselves on their own account. Before the establishment of shoe factories conducted by large capital, which is only of recent date, all New England farmers were shoemakers. There is scarcely a farm to-day without its building formerly devoted to this industry. It was then necessary, in order to enable the farmers to eke out a comfortable living, which their farms did not always insure. Young boys were bound out to farmers just as in other occupations, and devoted the winter months to the trade of shoemaking. Many men, who in after life became wealthy merchants, had the early training given by a trade.

In these days of much-talked-of prohibition it seems strange to look back to the time when our progenitors never looked upon water as made to drink. In fact, water was scarcely used by them as a common beverage. New England rum and cider were looked upon as the proper drink. Tea was a luxury, used in sickness or on special occasions of social gatherings. It was purchased by the ounce. Coffee was not in general use, and among farmers never seen on the breakfast table, as now. Two quarts of rum and a pint of molasses was the weekly allowance of the average family. This was independent of the frequent potations of flip,—a home-made beer of hops, heated by a flip-iron always at hand. The rum and molasses charges in the books of retailers and grocers in early days are a sight that would overturn the equilibrium of our Prohibitionists.

On Isaac Lamson's books is a charge for New England rum, brandy, and sugar against the committee of three chosen in town meeting to collect the minister's tax of £3 3s. 6d. When we consider that the best rum sold for thirty-seven cents a gallon, some idea can be formed of the wear and tear to which the committee was subjected in the performance of this religious duty. The women aided and abetted in the general use of wines and liquors, but their brew was of their own make. In every house could be found an abundance of currant, elderberry, and noyau wines. No visitor, however humble, was allowed to depart without an invitation to the sideboard or cupboard. To have overlooked this act of hospitality was an offence not to be forgotten or readily forgiven. Notwithstanding the universal use of spirits, confined to no one class and forming a part of all contracts between master and servant, there was little or no drunkenness, as we see it in its disgusting form in our day. The men drank hard, perhaps: they certainly drank often; but they worked hard, and black-strap was with them an article of food as well as drink.

The standing amusement among the neighbors of a rainy day, when outdoor work was impossible, was to congregate at the tavern and pitch cents. On one occasion, having become tired of that fun, one of the party made a bet that there was nothing in Dexter Stratton's store in Waltham one could ask for that he did not have. Joel Smith, or "Uncle Joel," as he was called by old and young, took the bet, and they all started for Stratton's, where they asked for all the impossible things they could think of, and Joel was called upon to pay up. But he had made up his mind what he wanted, and asked for an old pulpit. This Stratton reluctantly acknowledged he had not got, but his boy called out that the old Lincoln church pulpit was out in the shed; and there it was found, sure enough! Stratton was not so fortunate as to purchase the old Weston pulpit, for a townsman elevated it to the position of a barn ventilator. Having served its time as a vehicle of the wrath of God to the unrepentant sinner, it finally went up in a blaze of glory.

We have said that every farm-house had its shoe-shop attachment. So every farm had its cider-mill. Apples were not then, as now, a marketable article to any extent, and all apples were made into drink, excepting what were needed for pies. These were made at Thanksgiving in numbers sufficient to last the whole winter. The food used by farmers was largely brown bread and Indian pudding. Apples were introduced into Massachusetts by Governor Winthrop, and Governor's Island in Boston Harbor was given to him for this service to the State. The governor planted it all over with apple-trees. Boys and girls were brought up on brown bread and milk for breakfast and supper the year round, and they were lucky when they got enough of that. Meat was as little in use by our forefathers as is the case now in the old country. There were no butchers going about, as now. Farmers took turns in killing a cow or a calf, and the meat was distributed among the neighbors, generally without money consideration, but in exchange one with another. There is extant a note from Artemas Ward for a quarter of veal sent him by a neighbor. Bean porridge was also a staple article of food. Little is said, however, of the Yankee pork and beans.

At a town meeting held April 5, 1784, a protest was read from the Baptists against being taxed for the support of Rev. Mr. Kendal, since they paid their proportion of a tax for the support of the gospel ministry to the minister of their own church. A committee was chosen to examine into their grievances, consisting of Colonel Marshall, Captain Jones, and Jonathan Stratton. The names of the Baptist petitioners are as follows: Oliver Hastings, Jonathan Spring, Josiah Severns, Mary Ballard, John Hastings, Jr., James Hastings, Samuel Pratt, Samuel Train, Jr., Enoch Bartlett, Thaddeus Spring, James Stimpson, Joseph Severns.

At a meeting held April 5, 1786, it was voted to hear the report of the committee appointed to listen to the reasons that might be offered by the Baptist society relative to their paying the ministerial taxes. Here is their report:—

Your committee chosen the 6th of March last, to wait upon those who call themselves of the Baptist Society, to hear the reason they have to offer why they should be released from paying taxes to the Rev. Mr. Samuel Kendal for his services in the Gospel Ministry, report as follows, viz.: "That it is our unanimous opinion that those whose names were sent in to the Selectmen and Assessors of Weston, upon a schedule dated February 13th, 1786, signed by Oliver Hastings, Samuel Train, Jr., and Thaddeus Spring, Committee for said Society, should be released from paying taxes aforesaid for the reasons they gave us, except Messrs. Joseph Roberts, Samuel Seaverns, Jr., and Increase Leadbetter, whose reasons in our humble opinion are not sufficient to exempt them from paying their proportion of the Rev. Mr. Kendal's settlement and first salary at least."

In 1784 the town applied to the legislature for authority to raise the sum of £1,000 by a lottery, which petition was granted and a committee appointed by the town to dispose of the tickets. It does not appear how this venture turned out. The purpose for which the £1,000 was to be devoted was the widening of the Watertown bridge.

In town meeting held March 7, 1785, it was voted that the pews in the church be sold, and that the purchasers of said pews shall hold the same to themselves, their heirs and assigns, forever, so long as the present meeting-house shall stand. Eight pews were sold. The committee report that the pew then occupied by Mr. John Coburn was not sold, as the power to sell it was disputed by Mr. Coburn, who doubted the right the town had in it. The committee report that there were other pews in the same predicament. They were not inclined to give occasion for lawsuits, **and** state that the town should now settle the matter. The report is signed by Isaac Jones, Enoch Greenleaf, and Israel Whittemore. For a complete list of pew sales in 1772, a little earlier than the time we are now reviewing, see Appendix III.

At a town meeting held April 2, 1787, it was voted not to offer any bounty to men who marched in the "Shays rebellion." On January 1, this year, the limit fixed by the General Court for taking the oath of allegiance and for receiving pardon expired. At the time of the "Shays rebellion" the State debt was enormous, and the people were saddled with taxes beyond endurance. Farmers especially felt the burden, and many were sold out of their farms on account of not being able to pay their taxes and personal debts. Discontent was universal. Massachusetts' proportion of the federal debt was about £1,500,000. Private debts were computed at £1,300,000, and £250,000 was due to the soldiers of the Revolution. Dr. Samuel A. Green estimates that from 1784 to 1786 every fourth, if not every third, man in the State was subjected to one or more executions for debt. In 1784 there were over 2,000 actions entered at the court at Worcester, and in 1785 over 1,700 actions. Executions could be satisfied by cattle and other means besides money, thus putting the creditors at the mercy of the debtors. In 1786 Governor Bowdoin called a special session of the legislature, but the General Court failed to offer any relief to the people. Daniel Shays, who had been a captain in the Continental army, led a party of 1,000 men, took possession of Worcester, and closed the courts. Shortly after he closed the courts in Springfield and held the town, demanding the surrender of the arsenal. Governor Bowdoin finally decided on vigorous measures, and 4,400 troops and two companies of artillery were enlisted to serve thirty days. £6,000 was raised in Boston to equip the army. General Lincoln was given command, and Shays's forces were overthrown on January 25, 1787, by one discharge of grape-shot, which killed four men and scattered the rest. A reward of £150 was offered for the capture of Shays. It was not long before all were pardoned. Moses Harvey, who was then a member of the General Court, was sentenced to stand on the gallows an hour with a rope around his neck, to pay a fine of £50, and be expelled from his seat.

At the April town meeting the petition of Mrs. Abigail Woodward was read, setting forth her inability to pay the taxes that had been laid upon her since 1785, and praying to be excused from any in the future, as the circumstances of her family were such as to render her unable to discharge them, and her petition, having had several readings, was finally granted. December 10, 1787, Captain Abraham Bigelow was elected to represent the town in the convention to be held at the State House in Boston in January, 1788, to take into consideration the ratification of the Constitution, or form of government for the United States of America, as reported by the Convention of Delegates held at Philadelphia in the previous May. It is known that at the time of the Shays rebellion the governor of the State could place very little reliance upon the militia forces. The rank and file were to a very great extent in sympathy with those engaged in opposing the onerous taxation which was bringing ruin on the State. The officers (field and staff) were equally unreliable, and it was in consequence of this prevailing distrust that general officers were placed in command. At this period the "Independent Companies" were organized and received their charters. Among these were the Weston Light Infantry and Medford companies. The following letter will explain the organization of our Weston company:—

WESTON, January 16, 1787.

Sir,—In Conformity with your advice I have encouraged the raising of a Company of Light Infantry in the town of Weston, which has been so far carried into effect that a sufficient number have associated for the purpose of choosing their Commissioned officers: and did on Monday the 15th Inst: at a meeting appointed for the business elect Abraham Bigelow Captain, William Hobbs Lieutenant and Ebenezer Hobbs Ensign of said Company. I therefore make this return of the proceedings of said Company with a request that your honor would give information to His Excellency the Commander in Chief for the procurement of their Commissions. I am with respect Your Honors Obt Servt.

Samuel Lamson, *Colonel.*

To His Honor John Brooks, *Major General.*

This letter is indorsed as follows:—

It is my opinion that the formation of the above company will be for the advantage of the Commonwealth.

[Signed]   Jo. Brooks, *Major General.*

In 1770 there had been formed at Cambridge a voluntary association of the collegians, and Governor Hutchinson had ordered the commander at Castle William to deliver one hundred stand of arms for their use. The history of this college company is very interesting. It continued to exist down to the period of the charter of the Weston company, when, it being difficult to find arms for this company, Captain Bigelow obtained the written consent of Dr. Willard, the president of the college, and applied to Governor Bowdoin for permission to receive the arms belonging to the college company. This permission was granted on condition that a reasonable compensation for the arms should be paid to the quartermaster, General Davis, for the use of the Commonwealth. This was promptly done, and the arms removed from the college armory and delivered to the Weston company. The Weston company is reported to have joined the forces which passed through the town on their way to Springfield, but the town records make no mention of it, excepting that in town meeting the citizens refused to pay any bounty to the troops engaged in that expedition. The Weston Light Infantry continued in service till the 13th of May, 1831, when it was disbanded for insubordination at the muster-field in Watertown. The particulars of this affair, while not relieving them from the charge of conduct prejudicial to military discipline, will at least place their conduct in a light affording some excuse for their action on that day. The Weston company was attached to no regiment, reporting to the general of brigade. Its successive commanders were as follows: Abraham Bigelow, 1787; Artemas Ward, Jr., 1789; William Hobbs, 1793; Alpheus Bigelow, 1797; Nathan Fiske, 1800;

THE OLD JONATHAN WARREN PLACE, NORTH AVENUE.

Built prior to 1780 and occupied then by the Widow Wright, afterwards wife of Jonathan Warren, Sr., father of Jonathan Warren, Jr., and of Mrs. Jonas Hastings, and grandfather of Rufus Warren. This place was occupied successively by F. V. Stowe, Samuel Patch, and others, and is now owned by Francis H. Hastings.

THE FISKE HOUSE, NORTH AVENUE.

Built in 1845 by Alonzo S. Fiske, then taking the place of the ancient house that had formed the Fiske home for many generations. In 1912 it was bought by W. F. Schrafft. Until this date the Fiske estate had been in the family since 1673, and was originally a mile square.

Josiah Hastings, 1802; Isaac Hobbs, 1804; Thomas Bigelow, 1808; Nathan Upham, 1809; Isaac Childs, 1811; Isaac Train, 1813; Charles Stratton, 1814; Henry Hobbs, 1817; Luther Harrington, 1818; Marshall Jones, 1821; Sewell Fiske, 1822; Elmore Russell, 1828.*

A detail from this company was ordered, in the War of 1812, to guard the powder-house at Cambridge, namely: Sewell Fiske, Nathan Warren, Nehemiah Warren, Jesse Viles, Charles Bemis, William Bigelow, Henry Stratton, Jacob Sanderson, David Viles, Charles Morse.

Major Daniel S. Lamson, Charles Daggett, William Harrington, Deacon Isaac Jones, and Cooper Garfield also took part in this war. Major Lamson was of the Third Middlesex Regiment, of which his father had been colonel. He was lieutenant-colonel of the regiment when he died in 1824. Cooper Garfield lived to be over one hundred years old, and died in 1875, having spent the last thirty-six years of his life in the Weston poorhouse. The Weston Light Infantry, under Captain Sewell Fiske, attended the reception in 1824 given to General Lafayette at Concord.

* The muster-roll of the independent company at the time of its charter in 1787, under Captain Abraham Bigelow, is not at hand. The roll of the company commanded in 1797 by Captain Alpheus Bigelow is as follows:—

Captain Alpheus Bigelow.
Lieutenant Abijah Whitney.
Ensign Nathan Fiske.
Sergeant Josiah Hastings.
" Abraham Hews.
" Isaac Hobbs.
" Nathan Hobbs.
Music: Ebenezer Fiske.
" Enoch Flagg.
" Isaac Train.
Privates: William Bogle.
David Brackett.
Thomas Bigelow.
Jonas Billings.
Lot Bemis.
Ebenezer Bullard.
Nathan Child.
Solomon Child.
Samuel Child.
Jonas Coburn.
Jonathan Fiske.
Daniel Flagg.

Privates: Ephraim Allen.
Elisha Furbush.
Amos Hobbs.
Charles Hews.
Wm. Pitt Jones.
Samuel Lamson, Jr.
Amos Lamson.
Ephraim Livermore.
William Livermore.
Joshua Locke.
Charles Parks.
Joseph Parks.
Amos Pierce.
Thaddeus Peirce.
Isaac Peirce.
Abner Russell.
Josiah Starr.
Josiah Smith.
Nathan Spring.
Jacob Sanderson.
Jonas Sanderson.
Amos Sanderson.

A total of forty-four officers and privates. Captain Bigelow died in 1847 at the age of ninety.

The town vote for governor in 1788 gave 80 votes for John Hancock, but no other vote is recorded, which neglect occurred frequently. On May 9, 1788, news was received in Boston that the convention held in Philadelphia on the 28th of April had adopted the new constitution by a vote of 63 out of 74.

At a town meeting held December 11, 1788, the vote was taken for the first representative of this district in the Congress of the United States under the new constitution. John Brooks received 26 votes, and Hon. Elbridge Gerry 20 votes. The vote was also taken for presidential electors, and Hon. Francis Dana received 58 votes, and Nathaniel Gorham 41 votes.

In 1789 the town borrowed £50 of Harvard College and £50 of Hon. Francis Dana.

At a town meeting held September 3, 1789, a committee appointed at the spring meeting to fix upon a location for a new burying-ground reported that they had selected the south-east corner of Captain Jones's field; that a lane 3 rods wide ran upon the east end of said field, about 12 rods, to the burying-ground, which with the lane is to certain 1½ acres, valued at £20. At the same meeting it was voted to allow Artemas Ward and others to build a number of pews in the rear part of the church, and apply the proceeds of their sale to discharge the town debt. These pews were sold to Artemas Ward (£29 14s.), Elias Jones (£27 18s.), Nathaniel and Mirick Warren (£22 10s.), Nathan Hager (£20). Total, £100 2s., which sum was deposited in the hands of the town treasurer.

In October, 1789, General Washington, President of the United States, proposed a journey to the New England States, which he had not visited since the evacuation of Boston by the British army. He travelled in his own carriage, drawn by four horses, and was accompanied by Mr. Lear and Major Jackson, his secretaries, and six servants on horseback. Notice was given in Boston that the President would reach Weston on October 23. He passed the night at the Flagg tavern, now the residence of Mr. Emerson, and while at Weston he wrote Governor Hancock, accepting an invitation to dinner the next day. The letter is dated at Weston. On the morning of October 24 he was waited upon by the inhabitants of the town, and Colonel Marshall welcomed him in an address, after which the notables of the town were presented to him. Among these were officers who had served under him in the Continental army. He was escorted to Cambridge by the Watertown cavalry company. His progress through the towns of New England was one uninterrupted ovation, the people far and near flocking along his route. To those who had belonged to his army the visit was particularly pleasing. They were greeted by the general with affection and consideration. It was while in Weston that Washington kissed Hannah Gowen, then a child, and it was for her a matter of great pride and glory as long as she lived. (For a visit of President John Adams to Weston see end of this chapter.)

In 1791 the town ordered that the meeting-house be put in thorough repair and painted. The committee reported, April 4, that in their opinion the back side of said house should be new clapboarded, that the glass should be removed, and new window-frames with glass, and new window-heads, be made, etc. From the date of the incorporation of the town there had been elected each year an officer whose duty was the preservation of deer, but from 1791 the election of this officer ceases.

In 1792 Concord was made the shire town of Middlesex County, but Weston voted against it being so made. In 1791 and 1792 small-pox prevailed extensively throughout the town, and in 1792 the following houses were selected as pest-houses and places for inoculation: the Captain Fiske house on the north side, which was the first house built by that family, and stood on the hill back of the present location; Joel Smith's (this was probably the poorhouse given to the town by his father); the Parkhurst house, now that of Oliver Robbins; Deacon Fiske's, now of Henry White; Ephraim Livermore's; the widow Upham's, now in Loring Place; Josiah Starr's; Joseph Seaverns's; Amos Lamson's, now of James Upham. The alarm occasioned by this epidemic and the large number of deaths caused very stringent measures to be enforced by the Selectmen. The physicians were required to give bonds that they would not allow any person to visit the hospitals but those they were to see thoroughly smoked when they withdrew therefrom; and that they would uniformly cause themselves to be smoked; that there be a smoke-house erected at each hospital, and bounds set round about each hospital, to which those that had the distemper might come, and no further. There is no record of the number of deaths in Weston from small-pox. The dead were buried in the south-west corner of the old yard without ceremony and without headstones.

Pleasure carriages were not introduced until the close of the century. The sole way of travelling was on horseback, the pillion-saddle being most in use, the father in front, the mother and small children on the pillion, the boys astride the horse's back as far as the crupper. The first chaise seen in Weston was owned and probably made by Isaac Hobbs, inasmuch as he made nearly all the vehicles of this sort used in Weston and neighboring towns for many years.

In January, 1793, in honor of the French Revolution, a grand fête was held in Boston, in which neighboring towns joined. An ox was roasted whole, then decorated with ribbons and the flags of France and the United States, and placed upon a car drawn by sixteen horses, followed by carts loaded with 1,600 loaves of bread and two hogsheads of punch. The school children paraded, and cakes were distributed, marked "Liberty and Equality." A party of three hundred, with Samuel Adams, lieutenant-governor of the State, at their head, sat down to a dinner in Faneuil Hall.

In 1795 a petition was presented to the town for a road from Abraham Harrington's, now Perry's, over the flat lands, around the base of Ball's Hill, and coming out on the Concord road, thus avoiding the great hill. The town objected, and chose Artemas Ward and Thaddeus Spring a committee to defeat the project. A petition was also presented that four seats nearest the wall in the front gallery of the church be removed, and converted into two pews, "to be decently furnished for the use of the singing men and singing women that already have or may hereafter acquire skill in that sublime art, as shall qualify them to carry on that part of the public worship of God in a decent and becoming manner." Fifty dollars was voted to encourage the art of singing. It was also voted that a plan of the town be ordered made, with the length and direction of all the roads therein, with notice of all public buildings, etc. It is probable that this order of the town was not carried out, as no such plan is in existence, so far as can be discovered.

In 1796 is the first entry in the town accounts with substitution of dollars and cents for pounds, shillings, and pence. The change was slow and fitful. A sum of twenty dollars was voted for the relief of Samuel Livermore, Jr., who was reduced to straits by having his dwelling destroyed by fire.

In 1791, as we have seen, the town had ordered the meetinghouse to be repaired. In 1799 it was voted again to repair the house and erect a steeple on the tower, if the expense be paid by subscription. A committee was appointed to collect the subscription of the people for this purpose. The list is still in existence, and should be among the parish records.

There were sixty-eight subscribers for various sums, in all amounting to $414.75. The old bell was valued at $75.25, making total amount raised $490. The subscribers, however, make conditions that the additional expense for the spire and purchasing a new bell, to weigh not less than 800 pounds, shall be paid by the town. The subscribers who have a right in the old bell shall have credit for their proportion of the amount of its sale in their subscription. The new bell was purchased of Paul Revere, as I have stated in Chapter I. A copy of his bill to the town, traced from his ledger in his own handwriting, is now in the vestry of the church. The cost of repairing the church and building the cupola and pews was over $3,000, and the proceeds of the sale of the new pews was $1,066, leaving a balance paid by the town of $1,431.03.

The eighteenth century closed with great prosperity. The need of hard money was alone the drawback to large commercial ventures. *In 1790 the whole capital of the United States was only $2,000,000*, invested in Philadelphia, New York, and the Massachusetts Bank in Boston. In 1791 the National Bank of the United States was established with a capital of $10,000,000, but it did not commence business until 1794. The country at this time was thrown into political convulsions. The French Revolution was at its height, and the sympathies of Jefferson and his party were with the radical republicans of France. Among the Jeffersonians there was a feeling of gratitude for the assistance rendered to the colonies by France in the American Revolution. Washington and Adams realized from the first the difference between the French republic and our own, and they had little confidence in or sympathy with the hot-headed French radicals. The French Convention, acting upon a claim they pretended to have upon this country for the aid rendered by France in our Revolution, treated our ports as a part of their own dominion, and fitted out privateers sailing from the United States. The French minister Genet finally became so overbearing and insulting as to render his dismissal necessary. The settlement of the eastern boundary with the English, together with their impressment of American seamen on the high seas, added other grounds of enmity in the country, and war between the United States, France, and England seemed inevitable. Jay's treaty with England put off the evil day, which, however, followed a few years later. The debt of the United States in 1799 was $78,408,669.77.

We have already seen in the foregoing pages some account of the visit of President George Washington to Weston on his way to Boston in 1789, when he passed the night at Flagg's tavern. In 1798 we were visited by President John Adams, when he was on his way to Quincy. The Massachusetts *Mercury* of August 17, 1798, gives a full account of the visit and his reception by the citizens of the town. The *Mercury* states that,

Had it not been supposed here that the President of the United States had passed through a different road to his seat at Quincy, our company of Light Infantry, in complete uniform, would have met him at the line which divides East Sudbury from this town, and would have escorted him and his suite to Flagg's tavern, and have done him all military honors in their power. As the case was circumstanced, it was impossible.

The address delivered by Hon. Samuel Dexter is signed by the following prominent persons among many: Samuel Dexter, Thomas Marshall, Samuel Kendal, Isaac Jones, Artemas Ward, Amos Bancroft, and Caleb Haywood. The address delivered by Mr. Dexter on behalf of the citizens was as follows:—

To have the best government in the world, and that government administered in the best manner, is the distinguished lot of our happy nation. Ever since the adoption of the Constitution we have felt its benign effects: but in increased and increasing degree of late; since all have now learned the important lesson to respect themselves and despise foreign influence. This we owe, in a high degree, to your wisdom and patriotism. No longer ignorant of the devises of our enemies, acquainted with their true character, and with the means of defeating their nefarious designs, union and fortitude we are persuaded will be our impenetrable shield. In the town of Weston, Sir, there are no disorganizers. When called to elect public men, our suffrages upon every occasion have proved our federalism: and we pray you to be assured that, while we shall continue firm in the cause of our Country, and be ready to defend it upon all emergencies, we shall not cease to implore the Supreme Governor of the universe to "think upon you for good, according to all you have done for the people."

To this address President Adams made the following reply:—

Gentlemen,—I thank you for this Address, in which much excellent sentiment is expressed in a few words. If in any degree I have contributed to assist my Countrymen in learning the important lesson to respect themselves and despise all improper foreign influence, I shall not have lived in vain. I sincerely congratulate the Town of Weston on their signal felicity in having no disorganizers. Two or three of this description of characters are sufficient to destroy the good neighborhood, interrupt the harmony, and poison the happiness of a thousand families. A Town that is free from them will ever prove their federalism in election, be firm in the cause of their country, and ready to defend it in all emergencies. Upon all such towns may the choicest of blessings descend.

VIII.

A Record of Forty Quiet Years.

1800–1840.

On June 1, 1801, by a tripartite agreement between Watertown, Waltham, and Weston, the towns of Waltham and Weston ceased to have any further obligation in the matter of keeping in repair the Watertown bridge over Charles River, which had for years been a great expense and no little annoyance to those towns.

In 1802, complaints having been made that cattle were allowed to pasture in the old burying-ground to the injury of the graves and stones, a question arose as to the town's title to the land of said burying-ground. No record could be found of any deed, and Jonas Harrington, the then claimant of the soil, held that the town had no title to it, but only permission to bury their dead, the fee of the land remaining with him. In January, 1839, a deed of the land was, however, obtained.

The town voted this year for representative in Congress, and Rev. Samuel Kendal had 32 votes, Hon. Timothy Bigelow had 27, and Hon. Joseph B. Varnum had 21. It was also voted to build an armory and powder-house for the deposit of arms and ammunition, the Selectmen being a committee to build the armory. The building was placed in the north-east corner of what later became the second "God's-acre," where it stood until the latter part of the '30's, and after ceasing to be a powder-house was for a time used for the hearse.

In 1803 it was voted to pay Rev. Mr. Kendal $130 a year, in addition to his salary, instead of his twenty cords of firewood. The town was summoned before the Supreme Court about the highway from East Sudbury to Waltham. Five hundred dollars was voted for the repairs of said highway, and Isaac Fiske was chosen to make answer before the court on behalf of the town.

In 1804 Isaac Fiske was made town clerk. He held the office for twenty-four years, until 1828, in which year Dr. Benjamin

James succeeded him. Dr. Kendal's salary, which had been $300, was raised to $550, a sum that included his firewood. The electors-at-large for President and Vice-President of the United States were in two party lists, nineteen in each list. The first list of electors received 97 votes each. The second list received 38 votes. These two lists represented the federal and anti-federal parties. For representative to Congress Hon. Timothy Bigelow received 98 votes, and John Slack was elected representative for Weston at the General Court.

In 1805 Moses Gill, of Princeton, releases to Reuben Carver his pew in the church and his title to the shed, and also all his rights, title, and interest in and to the Baptist meeting-house or any money due from said meeting-house, or society. By this it would appear that the first Baptist church was built upon the Nicholas Boylston place, Moses Gill by marriage being an heir to that property. The question came up of the advisability of selling the old poorhouse. The committee reported it to be capable of repair, and they add:—

It having been argued that the town's owning such a house augmented their poor, we find among those who have been its inmates Mrs. Middlesex and Cornell, altogether objects of pity. Very few there are who would be willing to act the good Samaritan and administer to their wounds. There are others the town has to provide for by boarding or hiring a house for them. The poor we shall have ever with us, and it is for the interest of the town to have a house.

It was voted that, in the future, town meetings shall be warned by posting up the notice at the public meeting-house in the centre of the town. Before this regulation the constables gave notice of town meetings from house to house. It was also voted to lay out the Concord road from Dr. Bancroft's house, and $600 was appropriated for that purpose. It was voted to get a bath-tub for the town, probably for the poorhouse.

In 1808 the Worcester Turnpike Corporation was established from Roxbury to Worcester, through Framingham. This new route shortened the distance between Boston and Worcester considerably, and took off many of the stage-coaches which up to this time had run through Weston.

In 1810 a committee was chosen to contract with Waltham, Watertown, and Newton for a road from Stony Brook to Watertown bridge; and it was agreed that the town would appropriate $2,000, provided said road be laid out by the court. It does not appear that this project was accomplished until some time later. It was voted to employ a music-teacher.

It was voted in 1811 that the meeting-house be painted, the expense of the work to be drawn from the town treasury.

War against England was declared early in 1812.* It had been threatening for many years, and matters had arrived at the stage when the United States was forced to assert itself or become little else but a dependence of England. The great prosperity of the New England States, particularly of Massachusetts, since 1800, created strong opposition to warlike measures. The Embargo and Non-importation Acts of 1808 were bitterly opposed by this State. There was at this time fully as much disaffection expressed towards the general government as there was in the South previous to the breaking out of the Civil War in 1861. So strongly was this feeling expressed that it encouraged England to attempt to separate the Eastern States and have them unite with Canada. The party spirit between the federal and anti-federal factions was as bitter as we have seen was the case in 1795. A reference to the population and business interests of this section will explain the grounds of opposition to the war. By the census

* While the not over-glorious War of 1812 eventually gave this country commercial independence and the freedom of the seas, it developed during the war a system of inland transportation between the North and the South by wagon, due to the suppression of the coasting-trade by the blockade of our ports. Great canvas-covered wagons, drawn by double and triple teams of horses or oxen, wound their way like an Oriental caravan between Salem and Boston and intermediate cities to Augusta and Savannah. It was estimated that four thousand wagons and twenty thousand horses and oxen were employed in this transportation business. Two months went to a wagon-journey from Boston to Savannah; and what with the long time, the searches by customs officers for smuggled goods, and in New England the stoppage of Sunday travel by the tithing-men, and other mishaps of the way, the merchants became anxious for news of their ventures. So the wagons were named, and the teamsters instructed to keep a log of their meetings with other wagons, their destination and condition, and report to the newspapers of each town and city they passed through, the news to be published and copied by newspaper after newspaper for the benefit of the shippers. The journals entered into the spirit of the thing, and in the columns once devoted to shipping news recorded the wagon chronicles under such headings as "Horse Marine Intelligence," "Horse and Ox Marine News," "Jeffersonian Commerce." The wagons figured under such names as "Teazer," "Salt Hog," "Commerce Renewed," and "Old Times," "Sailors' Misery," "Cleopatra," "Don't give up the Ship," etc. One sample of the wagon "log" was this: "Port of Salem.— Arrived the three-horse ship Dreadnaught, Captain David Allen, 16 days from New York. Spoke in the latitude of Weathersfield the Crispin, Friend Allen, master, from New York, bound homeward to Lynn, but detained and waiting trial for breach of the Sabbath."

of the United States the population was 5,905,782, of which the
New England States and New York contained 2,615,587, almost
half the population of the Union. The exports in 1811 amounted
to $58,643,711, of which $27,045,425 was the amount from these
States. The tonnage of vessels was 1,424,000, and these six
States owned 882,005 tons. Massachusetts alone owned 496,000
tons, or more than a third of the total.* On the passage of the war
act the six States voted in the House of Representatives against
the war by a majority of 31 to 15, and in the Senate of 6 to 4.

In July Governor Strong appointed a day of humiliation, fasting, and prayer, and on the day appointed the pulpits everywhere resounded with bitter invective against the war. The governor was very lukewarm during hostilities, and refused the requisition of the general government for Massachusetts troops to go out of the State. It was only when danger threatened our territory or seaboard that he took any active measures. The State has no records at the State House of this war. All documents relating to the action of the State were sent to Washington, when the claim was made for money due the State in the war, and they never have been returned. The claim of the State against the government has not been paid.

In July a convention of the friends of the "Independence, Peace, Union, and Prosperity" of the United States (consisting of delegates from forty-three towns of Middlesex County) was held at Concord. Hon. James Prescott was made moderator, and Isaac Fiske, of Weston, was made secretary. There is no mention on the town records that he was a delegate of the town to the convention. A strong appeal to the people of the county was issued, and is still preserved.

It was voted in town meeting that Cambridge should continue to be the shire town and that the jail should be kept there.

Voted, That the soldiers, who volunteered and have actually been mustered shall draw from the treasury $3.25 each, and also those who shall hereafter be mustered.

Votes were taken for electors-at-large for President and Vice-President of the United States. The first ticket had 5 candi-

* This includes Maine, which was not set off as a separate State until 1820.—ED.

dates, and each received 93 votes. The second ticket had also 5 candidates, and each received 61 votes.

Voted, That proper gravestones be erected in memory of the Rev. Dr. Kendal, as large as those erected in memory of the late Mr. Woodward, at the town's expense.

Dr. Kendal died in 1814, after thirty-one years' service as pastor of the Weston church.

In town meeting held April 16, 1814, it was voted that the town pay the expenses of Dr. Kendal's funeral, including mourning apparel for the family, but they refused to print the sermon preached by Rev. Dr. Osgood at the funeral of Dr. Kendal. Isaac Fiske, Deacon Warren, Ebenezer Hobbs, Deacon Bigelow, and Captain Isaac Hobbs were chosen a committee to hire a minister to supply the pulpit, and granted $550 for that purpose.

Voted that the town accept the stove given by individuals, and that it remain in the meeting-house.

Voted to ascertain the bounds of the town's land (?) on which the meeting-house stands, and to erect monuments and make a plan thereof. No report is made, and no bounds set. The land goes to the church, and the town has no claim upon it whatever. The town passed a similar vote about 1784, and then failed to find any deed or bounds. The same is the case with the sheds land. It was voted this year (1814) that the Selectmen cause new sheds to be erected, near the town's pound, "where, or near where, the old horse-sheds now stand, with the right of having them remain there during the pleasure of the town" (it should be of the church), "and no longer, provided they can agree with the proprietors of said horse-sheds; and also that they be authorized to place an estimate of said pound upon the land of the heirs of Isaac Lamson deceased, and provided also that the whole shall be done without any cost to the town." The pound land and also the land upon which the sheds are built are all one, and the fee is in the Lamson heirs. In the deed to Jonas Sanderson it is stated that the sheds are partly on town's land (church) and partly upon land of the heirs of Isaac Lamson.

At a town meeting held December 27, 1814, it was voted to give Mr. Joseph Field, Jr., an invitation to settle in the ministry in the town of Weston, three only voting against it, as we have previously stated (see Chapter I., near end, for details of the ordination, etc.).

At the March meeting in 1815 it was voted to remove the pews on the lower floor of the meeting-house, and also the body seats, and to erect in their place long pews, so as to cover the whole floor, excepting space for the aisles and stove; to lay a new floor; and to provide a new door, to swing outwardly. It was voted not to send any representative this year.

At a town meeting held September 18, 1815, the Selectmen were empowered to agree and settle with the Boston Manufacturing Company for all injuries or damages that have been done or may hereafter be done to the bridge and causeway over Charles River (so far as the limits are within the town of Weston) by reason of the dam which said manufacturing company has erected, etc. This was important, since the bridge was carried away and destroyed some years later, and it was said that the dam of that company was the cause. It was an accident that may occur again.

It was voted in 1816 that all the inhabitants who shall pay their taxes within thirty days shall have an abatement of six per cent., within sixty days five per cent., and all within one hundred and twenty days four per cent. $1,000 was voted for Mr. Field's salary for this year, but the year following it is only the $800 agreed upon with him. The addition of $200 was probably for the expense attending his settlement. Voted to build a new schoolhouse in the South-west District. Voted that those soldiers who were drafted and served in the late war should be paid $14 per month for the time they served, and the same be allowed those of the Independent Light Infantry Company of Weston (who actually served) upon a return made by the clerk of the company.

In town meeting, March 3, 1817, voted to sell the old poorhouse and land, and purchase a site for a new poorhouse. Voted $60 for salary of town treasurer and collector.

In 1818 the committee appointed to purchase a site for the new poorhouse report that they have purchased of Habakkuk Stearns a farm on the northerly part of the town, containing about eighty acres with the buildings thereon, and have taken a deed therefor

for the sum of $2,513.27; that the expense for placing the aforesaid premises in condition for the use of the town was $1,550.62; that they have sold the old poorhouse and land to Samuel G. Derby for $230, leaving a balance due from the town of $3,835.89.

Voted in 1819 that the soldiers belonging to the town of Weston, whenever they are lawfully called to do military duty out of the town, shall each receive one dollar from the treasury, provided the clerk of the company shall certify that said duty was performed, said sum being in lieu of the powder now by law provided by the town when they are called to attend reviews.

Daniel S. Lamson was made town treasurer in 1819.

In 1820 $100 was voted for instruction in sacred music; also that a committee be appointed, consisting of three from the Congregational church, one from the Methodist, and one from the Baptist, who shall be authorized to draw said money for that purpose.

At a town meeting held August 21, 1820, to consider whether it be expedient that delegates be chosen to meet in convention for the purpose of revising or altering the constitution of government of this Commonwealth, the vote stood as follows: in favor of appointing delegates, 35; against the appointment, 15; and Isaac Fiske was appointed such delegate. At a town meeting held November 6, 1820, to choose electors-at-large for President and Vice-President of the United States, Hon. William Phillips had 47 votes; and Hon. William Gray, 47.

Dr. Benjamin James contracted with the town to inoculate the inhabitants of Weston with cow-pox for $50.

Voted in 1824 that there be appropriated to the use of the soldiers of Weston so much of the powder and ball as the law requires each soldier to be furnished with, the same, however, to remain in the powder-house. Electors-at-large in 1824 for President and Vice-President of the United States: Hon. William Gray, 91 votes; Levi Lincoln, 91 votes.

The contest in town meeting in 1826 over the election of a representative to the General Court was quite animated. Five ballots were taken, resulting finally in the election of Mr. Nathan Hobbs.

The town meeting held April 2, 1827, was held in the hall of John T. Macomber's tavern; but, as all the other warrants of town meetings are ordered to meet in the meeting-house of the town, it would appear there was a special meeting held at the tavern. It may be, however, that this was the first meeting out of the church. They were so accustomed to follow old formulas in the warrants that it may be the meetings were henceforth held at the tavern. The warrants, however, order meetings at the church down to 1840, when the church was ordered to be taken down. The contest over the election of representative occurs again this year. Four ballots were taken, and Alpheus Bigelow was elected. Mrs. Patience Lamson, widow of Daniel S. Lamson, applies for abatement of her taxes for 1825. The assessors report there was an error made. Her tax should be $9.15 instead of $23.63.

In 1828 Mr. Isaac Fiske ceases to be town clerk, after filling the office for a period of twenty-four years. He is succeeded by Dr. Benjamin James, who is also elected a selectman, assessor of taxes, and school committee man; and it was voted that the school committee should consist of three members only. In 1828 it was voted that a committee provide a place for holding town meetings in the future. No report is on the records.* The tithing-men, who had been elected each year since the incorporation of the town, from 1830 on ceased to be elected.

In 1830 a petition was sent to the County Commissioners for a road from Luther Harrington's house to Ball's Hill. The town opposed the road as prayed for, and the Selectmen were authorized to employ counsel. Mr. Hoar was engaged.

In 1832 to promote sacred music $100 was voted, and Charles Merriam, Uriah Gregory, and John Jones directed to spend the money.

Voted in 1833 to extend the stone bridge over the watering-place and the canal, near the house of the late Dr. Kendal, and make the same passable. There had been here up to this time a place to water cattle and a driveway through it, as may be still seen in places in town. In old times, when there were large droves

---

* No vote of the town is recorded this year, 1828, for painting the meeting-house, as had been the case up to this time in all pertaining to the church. The painting, however, was done by private subscription. There were sixty-eight subscribers, and the sum raised was $190. [A list of the subscribers found among Colonel Lamson's papers puts the total sum at $178.—ED.]

of cattle on their way to market, such places were not very far apart; and, where they were not near enough to each other, the farmers were induced to have wells and troughs for cattle near the road, and a certain abatement of taxes was made to induce the citizens to establish them. One of these pumps may still be seen in front of Mr. Frank Hastings's house. It was voted to build the road and bridge from a point near the barn of the late Abraham Bigelow to the centre of the brook at the Waltham line, so far as the same is within the limits of Weston, and $400 was appropriated for that purpose. Up to this time the road to Waltham had run over the bridge through the Sibley property back of the present main road.

In 1834 a tract of land was purchased by the town from Isaac and Stephen Jones, to enlarge the burying-ground on its northern side to the great road, and one rod in width upon the west side, extending from the great road to the southerly side; to cause the walls to be removed and suitable gates erected, provided the same should not exceed the sum of $300. Voted that an abstract of the treasurer's account be prepared and 220 copies printed for the use of the town. This abstract was printed on sheets of paper about eighteen inches square. The publication of this abstract was probably not continued, inasmuch as only the one dated 1834 can be found. They are now very rare, but one of them should be among the records. The publication of town reports in pamphlet form did not begin until the year 1844. In 1834 Charles Merriam was made town treasurer. Voted to enlarge the East Centre School-house about twelve feet, and procure a title to the land on behalf of the town. Voted that the Selectmen procure a new building for a hearse-house or repair the old one, which had been the old powder-house in the burying-ground; but in 1835 the powder-house was sold by auction, for the space was needed to enlarge the ground.

In 1835 the town authorized the treasurer to borrow $500 in anticipation of taxes. This is the first time authority was given to make any such loan.

In 1836 Dr. James was elected to fill six offices of the town. It was voted to make the road between Dr. Field's meeting-house and the house of Mr. Alpheus Cutter in accordance with the

THE SAMUEL PHILLIPS SAVAGE PLACE, NORTH AVENUE.

Probably built by Mr. Savage, who died in 1797. This place was owned and occupied a long time by Captain Thomas Bigelow, son of Josiah Bigelow, of Weston. It was later bought by Samuel G. Snelling, who extensively remodelled it about 1880. It is now owned by the heirs of Samuel Lothrop Thorndike.

THE WARREN HOUSE, LEXINGTON STREET.

The main portion of the house was built in 1743. The new part was built in 1810. This was known as the Benjamin Pierce, Jr., house previous to 1885, when it was bought by Francis H. Hastings, and by him sold in 1893 to George H. Ellis.

order of the County Commissioners. Starr bridge, or, as it is sometimes called, Stack bridge, and the causeway over Charles River were ordered rebuilt of wood or stone, in conjunction with the town of Newton; the structure to be not less than eighteen feet wide in the clear, and the cost to the town not to exceed $1,000. This bridge was carried away, as has been stated, and probably by ice.

The debt of the United States, which in the year 1791 was $75,463,476.52, was entirely paid off in 1835. The interest on this debt in 1816 was $7,156,500.42. In 1826 the interest was $4,000,000. After that year the government paid off, including interest, nearly $100,000,000 over and above current expenses; and so great was the general prosperity of the nation that the payment of this large sum was but little felt by the people.

In 1833 the six winter and summer schools cost the town $859.91; town treasurer's salary, $200; and the total expenses of the town were $1,468.95 with a population as large as that of to-day.

In 1837 the town voted to procure a new hearse and pall, such as would be decent in appearance and respectable for the town. This hearse was kept in the north-end church shed, which, when the town house was built, reverted to the Lamson estate, and in 1882 was sold by auction for $6.

In March, 1837, the legislature passed an act, distributing by instalments to the towns of the Commonwealth the surplus revenue of the State. The treasurer of Weston was directed to use the fund as he received it, and pay off the indebtedness of the town. Weston received from the State treasurer $2,259.17, which paid the town debt at that time and left a balance in the treasury of $9.17.

The city of Boston brought an action against the town for the support of Abijah Bemis, and the town defended the case. There is no record of the result, but later it was found that Bemis had been sent by the city to the House of Correction, and they applied to have him removed to the Weston poorhouse.

The vote for governor in November, 1837, was about equally divided between the Whigs and Locofocos. Edward Everett received 75 votes, and Marcus Morton 73 votes. Morton was elected governor of the State. There was considerable excitement throughout the State at this election, and party spirit was rife.

In 1837 great excitement prevailed throughout the State, growing out of the rescue of the slave Shadrach by a mob that forcibly entered the Supreme Court room in Boston, and took him from under the nose of Judge Shaw, and secretly conveyed him to Concord. Francis Edwin Bigelow, son of Converse Bigelow of Weston, had removed to Concord about 1836, where he worked at the trade of blacksmithing until his death in 1893. He was one of the original Abolitionists, who at that early date had begun to make themselves felt in the community. He harbored the fugitive Shadrach, and drove him at night to Sudbury on his way to Canada, having clothed him in a suit of his own clothes, including a hat of Mr. Nathan Brooks. Later Elizur Wright, Lewis Hayden, Robert Morris, and others were arrested and brought to trial for aiding the rescue of the slave. They were defended by John P. Hale, of Maine, and Richard H. Dana, Jr. The most curious part of this strange episode is that Mr. Bigelow was summoned as a juror from Concord to sit upon the case to be tried. The eminent counsel had little hope of an acquittal, the evidence against the accused being so strong. To their surprise, notwithstanding the judge's charge to the jury, they were acquitted. Some years after Mr. Dana, meeting Bigelow, asked how the jury could bring in such a verdict after all the evidence. "Well," said Mr. Bigelow, "*I drove the wagon that took Shadrach to Sudbury.*" Mr. Dana asked no more questions. When called upon to take the juror's oath, Mr. Bigelow said he felt some doubts, but, seeing an Abolition friend from Littleton take the oath, he thought he could do so, thus carrying out the "Higher Law" laid down by Theodore Parker.

In 1838 the town ordered a new road to be laid out between the house of Isaac Jones and the house of Otis Train. The old road was too narrow and circuitous. The petitioners for this new road were Alpheus Morse, Otis Train, Abijah Upham, Swift Leadbetter, Samuel Train, Jr., Adolphus Brown, Marshall Brown, Henry Leadbetter, and Tyler Harrington.

The great commercial and financial crisis of 1837 and 1838, the first of its kind since the Embargo Act of 1808, was seriously felt throughout the United States, and produced wide-spread ruin, but was not of a kind materially to affect the agricultural interests of our people.

The years 1838 and 1839 were noted for the great crusade against the indiscriminate sale of liquor. It was in fact a temperance movement. George W. Cutting was arrested for the sale of liquor, and taken to Cambridge jail. Joel Smith was summoned as a witness, but did not see fit to obey the summons. He also was arrested and sentenced to a week's imprisonment and a fine of $50 for contempt of court.

In 1839 took place the Dedham muster, locally famous in story and song. This was better known as the Striped Pig Muster, and was the last of the rollicking musters so famous in the old times. There was more of fun and frolic at these old meets than drilling, more of drunkenness than discipline; and yet there was this about them,—they kept up among the farmers and their sons military organizations now completely gone out of date. Towns that formerly had one, two, and three companies, now have none, and there are many towns that have not a single inhabitant belonging to any military company. The militia of to-day is made up of the inhabitants of large cities and manufacturing centres, to the utter exclusion of the yeomanry, and we shall be fortunate if we escape the realization of this error in the near future.

IX.

THE STORY OF THE TOWN FROM YEAR TO YEAR.
1840–1860.

With the close of the year 1839 that which can be called the ancient history of Weston closes. With the year 1840 begins a new era, within the memory of many now happily living. We cannot enter upon this period without making a few reflections in keeping with the subject-matter of this book. All that relates to the past of our town and country is hallowed to us of the present day by story and tradition, and a comparison with all that has gone before with that which follows is not in every respect to the advantage of the times we live in. Every period of time has its special defects, but it is essential that the moral element be kept at a high level, if these defects are to be safely overcome. As the American people progress in wealth, comfort, and luxury, and enjoy all those appliances in every-day life which were unknown to our ancestors, it is to be feared that the young men and women are losing sight of those sturdy moral principles which gave force and decision to the early settlers. Faith in God is not so firmly established in the minds and hearts of youth as was formerly the case. Education has become materialized, and the aims of life have taken in consequence a more sordid and vulgar level.

The marvellous progress of our country in every walk of life, unparalleled the world over, may be said to date from 1840, when railroads came in and horse chaises began to disappear. Families are not so large now, and perhaps we can say with equal truth that their virtues are less prominent. Time has become so valuable in the pursuit of wealth and comfort that it is thought wasted upon local affairs over which our sires fought with a tenacity little understood or appreciated to-day. People throughout New England do not love the town meetings as they used to do. Trivial matters, such as money grants, low taxation, sanitary measures, good order, and discipline, are left to the few ambitious of local honors, and the inhabitants transfer all responsibility and interest to the hands of those who will do the least work for the most pay. The result of all this is that the State is yearly encroaching upon the rights of towns that no longer care to preserve their liberties, the best guardians of which are the old town meetings, the corner-stone of the Constitution of the United States. While generous sums are being spent on education, our boys and girls are less able to cope with the labors and difficulties of every-day life than were their fathers and mothers before them, who little enjoyed the privileges purchasable by the plethoric purse of the tax-payer or the liberal State bounties. The fundamentals in education are being less thought of, and seem to be giving place to 'ologies and 'isms, which, while perhaps more ornamental, are but poor aid to people in the battle of life.

The majority of farm lads find themselves incapable of doing the work of the farms or unwilling to do it. Consequently, these are passing into the hands of the stranger or the foreigner. Young men flock to the cities, where the scramble for employment each year becomes greater, and where they sacrifice their independence to do the bidding of their wealthy employers, who rarely take them into their confidence. Unless young men, who go out from their modest, happy homes into large cities, are established in sound moral and religious principles, they become careless in their methods of life, and are easily led into unscrupulous business transactions. When the country loses $8,000,000 in one year by fraud and dishonesty, it is time to study a remedy; and this can be found in a higher standard of moral education rather than in the broad range of study which educates the mind at the expense of the heart.

The year 1840 opens with the taking down of the old church which stood upon the church green and the action taken by the town in connection therewith. Some of the steps taken will be new to many of us, and, although not carried out, it will be interesting to state them here as a part of the history of that period. Before doing so, however, the reader must be told of a feat performed by Joel Harrington and Elisha Whitney. They climbed to the top of the lightning rod of the church steeple, drank a bottle of wine on the top, and left their tumbler on the rod, where it remained until a hawk is said to have picked it off.

At a town meeting held May 4, 1840, the committee appointed at a previous meeting reported that they had conferred with Rev. Dr. Field's parish upon the subject of the construction of a new meeting-house in such a manner as should furnish a convenient place for holding town meetings and for other public purposes. They were to agree upon cost, making proposals to the committee of the parish as to the terms upon which the same should be done; and also to ascertain whether a convenient spot of land could be procured upon which to build a town house, and what a town house would cost.

Your committee was in conference with said church committee, who propose a building 60 feet in length and 46 feet in breadth, with a basement story, or hall, under it of the same dimensions, with one convenient room partitioned off for the use of the Selectmen, and another for the assessors of the Town, which they offered to do for $1,300, or whatever sum the contractors shall say will be the actual cost. That when completed to the acceptance of the Town, they will convey the same to the Town of Weston, will covenant to keep the same externally in good repair and will also covenant to pay over and refund to the said Town the original cost of the same whenever the said house shall be permitted to fall into decay, or cease to be occupied as a Meeting house for the Worship of Almighty God. The Committee of the Town are of opinion that a convenient spot of land and a building for the Municipal and other public purposes sufficiently capacious, durable, and comely would cost the town $2,500; they are therefore, on the principle of economy, of the opinion that an agreement be made with the Parish for the accommodation of the Town, or with some individual whereby the town may be permanently accommodated, and a committee of five was appointed with ample powers to effect the same.

ALPHEUS BIGELOW, Jr.,
ISAAC JONES,
EZRA WARREN,
AMOS WARREN,
Committee.

It was voted to accept the proposal of the parish committee, the expenses of which were to be determined by the contractors, together with Oliver Hastings, of Cambridge, and Samuel Sanger,

THE STORY OF THE TOWN FROM YEAR TO YEAR 133

of Brighton; and the treasurer was authorized to borrow the money and give his notes for the same.

The town meeting last held in the old church was on May 4, 1840. At the town meeting of April 6, 1840, the citizens voted for and against a proposed article of amendment to the Constitution, as follows: for, 35; against, 45.

In accordance with the militia law of the Commonwealth the town made a return of those inhabitants of Weston subject to military duty for the year 1840. They numbered 147 men. This law is still in force, and returns are made each year to the State. The votes this year for electors-at-large for President and Vice-President of the United States were William P. Walker, of Lenox, 116 votes; Ebenezer Fisher, of Dedham, 116; Isaac C. Bates, of Northampton, 83; and Peleg Sprague, of Boston, 83. The vote for governor was 118 votes for Marcus Morton, and 82 for John Davis. William Spring was elected representative to the General Court from Weston. Eleven guide-posts were erected in several parts of the town in 1840 in accordance with a law of the Commonwealth. The town debt in 1840 was $4,241.55. An inventory was taken of property belonging to the town, but no valuation of said property is reported.

In 1841 it was voted that the name of no person shall be retained on the jury list unless as many as 10 votes are cast in his favor, and that each shall be voted upon separately.

Samuel H. F. Bingham was elected to the General Court.

In 1843 an agreement was made by the committee appointed to contract for a place to hold town meetings, and they reported that a lease had been made with Marshall and John Jones for five years, at a yearly rental of $30, for the hall in the dwelling-house near Rev. Mr. Field's meeting-house, for the purpose mentioned and for other town business. Meetings had already been held in this hall since 1840.

In 1843 it was voted to have Town Reports printed in a pamphlet form, and a copy distributed to each family. This pamphlet appeared in 1844, and has continued to be issued in this form down to our own time.

In 1844 the town voted to build a barn on the poor-farm, 40 by 50 feet, and 16-feet posts. Five hundred dollars was appropriated for that purpose. The actual cost of the barn, when finished, was $828.50. The vote for governor of the State was: George Bancroft, 102 votes; George N. Briggs, 100. Edwin Hobbs was elected to represent the town in the legislature.

As early as 1845 a petition of Leonard C. Drury and others for the widening and straightening of the road between the meeting-house and Hobbs's Depot was sent in, but opposed by the town. It was done, however, on an extensive and expensive scale, costing the town about $8,000. This road is now called Church Street. The vote this year stood 49 for George N. Briggs and 60 for Isaac Davis. No representative was sent to the General Court this year.

At a town meeting held March 1, 1847, a vote of thanks was proposed, and unanimously carried, to be presented to Dr. Benjamin James for his long and faithful services as town clerk. He had held the position since 1828, a period of nineteen years. Dr. James was succeeded by Mr. Nathan Hager in the office. The school committee was directed to draft a plan for a high school.

In May, 1847, it was voted to build a town house, and Benjamin Peirce, Nathan Hager, and Marshall Jones were appointed a committee for said purpose. June 7 this committee reported:—

That the plan of a house, such as we think would be satisfactory when completed, should be 60 feet long, including the colonnade, 40 feet wide, and two stories high. The cost of such a house finished like those in neighboring towns would probably be about $3,000. Town Committee would recommend that the Town House be located on the northerly side of the meeting-house Common, which is now occupied by a pound and for horse-sheds and a highway, provided satisfactory arrangements can be made with the parish and the owners of the sheds.

It was voted that acceptance of the report be decided by a yea and nay vote. The result was: yeas, 76; nays, 46. A resolution was also carried that the committee be authorized to hire the money for all expenses pertaining to the building of said house.

December 13, 1847, the committee reported that the expense incurred in erecting and furnishing the town-house building amounted to $4,078.62, which amount was then due. At this meeting it was voted that any inhabitant or inhabitants of

Weston shall have a right to the use of the hall for singing or lectures or discussions on any subjects which are intended to diffuse useful knowledge in the community, provided they are free to all, and that they furnish fire and light. Voted that the next town meeting be held in this house. The vote for governor in 1847 stood 76 for George N. Briggs and 57 for C. Cushing.

At a town meeting held March 6, 1848, it was voted that the lower rooms in the town hall may be used for school purposes. Voted that all demands for abatement of taxes, heretofore passed upon in open town meeting, be henceforth referred to the assessors for their action thereon. In 1848–49 no vote is recorded for a representative to the General Court. Otis Train was sent in 1847.

In 1851 it was voted to build three new school-houses, one in the North-west District, one in the North-east District, and one in the West Centre District, which three houses cost $4,111.92.

At a town meeting held November 10, 1851, on the question "whether it was expedient that Delegates be chosen to meet in Convention for the purpose of revising or altering the Constitution of this Commonwealth," the vote was as follows: yeas, 58; nays, 94.

Again, in 1852, the same question arose as to the appointment of delegates in convention for the same purpose, resulting in a tie vote, 76 to 76, and Edwin Hobbs was chosen delegate.

In accordance with the law passed by the legislature in June, 1855, concerning the sale of spirituous liquors, the Selectmen appointed Joel Upham an agent for the purchase of spirituous and intoxicating liquors to be used in the arts or for medicinal purposes in the town of Weston.

At a town meeting held March 3, 1856, a breeze was created after the election of the Selectmen and town clerk. Objections were made by J. Q. A. Harrington to these officers being sworn, on the ground that the check-list had not been used in their election, as required by law. It was decided to go back and proceed to a new election. The vote, as declared, elected John A. Lamson town clerk, and Nathan Barker, Luther Upham, and Edward Coburn Selectmen, John A. Lamson acting as town clerk. Nathan Hager, who was undoubtedly legally elected town clerk and had been sworn as such, entered into the book of town record at the close of the meeting that "the proceedings of this meeting are irregular, informal, illegal, and do not form part of the Records of the Town of Weston."

At a town meeting held November 3, 1857, it was voted by the citizens assembled to establish a library, to be called the "Weston Town Library," for the use of the inhabitants thereof. They chose Isaac Fiske, Dr. Otis E. Hunt, and Rev. C. H. Topliff a committee to prepare rules and regulations for the organization and government of the library. This committee reported, December 21, 1857, "that the people of Weston, impressed with the necessity and importance of a public library, commenced a subscription in the several school districts for this purpose." The movement was initiated by a committee of twelve gentlemen and seven ladies, with the result of a subscription of about $500 in money and donation of books valued at about $70. It was voted to choose a library committee of six members by ballot, and Rev. C. H. Topliff, Otis E. Hunt, Charles Dunn, Nahum Smith, J. Q. Loring, and Isaac Coburn were chosen, with Marshall Jones as treasurer of the library.

In 1858 appears the first vote by district for representative to the General Court. George W. Warren, of Weston, had 74 votes, Nathan Barker 34, and Julius M. Smith, of Concord, 27.

In 1859 Mr. Charles Merriam donated $1,000 to be appropriated for the purchase of books for the town library. It was voted that this sum be securely invested, and no part of the principal be expended for the above purpose for a period of ten years. This money is still invested, and the interest alone devoted to the purchase of books.

Voted that the thanks of the town be tendered to Marshall Jones for his long and faithful services as town treasurer. Mr. Horace Hews at the same meeting was chosen town treasurer, which office he held until 1889, when in consequence of failing health he felt obliged to resign the trust which he had held for thirty years. Mr. Hews's resignation was much regretted, and sympathy was expressed for him by all.

X.

WAR VETERANS, RAILROADS, ETC.

1860–1890.

At the town meeting of April 2, 1860, the committee appointed to report on the condition of the poorhouse deposed that,

with regard to the plan of "letting out" the poor to board with the one who would do it the cheapest, we can only say that the time has gone by when a course so advisedly opposed to every good principle can ever again be adopted. We have considered it a settled policy of the town to support their poor upon a farm of their own. We believe they should be provided with a warm and comfortable shelter, with wholesome food and proper raiment. We do not feel that it would be wise or politic for the town to exchange the present location for another one. We believe a building might be erected at an expense not exceeding $2,500. It has been said that the town is in debt and that much money has been expended during the last ten or fifteen years. If money has been expended, it has not been wasted or squandered, but has been wisely and judiciously expended, giving us an equivalent in our neat and commodious public buildings.

Voted that Edwin Hobbs, Horatio Hews, Isaac Coburn, Alpheus Morse, and John W. Harrington be a committee to build the house on the town farm, for the best interest of the town, and that they be authorized to draw on the treasurer for the money. In November, 1861, this committee reported the building as completed, 32 by 40 feet, with an "L" 14 by 34 feet, at a cost of $2,450. School appropriation, $1,629.28. Town debt, $3,700. Treasurer's salary, $25.

The list returned to the State of those inhabitants of the town of Weston subject to military duty in the year 1860 formed a roster of 161 men. The vote for the governor this year stood: John A. Andrew, 100 votes; Amos A. Lawrence, of Boston, 39; Benjamin F. Butler, 4. In the fall of the year 1860, when the clouds were thickening over us, but before any overt act had been committed by the slave States, a Home Guard was organized by Captain D. S. Lamson for the purpose of drill and general preparation for future contingencies. The men purchased their own arms, which were deposited in the town hall. About fifty young men joined the company, and were drilled in the manual of arms and street marching. This company never entered a regiment as a whole, but all its members enlisted in regiments as they were later formed by the State.

In June of the year 1861 Mr. Lamson was appointed major of the Sixteenth Regiment, which was then forming at Camp Cameron, North Cambridge. The mustering into the service of the United States for three years took place July 13, 1861. The vote for governor this year stood: John A. Andrew, 74 votes; Isaac Davis, 80. In the same year the town treasurer was chosen to be collector of taxes. Heretofore it had been the custom, from the earliest period of the town records, to put up the duty of collecting the taxes to the highest [?] bidder, and the sums awarded for this duty varied from one cent and five mills to one cent and six mills on a dollar. Isaac Fiske, Esq., who had died, bequeathed three hundred dollars for the town library.

At a town meeting, July 19, 1862, it was voted to pay a bounty of $100 to each man who should enlist in the army of the United States for the purpose of fighting the South, till the quota of seventeen required of the town should be furnished, the bounty payable on presentation of a certificate that the volunteer had been accepted and mustered into the service. In August this bounty was increased to $200 "to all who enlist within ten days for nine months." The town further voted to give to each man now or hereafter to enlist $10. Twenty-six young men enlisted, and the town voted to pay them the above bounty, although the number exceeded the quota of the town. It was also voted that the treasurer give a note to any of the volunteers for his bounty, payable on demand at six per cent. interest.

At a town meeting, September 27, 1862, the following resolution was carried:—

That, whereas we have learned that Ralph A. Jones, one of our volunteers, has fallen in battle, and that others are known to be wounded, therefore *Resolved*, That the Rev. C. H. Topliff proceed to Maryland and recover, if possible, the body of said Jones or any others that have since died, and attend to the wants of the wounded men suffering in any of the hospitals. *Voted*, That in case of the death of any volunteers of the town whose families are entitled to State aid the same shall be continued to them.

At a town meeting, October 11, 1862, Rev. Mr. Topliff related the incidents of his journey to Maryland. A committee was appointed to make the necessary arrangements for the funeral of Ralph A. Jones. The following is the list of volunteers, in the service of the United States for three years, from the town of Weston:—

Daniel S. Lamson	Major	16th Regt.	Infantry
William Henry Carter	Co. H	26th "	Infantry
Ebenezer Tucker	" M	1st "	Cavalry
John E. Powers	" H	16th "	Infantry
Charles L. Field	Lieutenant	99th "	New York
Lewis Jones	—	1st "	Cavalry
Philip J. Meyer, Jr.	—	2d Battery Artillery	
John Robinson	Co. H	24th Regt.	Infantry
Warren Stickney	Corporal Co. H	16th "	"
Adoniram J. Smith	Co. G	22d "	"
Thomas Palmer	" H	16th "	"
Edward Banyea	—	5th "	Vermont
William G. Clark	Co. H	16th "	Infantry
Frank W. Bigelow	Sergeant Co. G	13th "	"
Henry H. Richardson	—	16th "	"
Thomas Fahey	—	9th "	"
David E. Cook	—	35th	" Sappers and Miners
John W. Drew	—	35th "	Infantry
John L. Ayer	Co. I	35th "	"
Lemuel Smith	" "	35th "	"
Charles Roberts	" "	35th "	"
Samuel Patch, Jr.	" "	35th "	"
Henry A. Tucker	" "	35th "	"
George T. Tucker	" "	35th "	"
Andrew Floyd	" "	35th "	"
Wm. C. Stimpson, Jr.	" "	35th "	"
Frederick A. Hews	" "	35th "	"
Joseph Smith	" "	35th "	"
George G. Cheney	" "	35th "	"
William Henzy	" "	35th "	"
Charles G. Fisher	" "	35th "	"
Ralph A. Jones	" "	35th "	"

140 HISTORY OF WESTON

Andrew C. Badger	Co. I	35th Regt. Infantry
Daniel H. Adams	" "	35th " "
Jabez N. Smith	" "	35th " "
James M. Fairfield	" "	38th " "
Daniel Keyes	" "	41st " "
Sefroy Britten	" "	3d Rhode Island Battery

The following are nine months' men under the call of August 4, 1862:—

Henry L. Brown	Co. I	44th Regt. Infantry
Charles E. Cutter	" "	44th " "
George E. Rand	" "	44th " "
Albert Washburn	" "	44th " "
Edward L. Cutter	" "	44th " "
Marshall L. Hews	" "	44th " "
Edwin P. Upham	" "	44th " "
James A. Cooper	" "	44th " "
Francis H. Poole	" "	44th " "
Samuel H. Corliss	" "	44th " "
George W. Rand	" "	44th " "
George C. Floyd	" "	44th " "
Isaac H. Carey	" "	44th " "
Herbert B. Richardson	" "	44th " "
Wm. C. Roberts	" "	44th " "
John Coughlin	" "	44th " "
Benj. A. Drake	" "	44th " "
James M. Palmer	" "	44th " "
George E. Hobbs	" "	44th " "
George J. Morse	" C	44th " "
Henry W. Day	" H	44th " "
Abner J. Teel	" "	43d " "
Saml. W. Johnson	" "	43d " "
H. Illingsworth	" E	43d " "
Fuller Morton	" "	43d " "
H. A. Whittemore	" "	43d " "
Walker W. Roberts	" A	43d " "
Caleb W. Lincoln	" E	6th " "
Ferdinand Dagsburg	—	16th " "

Making a total of thirty-eight three years' men and twenty-nine nine months' men. Of the thirty-three men drafted at Concord, July 18, 1863, twenty-eight were exempted, one commuted, two found substitutes, and two entered the service, one of whom (Lucius A. Hill) was killed, May 10, 1864.

The following 16 men enlisted and constituted the quota of Weston under the call of the President, October 17, 1863:—

Daniel J. Webber,	2d Mass. Cav'ry	William Chandler,	2d Mass. Cav'ry
Henry W. Ober,	2d " "	John Vaughn,	59th Reg. Infan'y
Joy Chandler,	2d " "	Peter Richie,	2d Heavy Artill'y
Walter Webster,	2d " "	Nicholas Besson,	2d " "
John Conners,	Heavy Artillery	Michael Durfee,	2d " "
John S. Doane,	5th Mass. Batt'y	Hugh J. Sharpe,	56th Reg. Infan'y
George Crosby,	5th Mass. Batt'y	John O'Connell,	1st Cav'ry
John W. Stowell,	7th Reg. Infan'y	Mchl. Cavanaugh,	56th Reg. Infan'y

The enlistment under the additional call of 200,000 men, fourteen being Weston's quota, was as follows:—

James Welch,	59th Regt.	Arthur Martin,	3d Cavalry
Charles H. Burton,	59th "	William Barry,	4th "
John Lund,	59th "	Charles A. Fitch,	5th "
Joseph Faybien,	59th "	John Robinson,	24th Regt.
Daniel Robinson,	56th "	William H. Carter,	26th Regt.
William C. Roberts,	55th "	William Carnes,*	U.S. Navy.
James J. O'Conner,	4th Cavalry		

The vote for governor stood: John A. Andrew, 78 votes; Charles Devens, Jr., 64. It was voted that "the Rev. Mr. Topliff be a committee of one to bring home the bodies of any of our soldiers who have or may hereafter fall in battle and render any assistance necessary to our sick or wounded soldiers."

The town debt as reported by the treasurer was stated to be $20,072.82. In April, 1863, bonds were ordered for $10,000 of the town debt, payable in ten years from May 1, at five per cent. interest. The bonds were to have interest coupons attached, signed by the town treasurer, payable semi-annually each year. These bonds to be issued in sums of $100, $250, and $500 each. In 1863 John A. Andrew had the entire vote of the town for governor. At a town meeting, November, 1863, Nathan Hager, town clerk, having died on the 14th of that month, Horace Hews was chosen town clerk *pro tem*. Mr. Hager had been town clerk for twenty years. He had filled various other offices of trust, and the town was indebted to him for his judicious management of their affairs. It was voted that the resolution passed March 7, 1864,

*Died in Andersonville Prison in 1864.

be transmitted to his family and entered on the records of the town.

Voted that a committee of six be appointed, one for each district, to assist the recruiting officer in filling the town quota of troops, and $3,200 was placed in their hands for that purpose. At a town meeting held on November 28, 1863, Horace Hews, clerk *pro tem.*, declined to serve longer, and Benjamin F. Morrison was chosen clerk *pro tem.* The Selectmen appointed Dr. Otis E. Hunt clerk until another should be legally chosen.

At a town meeting held on March 7, 1864, George W. Cutting, Jr., was chosen clerk. Three hundred dollars was voted for hay scales, which were to be of the size called ten tons. In May the town voted $125 a man, if necessary, "to aid in filling any and all calls that the general government has made or shall make upon this town for soldiers for the year ending in March, 1865."

In 1864 the quota of Weston for three years' men was twelve, and they were all hired by the town.

The number of men furnished by Weston during the War of 1861–65 was a hundred and twenty-six. Of these eight were killed, three died of wounds, and one in prison. The names of the killed are as follows:—

Ralph A. Jones, killed at Antietam, September 17, 1862, 35th Regiment.
James M. Fairfield, killed at Port Hudson, June 1, 1863, 38th Regiment.
William Henzy, killed at Knoxville, November 20, 1863, 35th Regiment.
Lucius A. Hill, killed at Laurel Hill, May 10, 1864, 22d Regiment.
John Robinson, killed at Drury Bluffs, May 14, 1864, 24th Regiment.
George T. Tucker, killed at Petersburg, July 4, 1864, 35th Regiment.
William H. Carter, killed at Winchester, September 19, 1864, 26th Regiment.
William C. Stimpson, killed at Poplar Springs, September 20, 1864, 35th Regiment.

The following soldiers of Weston died of wounds in hospital:—

Frederick A. Hews, 35th Regiment; died in Washington, January 5, 1863.
Fuller Morton, 43d Regiment; died in Kingston, N.C., January 6, 1863.
Edmund L. Cutter, 44th Regiment; died in Newbern, N.C., April 31, 1863.
William Carnes, United States Navy; died in Andersonville, June 13, 1864.

THE CUTTING HOUSE, LEXINGTON STREET.

This is on the original Warren estate, where John Warren, Sr., settled soon after his arrival from England in 1631. For over a century and since the marriage of Cynthia Warren to the senior John Cutting it has been the home of the Cutting family.

THE OLD DR. WOODWARD HOUSE, CONCORD STREET.

Built by Rev. Mr. Woodward when pastor of the church at Weston, preceding Dr. Kendal. It was later owned by Dr. Bancroft, the town physician, and here Dr. George C. Shattuck, of Boston, studied with Dr. Bancroft. It was bought by Augustus H. Fiske in 1848, and is still owned by his descendants.

The amount the town paid for bounties during the war was $9,025; the expenses attendant upon drafts were $3,524.90; a total of $12,549.90. To this total voted by the town must be added the money raised by voluntary subscription, amounting to $5,104.95, or a total of $17,654.85. To this amount must be added the sum paid for recovering the bodies of George T. Tucker, William H. Carter, and John Robinson, killed in battle ($416.03),—making a grand total of $18,070.88, which must be admitted as a very liberal and patriotic showing for a population of about 1,400. Nor is this all; for the town paid out for State aid the sum of $4,870.16 during the years from 1862 to 1868.

In October, 1864, a petition was addressed to Edwin Hobbs, Esq., justice of the peace for Middlesex County, as follows:—

Whereas the Methodist Episcopal Church Society in Weston, having for several years neglected to choose Trustees of the Society, and there being no clerk legally qualified to call a meeting, we, the undersigned members thereof, respectfully request you to issue a warrant, calling a meeting of the qualified voters of the Society agreeable to the provisions of the Revised Statutes.

The petition was signed by Franklin Childs, Amos Carter, Jr., Daniel Stearns, Abijah Gregory, and Abijah G. Jones. A warrant was issued accordingly, returnable November 7, 1864, and E. F. Childs was made clerk, and seven trustees were chosen.

In March, 1865, Mr. Charles Merriam, of Boston, addressed a letter to the Selectmen of Weston, enclosing bonds to the amount of one thousand dollars for the purpose of establishing a fund for the "silent poor of Weston," the interest of which sum shall be paid over to the "honest, temperate men and women who work hard and are prudent and economical and yet find it difficult to make both ends meet." Upon the reading of Mr. Merriam's letter, Mr. A. S. Fiske presented the following resolution:—

Resolved, That we tender to Mr. Charles Merriam, Esq., our sincere thanks for his munificent donation, presented to the inhabitants of the town.

Resolved, That we gratefully accept the trust, and that the fund shall be called the "Merriam Fund for the Benefit of the Silent Poor of Weston."

The trustees of this fund were chosen by ballot; namely, Edwin Hobbs, George W. Dunn, C. H. Topliff, Benjamin F. Cutter, Increase Leadbetter, and Alonzo S. Fiske.

Samuel Patch, Jr., of Weston, a soldier of Company I, 35th Regiment, Massachusetts Infantry, having been promoted to the rank of lieutenant of that company, the citizens of Weston presented him with a sword and sash. His letter of acknowledgment for the gift, dated in camp before Petersburg, Va., December 29, 1864, was read and recorded.

At a town meeting November 7, 1865, the following resolutions were presented by Rev. C. H. Topliff:—

Resolved, That we have heard with sincere regret and sorrow of the accident by which the valuable life of Charles Merriam, Esq., formerly a citizen of this town, and a noble-hearted and liberal benefactor to it, was terminated. By his generous gift for the foundation of a public library, and also by a similar generous gift for the relief of the "silent poor" of Weston, he had enshrined himself in the hearts of the people, and secured grateful remembrance for his name in all future years.

Resolved, That the above be entered in the records of the town and a copy transmitted to the family.

It was voted as the sense of the town that a monument should be erected in commemoration of our fallen soldiers, and that a committee of five be appointed to inquire the probable cost of a suitable monument and report at the March meeting. At the April meeting the above committee's report was, in substance, as follows:—

The object of a monument is not that it may serve as a tombstone on which to record the names and deaths of our valiant soldiers who offered their lives upon the altar of their country. Its design is to honor the fallen by inspiring the souls of the living with their noble deeds and their unselfish love of country. The necessity which at present exists, and in any event cannot long be delayed, of making some provision for the town library and the expediency of enlarging the town hall, our inability on account of our obligations incurred by the war to meet these outlays and build a monument also, have led us to the conclusion that a Memorial Hall will secure to us the additional room and conveniences needed, and will be the wisest plan for the town to adopt. These objects will be obtained by the addition of 20 or 25 feet to the westerly end of the town house. We find that the cost of the addition, which is put at $2,500, may be wholly provided for in the taxes of this year.

The report was accepted, and a committee of three chosen by ballot to carry out the recommendation of the above. Edwin Hobbs, Isaac Coburn, and Alonzo S. Fiske were duly elected.

The Library Committee reported that the number of books taken out from the library during the year was 5,207, and the number purchased and given was 93. The vote for governor in 1866 was 106 for Alexander H. Bullock, 15 for Sweetzer.

At a town meeting on March 4, 1867, the following resolution was voted: "*Resolved*, That the thanks of the town be presented to the Rev. C. H. Topliff for his long and faithful services in the various offices which he has held in town affairs, and that a copy of this vote be communicated to him."

The vote for governor in 1867 stood: Alexander H. Bullock, 149 votes; John Quincy Adams, 6.*

In 1868 an enlargement of the cemetery of the town was deemed necessary, and the committee chosen by the town, which consisted of Edwin Hobbs and Isaac Coburn, reported in favor of purchasing, for the sum of $900, the land west of the present cemetery, being about one and one-third acres, belonging to Mr. Charles Jones. Objections were made by the owners of property on the street to this selection, and a minority report was presented to the town by Mr. Horace Hews, in which these objections were fully set forth by him, and the recommendation was made for the purchase of twenty-three acres of land south of the present cemetery, which could be obtained for $2,300. The town voted to accept the minority report, and that measures be taken to secure the lot and take a deed. The vote for governor in 1868 stood 149 votes for William Claflin, of Newton, and 31 for John Quincy Adams.

At a town meeting held January 30, 1869, it was voted to reconsider the vote whereby the town voted to purchase the land of Marshall Hews for a burial-lot. The matter seems to have remained in abeyance until the May meeting in 1873, when the committee again reported in favor of the land on the westerly side of the present cemetery, "and, if it cannot be obtained by agreement with the owner, to petition the County Commissioners to adjust

---

* In 1867 Mr. Charles H. Fiske was elected in this district as representative to the General Court. He received 93 votes in Weston and 259 votes in Concord.

the damages." At a later meeting, held in June, better counsel seems to have prevailed, and the committee state that

> We have now three burial-grounds in town, and the creation of a fourth one widely separated from the others is quite objectionable. From many lips we have heard the expression, "Let us all lie near together when life's work is done and we are called to take our places with the slumbering dead." This feeling was beautifully expressed by the patriarch Jacob more than three thousand years ago, when he charged his sons, saying, "Bury me with my fathers in the cave that is in the field of Ephron the Hittite. There they buried Abraham and Sarah his wife; there they buried Isaac and Rebecca his wife; and there I buried Leah." Influenced by these considerations, we have sought a place as nearly connected with the present cemetery as to make it one and the same, this lot embracing seven to ten acres. It can be had for $250 an acre.

It was voted to accept this report. In 1874 $1,000 was voted to be expended on the new cemetery.

In 1869 it was resolved "that the citizens of this town do most earnestly remonstrate against the annexation of the city of Charlestown to the city of Boston."

The vote for governor in 1869 stood 82 votes for William Claflin and 19 votes for John Quincy Adams.

In town meetings of January 3 and February 14, 1870, it was

> *Resolved,* To authorize the town treasurer to subscribe to 500 shares of the Massachusetts Central Railroad upon certain specified conditions regarding depot accommodations for the town; and also that the road shall be an independent through line to the city of Boston.

A vote was taken by ayes and nays upon this resolution, and it was defeated by a vote of 72 ayes and 85 nays.

The vote for governor in 1870 stood: William Claflin, 80 votes; Wendell Phillips, 12; John Q. Adams, 19.

The Massachusetts Central Railroad, in its inception purely a speculative enterprise, has now come to maturity on a solid basis, after twenty years of incubation. Not one of the original officers had personally any practical experience either in building or operating railroads. They went to work blindly, and began their road "nowhere," and ended it in about the same place, as regards being within the reach of business. In 1868 an act passed the legislature incorporating the Wayland & Sudbury Railroad, which was to run from Mill Village in Sudbury to Stony Brook on the Fitchburg Railroad. This was the origin of the Massachusetts Central. In 1869 the bill incorporating the Central passed the legislature, superseding the act of the year before. The capital stock was fixed at $6,000,000, but the company voted to issue only $3,000,000. As the two years in which to file a location was about to expire, a special act was passed, extending the time to 1874. N. C. Munson, the contractor for building the road, failed, and all the sub-contractors failed with him. For several years the road was in a comatose condition. The cost of construction in the fall of 1878 amounted to $2,782,932.78, there was a funded debt of $995,000, and an unfunded debt of $37,428.76. Work was resumed on the eastern end of the road, and in October, 1881, the road was opened from Boston to Hudson, 28 miles; in June, 1882, to Oakdale, 41 miles, and to Jefferson, 48 miles. Governor Boutwell became president in 1880, remaining such until 1882, when he was succeeded by Hon. S. N. Aldrich, of Marlboro. Upon the failure of Charles A. Sweet & Co. work on the road was again suspended. In 1883 the road was sold under foreclosure to a committee of the bondholders,—S. N. Aldrich, Thomas H. Perkins, and Henry Woods. In 1885 they made a contract with the Boston & Lowell Railroad to operate the Central. It was in operation under this contract for one year. In 1886 the Lowell road leased the property to the Boston & Maine for ninety-nine years, the company issuing bonds to the amount of $2,000,000. The road has to earn $500,000 to meet the interest on the bonded indebtedness, and there is prospect of its doing better than that. The credit for rescuing the Central road from total wreck is due to the president, Hon. S. N. Aldrich, Assistant Treasurer of the United States. The road, running, as it does, through Middlesex County and central Massachusetts, has a great and prosperous future before it. If the directors follow in the footsteps of the Boston & Albany, they can in a few years create a suburban population along the route equal to that which now secures the yearly dividend of the Boston & Springfield branch of the Albany road. Weston, through which the Central runs, can by generous accommodation be made the centre of a large population. The present size of Weston is 10,967 acres by actual survey, and it has 155 acres in ponds. It is in general an uneven and, in some places, a broken tract of land. High cliffs, or ledges, of rock are found within its limits. The town is elevated above the common level of the surrounding country, and affords an extensive view of other parts. The soil is of a deep, strong loam, favorable to the growth of trees, for the beauty of which this section is noted. The hills are springy, and suffer but little from frost or drought. Brooks and rivulets abound on every side, and for the greater part rise within the limits of the town. The character of its inhabitants would not suffer by a comparison with those of any other town in the Commonwealth. Few towns within a radius of twenty miles of Boston have preserved the old-time characteristics, both as regards population and customs, as has Weston. The names of the descendants of the men of Concord and Lexington are to-day on the voting list of the town. Property and estates have changed owners but little within the past century. The finances of the town are managed with great care, while its roads and public buildings and general improvements are liberally provided for in the yearly grants.

In 1871 it was again proposed to sell the poorhouse farm and to purchase a smaller place, more centrally located. It was thought at the time that the people of the north side wanted to get rid of it in their neighborhood, and an effort was made to have the house located in the centre of the town. For this purpose the property now owned by Miss Marshall was proposed. No definite action seems to have been taken on this proposition until the May meeting in 1873, when the committee who had the matter in charge reported that they had examined several places, among them the farm of John A. Lamson, of 71 acres, valued at $8,000, that of Henry J. White, of 25 acres, valued at $8,500, and that of Nathan Barker, of 40 acres, with buildings valued at $8,000. None of these places being considered suitable for the purpose, the report was tabled. The vote for governor stood: William P. Washburn, 96 votes; John Q. Adams, 25; Robert C. Pitman, 7. Mr. C. H. Fiske was elected representative to the General Court.

The vote for governor in 1872 stood: William P. Washburn, 159 votes; Francis W. Bird, 12.

The vote in 1873 stood: William B. Washburn, 53 votes; William Gaston, 9.

In town meeting, March 1, 1875, it was voted that a committee of three be appointed to purchase a lot of land of Henry J. White, fronting the house of Oliver N. Kenny, for a site for a high-school building. This lot was duly purchased, and $500 paid to Mr. White. The committee consisted of George W. Dunn, Nathan Barker, and George B. Milton. The sum of $3,300 was appropriated for schools, and $600 for school incidentals. At the April meeting the town directed the Selectmen to establish a town pump near the town house, and they were directed not to dig the well when the springs were full, but at the proper time.

Voted to accept the invitation of the towns of Concord and Lexington to be present at the celebration of the centennial anniversary of the opening of the Revolutionary War.

A letter was received from General Charles J. Paine, donating a town clock, if the town would provide a site for the same. Voted that the clock be placed on the Unitarian church, if agreeable to the society; and a committee, consisting of Edwin Hobbs, Alonzo S. Fiske, and George B. Milton, was chosen to confer with the trustees of the church and also with General Paine regarding the matter. Voted a sum not to exceed $500 for placing the clock.

The vote for governor stood: Alexander H. Rice, 69 votes; John J. Baker, 10; and William Gaston, 13.

Edward Coburn was elected to the General Court. Weston gave him 83 votes; Concord, 178; and Lincoln, 66.

In town meeting, March 6, 1876, the matter of the high school came up, and a committee, consisting of James B. Case, George W. Dunn, and George W. Cutting, Jr., was appointed to construct the building. They were instructed not to expend above $9,000. On March 20, same year, the above was voted to be reconsidered and to be declared null and void. At a meeting held in April it was voted that a committee of three be appointed to procure plans for a high-school house and estimates of cost, and report at the March meeting. At this March meeting, held in 1877, it was again voted to build a high-school building, the expense of which should not exceed $8,500. The Committee on

Plans, Site, and Estimates were George B. Milton, Isaac Coburn, and Eli E. Fox. In April the committee reported that the lot at the corner of the Willow Lane and the main road presented more advantages on account of being near the post-office, library, and store, while the other was a commanding and cheaper site. The price asked for the corner lot was $1,500 for an acre or $1,000 for half an acre. The choice of sites was voted by ballot, but, before this vote was taken, a motion was made to reconsider the whole matter. This motion was lost, however, by a vote of 84 to 69. The vote on the site for the school-house being then taken, 66 voted for the corner lot on the main road, and 77 voted for the lot already purchased of Mr. White. The Building Committee chosen were George B. Milton, Edward Coburn, George W. Dunn, Henry J. White, and William N. Gowell.

The vote for governor stood: Alexander H. Rice, 121 votes; William Gaston, 33. In November, 1877, the town voted on a State Constitutional Amendment making it eligible for the president, professors, and instructors of Harvard College to hold seats in the Senate and House of Representatives of Massachusetts. This vote stood: yeas, 30; and no nays.

The vote for governor in 1878 stood: Thomas Talbot, 202; Benjamin F. Butler, 26. In 1879, John D. Long, 164, and Benjamin F. Butler, 21.

In 1878 Alonzo S. Fiske was elected representative to the General Court. The vote stood: Weston, 200; Sudbury, 124; Maynard, 129; Wayland, 149.

In May, 1884, the charter of the Henry A. Upham Lodge, No. 52, of Weston was granted by the Ancient Order of United Workmen, Grand Lodge of Massachusetts, to Luther F. Upham, Nathan Barker, Jr., Edwin A. Newbury, Oliver L. Sherburne, Merrill French, William N. Gowell, E. O. Clark, Elias King, Charles Wark, and Charles A. Moody, and to their successors. This society of workmen has for its purpose the encouragement and support of the brothers of the order when in sickness and distress, and has the further purpose of securing to the family or heirs of the brother, in case of death, two thousand dollars. Other objects are "the practice of charity, the inspiration of hope, and the protection of all good and true brothers." In 1887 there were fifty-three members of this lodge in Weston.

WAR VETERANS, RAILROADS, ETC.

There is nothing of especial interest connected with the town and its affairs from 1880 to 1890 worthy of being noted here. The town has gone on during these last ten years in the even tenor of its way towards development and liberal management.

It may prove interesting to my readers to know the increase of voters and of personal and real property during the past century:—

	1773.	1876.	1888.	1911.
Number of polls	218	379	468	602
" " horses	142	372	415	453
" " cows	535	742	946	846
" " oxen	167	12		
" " sheep	279	—	19	
" " swine	225	297	137	
" " dwellings	—	—	286	472
" " slaves	16	—	—	
Value of personal estate	£2,128 7s.	$753,683		$4,388,934
Value real estate	5,241	875,400		3,393,298
Total	£7,369 7s.	$1,629,083	$2,076,600	$7,782,232

Debt of the town (1889), $5,695.93. Rate of taxation, $6. Number of deaths, 14, including six persons of seventy years and upwards, viz.: Mary Warren Hastings, seventy-seven years; Amanda Cheney, eighty years; Louisa K. Gregory, seventy-one; Martha Derby, eighty-three; Isaac H. Jones, seventy-nine; Beulah R. Livingston, eighty-four.

In 1911 there was no town debt. The rate of taxation was $11.30.

XI.

BUSINESS INTERESTS OF THE TOWN.

The early industries, commerce, and trade of Weston, from the date of its settlement, were quite extensive for so limited a population. Almost every trade was to be found within its limits. To enumerate some of them will give the reader an idea of the extent of the business interests of the town before the introduction of railroads. Among these was a brewery, or malt-house, numerous groceries, dry-goods stores, clock-makers, hatters, straw-braiders, grist-mills and saw-mills, machine-shop, pottery, cabinet-making, wheelwrights, shoemaking, tannery, and apothecary shop. All this activity seems strange to us to-day, when, until a few years ago, we were reduced to a blacksmith-shop, one grocery, and a grist-mill. We have seen how prosperous and numerous were our taverns, and how speedily they succumbed, one after another, upon the introduction of railroads. All the above enumerated industries followed the example of the taverns, and after a few years of fitful existence disappeared. Many Westonians who were storekeepers here in the early years of this century became prosperous merchants in Boston.

The oldest store of which we have any record is that of Elisha Jones, who was followed by his son Isaac. The original residence of Lieutenant Jones was opposite the Baptist parsonage. It is probable that the store, which was east of the present house, was built at a very early period. This building was moved some years ago to the rear of the house, and fell into decay. The date of the ledger of this store is 1745. Here was carried on one of the most extensive businesses outside of Boston. It included many lines of goods,—groceries, liquors, dry goods, etc. Judging from the books, Mr. Jones provided all the taverns far and near with their rum, brandy, and molasses. He was the banker of the town also, and his credit in Boston was perhaps better than that of his obscurer neighbors. He carried the notes of the town clergyman and farmers, all of whom borrowed money of him and gave their notes for loans and goods. We have seen that Colonel Ephraim Williams purchased his military outfit for the campaign of 1753–54 of Mr. Jones, and during the latter part of the War of the Revolution he had extensive dealings with the army on the Hudson, shipping large quantities of clothing. We have the receipts for nine hogsheads of blankets carried by ox-team 215 miles, and Ezekiel Moore receipts for another lot teamed to Fishkill (£27 12s.). The old account books are extremely interesting and of historic value. James Otis, the patriot, was attorney for Mr. Jones, and his bold, handsome signature appears as such attorney, followed by that of Harrison Gray Otis. It seems to have been the custom in early days for both the debtor and creditor to receipt for settlement of accounts in the ledger in sign of satisfaction. Consequently, we have an uninterrupted series of autographs of the early settlers and inhabitants of Weston, and also of those living in adjoining towns and counties. Many of these autographs are valuable to-day. The present house, or what is known as the Golden Ball Tavern, was built in 1753–54, as is shown in the ledger. At this time Mr. Jones vacated his old house; and Colonel William Williams, who had married Mr. Jones's daughter, moved from Newton into the old house. Colonel Ephraim Williams, his son, came with his father, and remained until they both took up their residence at Stockbridge. The landed possessions of Lieutenant Jones and of his son Isaac were very extensive, both in Weston and in towns adjoining, and particularly in Berkshire County. The Berkshire property was a grant from the crown, as was also true in the case of William and Ephraim Williams. Mr. Jones's book shows purchases of farms and lands in Barre, Templeton, Framingham, and other places. It looks very much as if some of these properties were taken in settlement of outstanding accounts. Elisha and Isaac do not seem to have been disagreeable creditors, judging from the fact that several years' accounts were allowed to run without a settlement, although interest was charged in some cases.

In the accounts of the different stores in Weston it is impossible to make any distinction between groceries and dry goods. There was nothing properly called "dry" in former days, and the people never went dry long or when they could help it. All dealers were licensed as retailers.

It has also become difficult to classify the different stores in the date of their establishment. Peter Jennison seems to have been a tailor here in 1750, but there is no mention of any other until 1800, when Hugh McPherson takes that position. All women were more or less tailors everywhere in country towns, and so continued down to about fifty years ago.

In 1782 Isaac Lamson, son of Colonel Samuel Lamson, kept a grocery on the site of the present Cutting store. He died in 1806. His books are in excellent condition to-day.

Ralph Abrahams, of the Isaac Jones family, kept a store on what is now the Minor property. The store stood east of the present house. In 1820 Abrahams sold the property to Alpheus Bigelow, and Bigelow sold to Oliver Shed, who remained until 1830, when the store was destroyed by fire.

In 1804 George W. Smith opened a grocery store where now stands the Cutting house, then the property of Joel Smith, his father. Upon the marriage of George Smith with Clarissa Lamson (sister of John and Daniel S. Lamson), Joel Smith gave his son George the estate now of Mrs. Robbins, and the store was moved to a position about where the driveway of that estate now is. It remained in this position until the death of Mrs. Smith in 1852, when it was bought by Mr. Cutting, and again moved to its original place. Mr. Cutting kept the store at this place for a short period, and then it was altered into the present dwelling-house in 1867. Previous to the last removal Captain Smith leased the store to William S. Barker, of Medford. He remained until 1828, when Mr. Smith again took the store. He died in 1829, and was succeeded by Jonathan P. Stearns, the business being conducted by Mr. George W. Cutting, who came to town from Wayland in 1822. In 1830 Mr. Cutting bought out Mr. Stearns, and remained the leading and deservedly popular storekeeper of Weston until his death in 1885. In 1852 the old Lamson stand, with the house and barn adjoining, which had been occupied as a store for a century, came into the possession of Mr. John Lamson, who took down the old buildings and erected the present store. It was leased to Charles Johnson, who with his son, Byron B. Johnson, later the first mayor of Waltham, kept both a grocery and dry-goods store until 1856, when Mr. Cutting took the lease, and in 1875 purchased the store of Mrs. E. T. Lamson. Mr. Cutting was succeeded by his son, G. W. Cutting. The old store above mentioned, and the one occupied by Isaac Lamson in 1782 (died in 1806), were taken about 1810 by Daniel S. Lamson as a dry-goods store. Under his management this store became one of the most important in Middlesex County. The business was very extensive, taking in all the towns west of us to the Vermont and New Hampshire line. It was the custom in old times for women to make their purchases in the spring or fall for the whole year. They would drive down from long distances in their "one-horse shay," put up over night at the tavern, returning home the next day. No one ever thought of going to Boston to buy goods. Waltham ladies came to Weston to buy. Cloths of all sorts were to be had. But, complaint being made that there was no one to make up the cloths, Mr. Lamson built the little shop about 1817, and installed a tailor. Mr. Lamson died in 1824, leaving what was considered a handsome fortune in those days, all of which he had made in Weston. Mr. Charles Merriam, who had served his time with Mr. Lamson, coming to Weston in 1821, was very popular. He succeeded Mr. Lamson in the business, and maintained the reputation of the store to the last. In 1836 Mr. Merriam, with Mr. Henry Sales, established the large business house of Sales & Merriam. Mr. Merriam died in 1865, leaving a large fortune. He was succeeded in Weston in 1836 by Henry W. Wellington, who remained until 1838. He is now of H. W. Wellington & Co., Chauncy Street, Boston.

With the departure of Mr. Wellington the prestige and glory of this store and business began to decline. The days of railroads had begun. George W. Smith kept the store for a while, but the profits of the business had gone to Boston. George W. Bigelow opened a store in the west end of Mrs. John Jones's house, but he was not one to recall the halcyon days of those who had gone before him. Both Bigelow and Smith went down at the whistle of the steam-engine. Mr. Merriam, when here, built the house now belonging to E. O. Clark; and here Charles

Merriam, the present wealthy Boston merchant, was born in 1832.

In 1791, 1792, and 1793 Wareham Woodward, son of Rev. Mr. Woodward, kept a store in the west end of what was later the paint-shop of M. & J. Jones. Mr. Frank Kendal, son of Rev. Dr. Kendal, appears to have been associated with him for a while. There was a small store next the west wall of the bake-house property, at one time used as a school and also as a shop. This building was moved to property now owned by George W. Dunn. The farm-house on the Lamson estate was at one time a hat store. Hats were manufactured here by Royal McIntosh. He sold this bake-house property to Benjamin Peirce in 1816, and in 1859 Mr. Peirce conveyed it to Mrs. E. T. Lamson. In 1823 and 1824 Sarah Woodward kept a store in the building formerly occupied as a store by Woodward and the Kendals. Abraham Hews built the Marshall Jones house somewhere about 1765.

At one time, with Ralph Plympton, Mr. Hews carried on the manufacture of chairs and other cabinet-work. Many of the chairs are still in use in the town, and were so faithfully and substantially put together as to promise a lasting existence. Mr. Hews sold this property to Plympton when he removed to his new house and pottery works, now belonging to Marshall Lamson Hews. Plympton sold to Marshall Jones in 1824.

In 1765 Abraham Hews established the pottery business, said to have been the first industry of its kind in New England. This business was transmitted from father to son in Weston from 1765 to 1871, a period of one hundred and six years. In 1871 it was found necessary, owing to the rapid increase in the business, to remove the works nearer the central market, and a large factory was erected at North Cambridge, at which time the name of the firm was changed to that of A. H. Hews & Co. The pay-roll of 1871 contained fifteen names; that of 1889, from eighty-five to one hundred. In 1871 800,000 pieces of pottery were required by the trade; in 1889, 7,000,000 are needed. The account books of the concern from 1769 are still preserved. The quaint charges and small beginnings of those early days make interesting reading to-day. It seems to have been the custom to mix up family affairs and general running expenses with the work of the business; for instance: "Samuel Brocett to my horse to Framingham, 12 miles, three shillings"; "Samuel Lamson, to my horse to Concord, two shillings"; "Isaac Lamson, to my horse and cart to Boston to bring Samuel's wife and children up to Weston, twelve shillings"; and so on. Dr. Gowen, at one time in the last century, had his office and apothecary shop in a building in front of the present school-house on Highland Street. This building belonged to the Isaac Jones estate, and was removed to their house. A grocery and dry-goods store was located in the William Hastings house. D. G. Ingraham kept it for some years, followed by Enoch Greenleaf in partnership with Caleb Hayward. Adjoining the Hastings place on the west was that of Ralph Abrahams, who was one of the Jones family. He kept a store in a building east of the present Minor house from 1802 to 1821, when he sold the property to Alpheus Bigelow; and he in turn, in 1824, sold it to Oliver Shed, who kept a grocery and retail liquor store until 1830, at which time the store was destroyed by fire.

The next place was that of the Livermores, who owned and operated the malt-house. It has been found impossible to discover the actual date when it was so operated and how long. The Livermores sold to Alpheus Bigelow, and he sold later to Mr. Cutting. Bigelow again purchased it some years later, and sold it to Jane Caswell, and Mr. Caswell still owns it. One of the first school-houses of the town stood about where the Caswell barn now stands. The Simeon Brown farm was owned by Marshall and Josiah Livermore, who sold it to Mr. Brown in 1836.

Henry Flagg kept a dry-goods store on the east corner of the estate now of Mr. Bennett. The building was moved, and is now the Bigelow farm-house. In the early part of this century there was a clock-maker in town named Cutter. Mr. Cutting has a handsome parlor clock made by Cutter. His shop was afterwards owned by Mr. Bingham, who invented the butter and cheese drill, since so generally in use. Orders came to him for these implements from all over the country, and they were in such demand that he had difficulty in filling his orders. Mr.

Bowen succeeded Mr. Bingham in this business, and continued in it to the time of his death in 1860.*

It was a custom throughout the State, in early days, to locate houses and people in Weston by the distance from the tannery. Bark was brought to the tannery from Vermont and New Hampshire, and as late as 1795 vessels loaded with bark from Maine came to Watertown. Thence the material was teamed to the tannery. Old bills for all this kind of work abound.

It has been difficult to fix the exact date when the Weston tannery was established by the Hobbs family. It has only been by overhauling the family papers that anything like a clear statement has been possible concerning this ancient industry. Perhaps a sketch of the Hobbs family in this connection will not be out of place, the better to understand the business, probably one of the first established in this country.

Josiah Hobbs came to Weston from Boston in 1730, and the same year purchased large tracts of land, a part of which is now owned by Mr. Edward Brown and Mr. Gowing. The deed of this property, bought of Cheeney, is dated October 4, 1729. Josiah Hobbs died in 1779, aged ninety-four. He had eight children, all born in Boston, excepting Nathan, who first saw the light in Weston in 1731. Ebenezer Hobbs, the eldest son of Josiah, born in Boston in 1709, is the ancestor of all the Hobbs family in Weston. He had nine children. He is mentioned as a shoemaker in old records as early as 1750. Isaac Hobbs, the eldest son of Ebenezer, was born in 1735. He married Mary Sanderson, of Waltham, in 1757. Isaac built the double house, one-half of which was occupied by his grandson, Captain Samuel Hobbs, and the west end by Captain Henry Hobbs. Isaac Hobbs was a deacon in the Weston church, and filled the office of town clerk

---

* The following note about Messrs. Cutter and Bingham appears in the papers of Colonel Lamson:—

Ezekiel Cutter bought the place known as the Bingham place of Abel Rice, of Sudbury, who was a school-teacher at East Cambridge in 1827. There was previous to this purchase a grist-mill on the premises, run by one Sanderson. Cutter was a clock-maker, and George W. Cutting bought his parlor clock of him when he married in or about 1830. The clock is to-day in good condition. Bingham succeeded Cutter, and made machinery for the manufacture of coarse woollen goods, purchasing the property about 1830.

Between 1835 and 1840 the United States government contracted with John Cutting, of Weston, to manufacture the plumbago for the government crucibles, to melt the gold and silver of the mints. While the material was baking, the mill took fire and was destroyed and not rebuilt. The work was being done by Mr. Hews, of Weston.—ED.

THE DEACON URIAH GREGORY HOUSE, MERRIAM STREET.

Said to have been one of the oldest houses in Weston. The property was in the Gregory family for over two hundred years. It was torn down in 1885.

THE ABRAM BIGELOW HOUSE, CONCORD STREET.

Mr. Bigelow was one of the selectmen of Weston, and a prominent man in the history of the town from 1757 to 1771. He was the original of "Deacon Badger" of Mrs. Stowe's "Oldtown Folks." In recent years it was bought by John Poutas, whose descendants still own and occupy it.

for forty years. He died in 1813, at the age of seventy-eight. Matthew Hobbs, the sixth son of Ebenezer Hobbs, was an active promoter of the Revolution. In 1780 he was captain of the Weston Company, the men enlisting under him for three years, or the war. Isaac Hobbs, the third son of Isaac, was born in 1765, and married Mary Baldwin in 1790. He died in 1834, aged sixty-nine. The Hager house was built by Isaac Hobbs, in 1786, for his sons Isaac and Ebenezer. Ebenezer, by his will dated October 13, 1762, bequeathed to his son Isaac all his stock in leather and hides, and also his tan-houses and bark for tanning. So far as can be gathered by records, the tannery was started between 1750 and 1760. Captain Henry Hobbs, son of Captain Matthew Hobbs, was born in 1784. He died in 1854, aged eighty. Henry was a harness-maker, and occupied the building which stood on the south-east corner of the double house, later the shoe factory of Hobbs & Hager. Henry was also a carriage-maker, and occupied for this business the sheds which formerly stood on the south-west end of the Hager barn. The first chaise ever seen in Weston was owned by him, and was probably of his make. In 1795 he took out a license for this chaise, for which he paid three dollars. The license mentions "a two-wheel carriage, called by him a chaise, to be drawn by one horse and to carry two people." Henry owned the land now of Curtis Robinson, and the little building formerly Dr. Kendal's study was moved to this property and is now the Robinson shoe-shop.

Nathan Hager owned and lived on the present Eldridge farm. His son Nathan married in 1832 Mary Ann Hobbs, daughter of Isaac Hobbs. Nathan Hager, Jr., owned and lived on the farm now of Mr. Frank Hastings, where he lived after his marriage. On the death of Isaac Hobbs in 1834 Nathan Hager moved over to the present Hager house, and formed the partnership of Hobbs & Hager. Mr. Hager sold his farm to Captain Dickinson, whose daughter married Mr. Hastings. The shoe factory was given up about 1850, and a short time before Mr. Hager's death, in 1860, the tannery also ceased to exist. Mr. Hager served as town clerk for twenty years. David Jacobs worked in the tannery for over forty years. Thus we see the tannery was in operation for a century, and the shoe factory about fifty years.

The business of cutting and selling barrel hoops would seem to have been quite extensive, if we may judge from the partial returns on record from 1764 to 1770, a period of five years only. The figures represent the returns of the several farmers employed in this industry, and are only partial. For instance, in 1763 there were made and sold 18,940; in 1764 the figures are 9,300; and in 1766 they are 11,080, etc.

One of the most important industries of Weston is that of the Stony Brook mills. This water power was rendered effective by one Richard Child, who in 1679 erected a corn-mill and later a saw-mill.* The grist-mill remained standing until about the year 1840. It was at the saw-mill that a great part of the timber was sawed for the early houses of the town. This property was sold in 1802 by Isaac Lamson, executor of Amos Bigelow, and was bought in by the heirs. At the time of the sale the property consisted of the mills, a dwelling-house, and two acres of land. Washington Peirce leased the mills, but, upon his marriage with the daughter of Joel Smith, removed, and kept the tavern. Coolidge, Sibley & Treat bought the property of Abraham Bigelow in 1831. They erected a machine-shop, and operated for a number of years the grist-mill, and also a mill for the manufacture of cotton yarns. In the machine-shop for many years the specialty was the manufacture of cotton machinery, looms, etc. They supplied the factories of Lowell, Lawrence, Lancaster, and Clinton, besides which they manufactured extensively for mills in New York. Here was also made the first machinery for cotton mills in Alabama and Tennessee. Here also later were made large quantities of door-locks, expanding bits, and other articles of steel and iron hardware. In 1859 was begun the manufacture of wood-planing machines, the Sibley dovetailer, and the Sibley pencil-sharpeners for schools, now in use from Maine to Alaska.

---

*The third grist-mill, or corn-mill, erected in the Watertown district, was that at Stony Brook. At a town meeting held January 5, 1679, it was "granted that the new mill now set up and to be finished at Stony Brook be freed from rates for twenty years from date." In 1684 it was owned by John Bright and others. For many years it was known as Bigelow's Mill. Lieutenant John Brewer's Mill, established about the same time, was in the northwestern part of Weston, now a part of Lincoln, and is at present operated by Mr. Harrington as a grist and saw mill.

Sibley became the owner of this valuable property, having bought out both Coolidge and Treat.

Near these machine-shops was the little cañon, enclosing the pool out of which the cascade fell. From above, the waters of the brook came down the rapids white with foam, the banks covered with mosses and ferns, the oaks and hemlocks overarching the stream. Altogether it formed one of the most beautiful bits of natural scenery to be seen this side of the White Mountains, the delight of artists and the admiration of all beholders. All the available portions of this valuable plant have now been completely destroyed by the Cambridge water board, who have seized the mills and rendered its future usefulness as a factory impossible. This act of the Cambridge authorities wipes out all this important factory privilege and destroys the taxable value of this industry for the town. It is time our people should realize the immense injury to farms and manufactories which the free and easy grants of the legislature of late years to water companies are doing. They are giving away for the asking the control of springs and waterways, which bids fair to destroy the value of our farms and property. In 1833 a furniture factory was built over the dam on this estate belonging to Mr. Sibley, and was leased to Joseph H. Cummings. This building was destroyed by fire about 1850. George W. Cutting, Jr., worked for Mr. Cummings when a young man.

In 1852 Dr. Otis E. Hunt and Nathan Barker together purchased the Harrington farm, and in the year 1854 sold a part of the property to Mr. Samuel Shattuck. This gentleman established a chair factory there, which eventually did a large business. In 1875 Oliver Kenney succeeded Mr. Shattuck. The firm is now engaged in the manufacture, on a large scale, of school furniture, and employs a number of hands.

Marshall Jones, who was born in the Hannah Gowen house in 1791, bought the old Abraham Hews property in 1824. It was then in rather a dilapidated condition, and had never been painted since its erection in 1765. Mr. Jones had served his apprenticeship in the harness business with Mr. Hobbs at the north side of the town, and here established the paint and harness business. His brother, John Jones, worked with him as a journeyman until taken into partnership, the firm then taking the name of M. & J. Jones. This business became very extensive, and the brothers became men of considerable wealth. Marshall Jones died in 1864, and Colonel John Jones in 1861, being killed while lifting a rock out of the ground on his estate. Colonel Jones was highly esteemed throughout the county, and was largely engaged in the settlement of estates in the town, so great confidence had our people in his ability and integrity. In 1825 he succeeded Colonel Daniel S. Lamson as lieutenant-colonel of the Third Middlesex Regiment.

David Brackett, a blacksmith of the town, had his forge on the main street in 1788–89, on the site of the Upham shop. He was succeeded by his son David, Jr., followed by Isaac Bigelow, son of Deacon Thomas Bigelow, who at that time owned the property. He was followed by Whitten and John Parks, and in 1830 Joel Upham bought the house and shop. Mr. Upham retired from the business in 1887, at the ripe age of eighty-five. John Hobbs, sixth child of Nathan Hobbs, born in 1771, was a blacksmith on the north road in a shop west of Mr. Edward Brown's barn. In 1802 he was bitten by a mad dog, and died of hydrophobia. Jonathan Warren was a shoemaker, and a maker of ploughs on property now of Mr. Hastings. Ebenezer Tucker was a blacksmith in the old shop still standing near the Garfield wheelwright-shop. Converse Bigelow, also a blacksmith, had a smithy on property now of Mr. Coburn. Park Boyce was a blacksmith near the Daggett tavern. George and Nathan Upham erected a blacksmith-shop on property of General Derby, facing the house and land they purchased in 1839 of the heirs of John Lamson. Luther and Quincy Harrington had a machine-shop where the shoddy mill stood, near Kendal Green station. Abijah Upham, son of Lieutenant Phineas, born in 1747, built the house now the property of Abijah Coburn, and had a blacksmith-shop at this place. He moved to the old place when his father died.

Lieutenant John Brewer, who died in 1709, left a farm and 216 acres of other land, together with a saw-mill and grist-mill. His widow, Mary Brewer, in 1715 entered into a copartnership or agreement with Richard Parks for the purpose of carrying on the saw-mill, provision being made in the articles of agreement that this work should not interfere with the running of the gristmill in possession of said Mary Brewer. These mills are still in operation, and are now owned by Mr. Harrington. The store of Henry Fiske on the north road was built in 1815, and the business was conducted by Henry and Sewell Fiske, John Williams, and Alonzo S. Fiske until 1852. Abijah Stearns was a clerk to Henry Fiske. Thaddeus and Abijah Peirce were wheelwrights, and in early days all such mechanics were also housewrights, or carpenters. Benjamin Rand was a housewright previous to 1800. He signs a "covenant, bargain or agreement made and concluded with Benoni Garfield, Benjamin Brown, James Jones, and Ebenezer Allen, of Weston [other names to contract lost], in behalf of the town of Weston for the building of the second church erected in Weston." The contract is signed by Randall Davis and Benjamin Rand, and is dated 1720. This interesting paper (the original) is badly torn, and only a part of it is decipherable. When Mr. Rand died, the town was in his debt over £300 for building this church. Daniel Rand, a wheelwright, began business in 1800 on the farm now owned by Mr. Caswell, and died in 1851.

The organ factory in the north part of Weston, now called Kendal Green, on the line of the Fitchburg Railroad, was established here by Mr. Francis H. Hastings in 1888. He moved his factory from Roxbury on Tremont Road, or Street, to Weston. It had been in operation there for forty years. In the year 1827 Mr. Elias Hook began the building of organs in Salem with his brother George Hook. They removed to Boston as E. & G. G. Hook. In 1855, when nineteen years old, Mr. Hastings entered their service, and in 1865 was admitted as a partner. Later the name of the firm was changed to "E. & G. G. Hook and Hastings," and in 1880, after the death of Mr. G. G. Hook, it was again changed to Hook & Hastings. In 1881 Mr. Elias Hook died, since which time the business has been conducted by Mr. Hastings. The business dates back over sixty years. Mr. Hastings has devoted himself to the building of church organs for thirty-five years. His relations with eminent European builders, the employment of experts trained in their factories, the ingenuity and skill of our American workmen, and his constant endeavor to advance the standard of his work have enabled him to obtain and to hold the highest place in his craft. The work of the house is found in every part of the country, and has a world-wide reputation. The large new factory at Kendal Green is situated on the Fitchburg Railroad, twelve miles from Boston. Trains stop at the factory for the accommodation of workmen and visitors. Mr. Hastings built this factory on land which formed part of the old Hastings homestead, and which has been in the family for four generations. He has built cottages for his workmen, and a club-house and hall, with reading-rooms attached, for public use. At stated times, lectures are given in the hall, together with musical and other entertainments fully appreciated by the workmen as well as by the townspeople generally.

XII.

Schools and Teachers.

The earliest mention of the pay of a schoolmaster was January 6, 1650, when £30 was voted to Mr. Richard Norcross. This sum continued to be the salary for about seventy-five years. In 1683 it was agreed that those who dwell on the west side of Stony Brook be freed from the school tax of 1683, that they may be the better able to teach among themselves. Mr. Norcross was employed in 1685–86. Those who sent children to school were to pay threepence a week each, and all short of £20 the town would make up to Mr. Norcross; the town to pay for such children as their parents were unable to pay for, the Selectmen to be the judges. November 16, 1690, the town allowed £15 for the schoolmaster's maintenance. The rate parents were to pay for tuition was established at threepence a week for English, fourpence for writing, and sixpence for Latin.

The town rates for 1687 were: rye, 4 shillings; Indian corn, 3 shillings; oats, 2 shillings. In 1691 the prices were: rye and barley, 4 shillings; Indian corn, 4 shillings. Two shillings in money were to be taken as 3 shillings in grain. In 1697 oak wood was 7 shillings; walnut, 8 shillings. In 1703 carpenters working in the water were allowed 3 shillings a day, laborers on land 2 shillings and 6 pence, and teams 5 shillings per day.

In 1690 Nathaniel Stone was chosen schoolmaster at £15, which was granted by the town, 20 persons agreeing to pay 50 shillings a quarter in addition. In 1693 Richard Norcross was chosen for one year to keep a month at the school-house, when, if a considerable number of scholars did not appear, he had liberty to keep all the year round at his house, the town to pay him £5 additional. If he finds the scholars to increase, then from April to October in the school-house and the remainder of the year at his own house. He was also to catechize the children and all others sent to him. In 1696 Edward Goddard was invited to teach the school. He replied, if the town would repair the school-house and give him £20, he would accept; but the town refused his terms. The result was the town was fined at General Sessions for not having a school. In 1696–97 the town refused to have a grammar school, and appointed a committee to estimate the cost of repairing the school-house. Two of the committee reported the cost at £3 to £4. The others reported from 30 to 40 shillings, and 40 shillings was granted. In 1697 Mr. Goddard was again asked to keep the school, but it does not appear whether he accepted or not. In 1699, however, he did agree to keep the grammar school. The next year he obtained his £20 salary and the rates from the "parents and owners of children." Mr. Goddard could not have continued long at his post, for in 1700 Rev. Samuel Parris agreed to keep the school at his place of abode until some other person could be chosen. In September, 1700, Mr. Norcross again becomes the schoolmaster at £10 and the usual rates from parents, they agreeing to send one-quarter cord of wood in winter. At this time Mr. Norcross had been a schoolmaster forty-nine years, and he was seventy-nine years old. In November, 1700, it was voted to keep the school in the first and third quarters at the old school-house and the second and fourth quarters in the middle of the town. In 1705 £30 was voted for schools.

In 1706, Mr. Mors having ceased to be the minister of the church in Weston in consequence of difficulties in the settlement, he was invited to keep the school and to be helpful to the minister for £40, and fourpence a week for all who sent their children. He accepted. This school was kept at Mr. Bigelow's house at Stony Brook. Mr. Mors removed to Dorchester in 1707, and died at Canton in 1732. In 1707 and 1708 Thomas Robie, who was graduated at Harvard in 1708 (probably the same who later is known as Dr. Robie of Wayland), engaged to keep the school half a year for £15,—the first quarter, seven hours, and the second quarter, eight hours, a day. Benjamin Shattuck followed in 1709, and continued to be the schoolmaster for six years, until 1714. In 1714 the town is presented at General Sessions for not having a writing-school, and the Selectmen report

SCHOOLS AND TEACHERS 167

they have chosen Mr. Joseph Woolson for such a master, and that he is acceptable to the town. The presentment was dismissed with costs. In 1714 the Selectmen visited the president of Harvard College in search of a schoolmaster. He informed them "they could not have any student to keep their school." The teacher whom the town reported to the General Sessions they had procured was Abraham Hill, who married Thankful, daughter of Ebenezer Allen, of Weston. Mr. Hill was graduated at Harvard College in 1737.

In 1737 the town was again presented at General Sessions for not having a grammar-school master, but the Selectmen made return that they had provided one. The case was dismissed with costs. The town records being lost from 1712 to 1754, it is impossible to give a history of the early progress in schooling for these years, but from other sources we find that from 1714 to 1751 (or thirty-seven years) there had been 14 teachers, some of them serving for three and four years each. They were all graduates of Harvard College. Benjamin Brown, in his diary for 1718, charges the town for schooling 4 boys one week 10 shillings; 2 boys five weeks, 5 shillings; and 1 boy four weeks, 2 shillings.

The first mention of schools in the second volume of town records, dated March, 1754, is the vote to pay Schoolmaster Cotton his last quarter, £6 6s. 11d., and to Nathaniel Williams £3 9s. 4d. for boarding Mr. Cotton. The town refused to grant money for a reading and writing school. They voted that the school shall be kept two months on the north side at Josiah Hobbs's, and two months at Benjamin Bond's.

In 1755 the town voted £40 for schools. This probably does not include the board of teachers, which the town paid.

In 1760 the town votes £100 for schools. Beginning with 1761, the citizens vote £160 for the same and for other town charges, so that it is found impossible to keep informed of what sum was paid for schooling. This system continued down to a very late period. Many of the townspeople, both men and women, kept school, and all took turns in boarding the schoolmaster, being paid by the town for so doing. The minister took his turn with the other inhabitants, and was probably glad of the addition to his slender salary. During the period of the Revolution the school-houses seem to have been very little in use, for we find at the close of that period that the buildings had been allowed to go to decay. Whatever schools there were during this time of trial were at private houses. Mr. Woodward and Dr. Kendal both kept school, and were paid by the town. Dr. Kendal received at his house the boys who were "rusticated" by the faculty of Harvard College for offences against discipline, and kept them up in their studies with the college classes. As we have elsewhere stated, many names of those who in after-life became distinguished men in Boston passed periods of punishment in Weston. The small allowance of wood for the schools in winter strikes us to-day as almost cruel.

In the year 1782 a committee, appointed by the town to select a spot for the Centre District School-house, reported that the south-east corner of the Eaton land would best serve the purpose, and it was voted that Major Samuel Lamson, Captain Isaac Jones, and Jonathan Fiske be a committee to purchase the land and build the school-house. This land measured forty by sixty feet. It was bought of Daniel and Ebenezer Eaton, who then owned as far as the Benjamin Peirce place, and the school was situated just west of Joel Upham's blacksmith-shop. The land was bought for £12, and the town gave the Eatons its note for the purchase money; but as late as 1812 the note was not paid, and the town refused to pay it. This central school-house continued in use until 1793, when Isaac Jones gave land twelve rods square for a building on Highland Street, somewhat back of the present school-house. In 1793 Dr. Kendal gave land for a school building on Wellesley Street, and he received the thanks of the town. In the year 1795 all the school-houses were overhauled. They were clapboarded, porches were added, and new benches and stoves introduced. In 1795, the old Eaton school-house being no longer occupied, Artemas Ward and others petitioned the town for the use of the building for a private school, which was granted. It would seem that at this early day it was as difficult to satisfy both parents and scholars as is the case to-day. The town officers receive a list of six charges brought against a teacher, signed by ten parents of children, who ask the dismissal of the teacher, as the money paid him is thrown away. The charges are worthy of a place here:—

1st. You are requested to make the boys get their lessons, if not to thrash them and make them get them.
2d. That you ride down hill upon a hand sled with your largest scholars, and that you break the sled.
3d. You are charged with having severely punished the boy who owned the sled, without sufficient reason.
4th. You are charged with using insulting language and gestures to Miss ——.
5th. You are charged with partiality.
6th. You are charged with talking and laughing for a very considerable time together with your largest scholars.

The final result of these charges is not recorded.

In 1796 the town voted $1,000 to build a school-house in the North-west District. The old school-house in the North-east District was sold by auction, and bought by Joseph Russell for £6.

In 1803 $25 is appropriated to each district for a woman's school, $600 for the support of schooling, and $40 for each district for painting and repairing school-houses. In 1804 the appropriation is $125 for each district, a total of $750. In 1805 $150 for each woman's school and $750 for men's schools. In 1806 Dr. Bancroft, Isaac Fiske, and Dr. Samuel Kendal were chosen a committee to examine persons who apply to become school-teachers.

In 1807 a census of school-children between the ages of four and eighteen was taken as follows: whole number, 374,—East Central District, 71; West Central District, 71; South-east District, 58; South-west District, 37; North-west District, 54; North-east District, 83. It was voted to enlarge the North-east School-house. Voted $716 for the reading and writing schools and $200 for the women's schools. In 1810 voted to employ a music-teacher. In 1812 voted to build a new school-house in South-east District.

Dr. Kendal in his centennial sermon, delivered in 1812, says:—

Our schools in general have been well taught; the youth in this place have been as fully prepared for active service and usefulness as in any town of equal size in this Commonwealth. The schools are the hope of our country. The culture of young minds, especially in religious and virtuous sentiments and habits, is of vast importance, not only to individuals, but to the community at large.

In 1813 the town had six school districts, each provided with a school-house.

In 1816 a new school-house was built in the South-west District. In 1817 $650 was appropriated for schools and wood, and $200 for women's schools. This appropriation continued down to 1837, with slight variation. In that year $1,000 was voted for schools and wood. In 1834 $50 was appropriated to purchase maps for the schools. In 1839 no teacher was allowed to keep an evening school without a vote of the majority of the inhabitants of the district. In those days, children were not allowed to wander about at night under any pretence whatever, and in many schools it was a rule for the scholar to report to the teacher the hour he reached home after the school of the day before.

In 1832 and 1833 Mr. Andrew Dunn taught the South School. He next taught in Wayland until 1836 and 1837, when he kept the winter term at the school "on the rocks" (so called) in Weston. In 1838 Mr. Dunn held a school in the hall in the Jones tavern, now the dwelling of Mrs. John Jones. This was probably a private establishment, answering to what later on became our "High School." This school was very largely attended, numbering about fifty scholars of both sexes. The charges were three dollars for the common course; higher English and Latin, four dollars. In the winter of 1838 Mr. Dunn taught the school on the north side. He was a most painstaking teacher, a strict disciplinarian; and to those who were refractory or idle he applied liberally the essence of birch, sending the boys to the Willow Lane, so called, to cut and bring in to him the rods which were to be applied in corrective measures. Mr. Dunn is still in active life and a clergyman in the Baptist church.

It was voted in 1839 "that a female teacher shall be employed in every school containing fifty scholars as the average number, also that the Selectmen report such measures as ought to be adopted to prevent the scholars from cutting, mutilating, defacing, and otherwise injuring the school-houses in the town and what punishment ought to be inflicted or penalty incurred for such offences."

In 1834 the State School Fund Act was passed under Governor John Davis. This fund was to be derived from the sale of lands in the State of Maine and from the claim of the State on the government of the United States for military services, provided, nevertheless, that said fund shall not exceed $1,000,000. A census of the population of Weston was taken by order of the Commonwealth concerning the disposal of the surplus fund, and the return of the assessors gave a population of 1,051. A return was also made to the town of the number of scholars in each school district in the town. The schools were kept fifteen weeks in winter and fourteen weeks in summer. The wages paid the female teachers was $2.75 per week; the master, $26 per month if he boarded himself, or $18 if boarded by the town. The female teachers were paid $10 a month if they boarded themselves, or $5 a month if boarded by the town.

		Men's School.	Female School.	Total Pupils.
South-west District	. . . .	27	19	46
South-east "	. . . .	37	19	56
North-east "	. . . .	36	24	60
East Centre "	. . . .	22	17	39
West Centre "	. . . .	27	33	60
North-west "	. . . .	16	16	32

Average in winter school attendance, 30; summer school, 10. 155 scholars in men's school, 128 in female; total, 283 scholars. The books directed to be used by the School Act of the legislature were: American First Class Book, Walker's Dictionary, Wilkins's Astronomy, Almy's Geography, Smith's Grammar, Emerson's Arithmetic, Goodrich's History of United States, Perry's Spelling Book, Parley's Geography. The money grant from town for schools was $1,000, with $200 for women's schools in addition; and this sum continues down to the year 1840.

In 1846 $1,050 was voted for schools, including fuel, and $300 for summer schools, increased in 1849 to $1,100 and $350. In 1851 three new school-houses were built at a cost of $4,111.92. In 1852 the West Centre School-house was built, one-quarter of an acre being purchased of Miss Martha Jones for $50, but twelve rods more were taken, amounting to $72, upon which sum interest was to be paid, as there were too many heirs to obtain a deed. It was again found necessary to form rules and regulations concerning the use made of the school-houses by the scholars.

In 1853 new school-houses were built in Districts 5 and 6 at a cost of $3,198.68. In 1854 a grant was made of $150 for a high school, and $5 to each school district, to be applied to the care of the school-houses and in making the fires. Mr. Ebenezer Gay was the first high-school teacher (one year, 1854–55). Mr. Train followed in 1855–56. He died in October, 1858. He taught the grammar school in Watertown in 1856 and 1858.

In 1857 $500 was appropriated for summer schools out of the total sum of $1,400 appropriated. In 1860 the sum set aside for schools was $1,629.28; in 1870 it was $2,934; in 1880, $4,149.61; in 1889, $6,900.

In Chapter X. (pp. 149, 150) details have been given of the construction of the high school. At a later date an additional plot of ground was purchased by the town from Henry J. White for a playground to be attached to this school. The sum of $400 was paid therefor.

XIII.

EVANGELICAL CHURCHES IN WESTON.

The history of the original Puritan church of Weston (which, like so many others of New England, gradually and almost imperceptibly merged into Unitarianism, and is now represented by its direct descendant, the First Parish Unitarian Church of the town) is almost identical with the history of the town itself in the first century of its existence. The town was a theocracy, and the records of the early settlement and of the later town proper are, as we have seen in previous chapters, thickly sprinkled with the records of the church. The old Puritan church was *the* church of the place, the established church; and for over a century or a century and a half no other denomination had any following, or at any rate any objective existence in the shape of buildings and organized corporations.*

Of other sects the *Methodist Episcopal Church* (or society, as it was first called) was organized about 1794, the first preacher being Rev. John Hill. A chapel was erected in the rear of the present church on the Lexington road. It was a very modest building, without paint or plastering, having neither pulpit nor pews. This chapel was in the old Needham circuit, which consisted of Needham, Marlboro, Framingham, and Hopkinton; the whole under the charge of one preacher, afterwards increased to three. The original society consisted of twelve members, and the first trustees were Abraham Bemis, Habakkuk Stearns, Jonas Bemis, John Viles, and Daniel Stratton. The membership of the church consisted of Ephraim Stearns, Susannah Adams, Jonas Bemis, Tabitha Bemis, Abraham Bemis, Abigail Bemis, Daniel Stratton, Elizabeth Bemis, Mary Bemis, Elizabeth Adams, Martha Stratton. The present church building was erected in 1828. In 1833 this church became a station with a regularly appointed preacher, which included Waltham and Lincoln. In 1839 Wal-

---

* Readers of this volume who are interested in the old church should read the interesting and scholarly volume of addresses published on the occasion of the celebration of the two hundredth anniversary of its existence in 1898.

tham was detached, thereby reducing the membership of the Weston society from 141 to 83, and it has not materially increased since that date. From 1794 to the present time this parish has had 107 preachers. In March, 1888, George Weston, of Lincoln, died, aged eighty-eight. He had been a member of this society for seventy years.

In October, 1864, the following petition was addressed to Edwin Hobbs, Esq., justice of the peace for Middlesex County:—

Whereas the Methodist Episcopal Church Society in Weston, having for several years neglected to choose trustees of the Society, and there being no clerk legally qualified to call a meeting, we, the undersigned members thereof, respectfully request you to issue a warrant, calling a meeting of the qualified voters of the Society agreeable to the provisions of the Revised Statutes.

The petition is signed by Franklin Childs, Amos Carter, Jr., Daniel Stearns, Abijah Gregory, and Abijah G. Jones. A warrant was duly issued accordingly, returnable November 7, 1864. E. F. Childs was made clerk, and seven trustees were chosen.

The following interesting printed account of the Methodist society in Weston, clipped from some magazine apparently, and not signed, was found with the manuscript of this book after its author's decease. It is styled "A Brief History of the Methodist Episcopal Church, Weston (Kendal Green), Mass."

The first house for public worship was erected in the year 1797, and stood in the pasture now owned by Mr. Fiske, to the right of the road leading toward the "poor farm." The structure was not imposing, but it was often filled with devout worshippers, and as a very aged member of the church told the writer of this article, though there were no stoves to warm them in winter, and they had but slabs on which to sit and hear the word of God, still the services were very helpful, very spiritual, and seasons of refreshing from the presence of the Lord.

Difficulties which we need not mention and opposition of which we need not speak were successfully met and overcome, and the society steadily grew until the place of meeting became "too strait" for them, and they began to agitate the building of another church. The old record refers to various meetings held in which the building of the "New Church" formed the main subject of discussion for the meeting.

It was not, however, until the year 1828 that the arrangement was finally made and the church put under contract. On February 20 of that year an agreement (the old records say) was entered into between Francis

THE RIPLEY HOUSE, WHEATON LANE.

Built prior to 1740 by Dr. Wheaton. Here the Tory doctor secreted the British spy in 1775. The place was confiscated, and later came into the possession of Dr. Bancroft. It is now owned and occupied by Mr. Francis B. Ripley.

THE WILLIAM H. HILL HOUSE, WELLESLEY STREET.

In his oration of July 4, 1876, Mr. Charles H. Fiske said that the house was then supposed to be from one hundred and fifty to two hundred years old. There is much in its appearance to justify the greater age. It is supposed to be the oldest house still standing in the town to-day.

EVANGELICAL CHURCHES IN WESTON 175

A. Pickering, Emery Bemis, George Weston, Thomas Jenkins (all of the town of Lincoln), and Marshall Jones, of Weston, on the one part, and Whitman Peterson, of Duxbury, on the other; said Peterson to furnish materials and build a "meeting house" for the Methodist Society in Weston, on a lot of "land not far from the old meeting house." And the said Peterson to receive for his work the sum of one thousand seven hundred dollars ($1,700). Mr. Peterson entered at once upon his work, and the church was completed the following November, the church being dedicated January 8, 1829.

The dedication was a great event, the Methodist people coming from near and far to join in the celebration. The singers seem to have been held in special favor, for at a meeting of the trustees it was voted that those assisting in the singing "on the day of dedication" shall have something to eat and something to drink at "Milton Dagett's Tavern"; and that the expense shall be paid by the building committee. And there is a bill placed in the old record in which so much is charged for brandy, wine, and loaf sugar. It really looks as if our fathers were not quite as sound on the temperance lines as we are to-day.

It would appear from an old subscription paper of the date July, 1828, that it was in the thought of the builders of the church proper to erect also a chapel for prayer and social meetings, and the names are given of quite a large number who pledged money for the purpose, but for some reason not given the chapel was not built.

As the years went by, the necessity of a "Preacher's house," as the parsonage used to be called, was more and more apparent, and various meetings of the trustees and stewards are recorded in which the matter was agitated; but it was not until the year 1850 that it was deemed "specially necessary" that a parsonage be built on "this station," and at a meeting held at the house of Brother Marshall Smith, May 14, it was finally voted to build a house for the preacher. Rev. H. C. Dunham presided at the meeting. Prayer was offered by Brother J. Whitman. Brother Hagar was appointed to secure a suitable "building lot." At an adjourned meeting the report of Brother Hagar was received, and it was voted to accept the offer of Captain S. Fisk, and take 48 rods of land on Marshall Smith's line, 4 on the road, and 12 in the rear, and pay the sum of $100. It was further voted to build an "upright" house, 28 by 22, with an ell 24 by 14.

Brothers H. C. Dunham, Joseph Whitman, Ephraim Brown, Rufus Babcock, and Franklin Childs were the building committee. The committee proceeded at once with their work. The cellar was dug and stoned without charge. Mr. Samuel A. Willis, of Sudbury, contracted to build the house for $800. He commenced the work in July, and finished about the 1st of October. It has been occupied as a parsonage ever since.

Repairs have been made on the church from time to time as it has needed, some $600 the last year of the pastorate of Rev. Mr. Noon and quite extensive during the pastorate of Rev. C. C. Whidden. It was at this time that the vestry over the vestibule was built, which is very convenient for the weekly meetings and the various social gatherings of the church.

The church has been remembered recently by will in the gift of some $600 by the late Mr. Joseph Whitman, a former member of the society, and gift of an organ from Mr. Hastings's factory has just been presented to the church by Mrs. George F. Harrington. This latter gift is given in memory of Mrs. Harrington's mother, who for many years was a most faithful and devoted member of the church and deeply interested in its prosperity.

The society has been favored with a succession of most worthy and faithful ministers, who have found their chief joy in declaring the glad gospel and doing what they might be able for the people in the ways of righteousness.

The list following dates back to the year 1794:—

1794, John Hill.
1795, John Vanneman.
1796, Joshua Hall, George Pickering.
1797, Daniel Ostrander, Elias Hull.
1798, David Brumley, Epaphras Kibby.
1799, Stephen Hull, Elijah R. Sabin.
1800, Nathan Emory, John Finnegan.
1801, Joseph Snelling.
1802, Joshua Soule, Dan Perry.
1803, Reuben Hubbard, Thomas Ravlin.
1804, Nehemiah Coy, Joel Wicker.
1805, Clement Parker, Erastus Otis.
1806, John Gove, Thomas Asbury.
1807, Benjamin Hill, Isaac Scarrett.
1808, John Tinkham, Isaac Locke.
1809, Benjamin R. Hoyt, Nathan Hill.
1810, Isaac Bonney, Robert Arnold.
1811, Isaac Bonney, Elias Marble.
1812, Elisha Streeter, John Vickory.
1813, Orlando Hinds, Vanransalear R. Osborn.
1814, Orlando Hinds, Zenas Adams.
1815, Vanransalear R. Osborn, Bartholomew Otheman.
1816, Orlando Hinds.
1817, V. R. Osborn, B. Otheman.
1818, John Linsey, Isaac Bonney.
1819, David Kilburn, Isaac Stoddard.
1820, V. R. Osborn, Nathan Paine, J. W. McKee.
1821, Benjamin Hazeltine, J. W. Case.
1822–23, Erastus Otis, George Fairbank.

EVANGELICAL CHURCHES IN WESTON

1824, Benjamin Hazeltine, Ira Bidwell, John E. Risley.
1825, John Lindsey, Hezekiah S. Ramsdell, and Jared Perkins.
1826, Joel Steel, Leonard B. Griffin, and Jared Perkins.
1827, Ephraim K. Avery, Giles Campbell.
1828, Ephraim K. Avery, Louis Jansen.
1829–30, Daniel Fillmore, Isaac Jennison, and A. B. Kinsman.
1831, Jacob Sanborn, Sanford Benton, and Samuel Palmer.
1832, Abraham D. Merrill, Samuel Coggshall.
1833–34, Ames Binney.
1835, Benjamin F. Lambord.
1836–37, Epaphras Kibby.
1838–39, Nathan B. Spaulding.
1840–41, George Pickering.
1842–43, William R. Stone.
1844–45, Henry E. Hempstead.
1846–47, Kinsman Atkinson.
1848–49, Thomas Hicks Mudge.
1850–51, Howard C. Dunham.
1852–53, John Cadwell.
1854–55, John S. Day.
1856, Abraham M. Osgood.
1857–58, Moses P. Webster.
1859–60, John M. Merrill.
1861–62, Oliver S. Howe.
1863, Nathan A. Soule.
1864, William A. Braman.
1865, Jabez W. P. Jordan.
1866–67, Porter M. Vinton.
1868–69, George Sutherland.
1870–71, William F. Lacount.
1872–74, William H. Meredith.
1875, S. O. Dyer.
1876–77, George E. Sanderson.
1878, William Merrill.
1879, William P. Blackmer.
1880, William H. Adams.
1881–84, Samuel H. Noon.
1884–85, J. W. Adams.
1886–87, Charles Nicklin.
1888–91, E. H. Thrasher.
1891–92, A. A. Loomis.
1892–94, C. C. Whidden.
1894, Samuel H. Noon.

The first *Baptists* in Weston began to gather together about 1776, meeting at each other's houses, under the lead of Deacon Oliver Hastings, who was baptized in Framingham in 1772. March 29, 1784, four young men—Justin Harrington, Samuel Train, Jr., James Hastings, and Joseph Seaverns—contracted to build a meeting-house thirty-one feet square. This building was first occupied in 1784, and finished in 1788. It was erected on land belonging to the Nicholas Boylston estate. As we see by the deed of Moses Gill, he releases "all right, title, and interest in and to the Baptist meeting-house in Weston, or any money due from said meeting-house or society, to Reuben Carver." Moses Gill was an heir to this property through his marriage with Rebecca, daughter of Thomas Boylston.

In 1789 a church of sixteen members was recognized by the ecclesiastical council. When the Baptists and Methodists began to erect places of public worship in the town, they signified their intention to "sign off" (so termed in those days) from the established church, as it may very properly be called. But, before they could be released from paying their taxes to this town church, they were required to produce, to the satisfaction of the Selectmen of the town, a certificate from the Baptist or Methodist church, testifying that they paid the tax for the support of the gospel ministry in their respective churches. This was done in the following manner:—

This may certify that Mr. Samuel Bingham and Jacob Leadbetter have attended public worship with the Baptist Society in Weston, since March, 1788, and pray to be excused from paying tax to the other religious society, as they bear their part in supporting the gospel with the Baptist Society.

In 1788 a protest was presented in town meeting concerning this matter of town taxation for the support of the minister and repairs of the town church, as being against the "bill of rights" and illegal. The town does not seem to have paid any attention to this protest, as there is no action recorded on the town records, and the protest cannot be found among the town papers.

The Baptist society had no settled minister till 1811, at which time they ordained Charles Train as pastor of this church, and a branch was formed at Framingham that year. The Weston church from 1811 to 1826 was known as the Weston and Framingham church; but in 1826 the Framingham branch became a distinct church, retaining Mr. Train* as their pastor until 1839. The Weston church numbered about forty members.

The present church, near the centre of the town, was erected in 1828, Mrs. Bryant giving $1,000 to the parish for that purpose, and Mr. Hews giving the land. The material of the old church was used in erecting the parsonage in 1833. In 1830 Rev. Timothy P. Ropes, a graduate of Waterville College, was ordained as pastor of this church, remaining three years. At the twenty-fifth anniversary of the Boston Baptist Association, held at Newton in 1832, mention was made of the growing church in Weston, and of the fact that a sister had given a thousand dollars to the society and a brother had given the land. At the twenty-sixth anniversary of the association the delegates from the Weston church were Joseph Hodges, Jr., Deacon Uriah Gregory, Isaac Jones, and John Dunn.

In 1835 candidates who were preparing for the Baptist ministry, and belonged to the Weston church, were Andrew Dunn, Elbridge Smith, and Benjamin W. Roberts.

In 1822 a second protest was made in town meeting as follows:

The undersigned members of the Baptist and Methodist Societies in Weston, having been compelled in years past, by illegal assessments, to defray a proportional part of the expenses annually recurring in the Congregational Society of said town, such as the making and collecting the ministerial tax, ringing the bell, providing wood, abatement of parish taxes, repairing the meeting-house, &c., do earnestly petition that some

---

*Charles Train, the third child of "Deacon" Samuel and Deborah (Savage) Train, was born January 7, 1783. Receiving his elementary education in the Weston district school, he completed his preparation for college with Rev. Samuel Kendal. He graduated from Harvard with distinction in 1805. At first he intended to become a lawyer, having aptitudes which enabled him to perform distinguished service in civic affairs. But in 1806 he decided for the Baptist ministry. At this time, through particular interest in his native town, he united with the Baptist church, and thereafter he continued to preach to this church until 1826, dividing his time between Weston and Framingham. This was due to his attachment to his native town and church. Although living and working mostly in Framingham, he continued his double service, and caused the society at Framingham to be a branch of the Weston church. He served several terms after 1822 in the House and Senate of the State legislature, being prominent in the formation of the State library and in revising the laws relating to common schools. Not least was his championship of religious liberty and social improvement. For a considerable period, while serving as the first pastor of the Baptist church, this son of Weston enjoyed a high reputation and wielded a large influence in civic and religious concerns.

measure may be taken by the town effectually to prevent the like imposition in future; that the aforesaid Baptist and Methodist Societies may be entirely exempt from all unjust charges and unlawful taxation.

This petition was signed by twenty-two members of these societies. But the evil they complain of does not seem to have been effectually done away until the year 1840. Those who succeeded Mr. Ropes in the ministry of this church are as follows: Rev. Joseph Hodges, Jr., settled in 1835, resigned in 1839; Rev. Origen Crane, settled in 1840, resigned in 1854; Rev. Calvin H. Topliff, settled in 1854, resigned in 1866; Rev. Luther G. Barrett, settled in 1867, resigned in 1870; Rev. Alonzo F. Benson, settled in 1870, died in 1874; Rev. Amos Harris, settled in 1875, resigned in 1890; Rev. Charles S. Hutchinson, settled in 1891, resigned in 1892; Rev. J. Mervin Hull, settled in 1893, resigned in 1899; Rev. Frederic E. Heath, settled in 1900, resigned in 1904; Rev. Harry E. Hinkley, settled in 1905, resigned in 1911; Rev. James M. Leub, settled since August, 1912, the present pastor.

(For more details as to the protests of the Baptists against paying money to support the all-prepotent Puritan, or First Parish, church in the town, see Chapter VII.)

The first meeting of the *Congregational Society* as a constituent part of the Congregational denomination, or sect, was held in Weston Town Hall, January 4, 1891. In September following, by a cordial invitation of the First Parish, the meetings were transferred to the chapel of that society. On October 29, 1891, the society was duly organized by the ecclesiastical council of the Congregational churches through the admission of Francis and Mary Hastings, Lucy Sherman, George A. and E. J. Hirtle, F. T. and Ella J. Fuller, Mary and Voluny Poor, H. F. and N. F. Davis, A. S. Burrage from Park Street Church, Boston, of Mrs. Burrage from Lancaster, of Mrs. Nathan Upham, John Schwartz from Bangor, Me., of Mrs. Harriet Warren from Weston Methodist Church, of Mrs. John McDonald, and Mrs. A. M. Upham from Boston.

The reception sermon was preached by Rev. Dr. Sturgis, of Natick. At a meeting the same day a call was extended to Rev.

R. F. Gordon, and accepted by him. At a meeting held December 8, 1892, steps were taken for the incorporation of the church. Land was purchased from Mr. A. H. Hews on Central Avenue, containing 21,150 square feet, and thereon a chapel was erected. The first service in the new chapel was held December 18, 1892. The following is the list of the church officers: clerk of the parish, Mrs. F. C. Burrage; treasurer, A. S. Burrage; standing committee, H. F. Davis, E. J. Hirtle, A. S. Burrage, senior deacons, H. F. Davis, Francis Hastings; junior deacon; G. A. Hirtle.

XIV.

The Medical Profession.

Robert Jennison would appear to have been the first doctor in Weston (in 1750), so far as any record can be discovered. It is probable that the physicians who visited Weston at an earlier period were from other towns. Dr. Jennison's charge for pulling a tooth was sixpence, or ninepence for two teeth! Peter, the doctor's brother, was tailor in Weston in 1750.

In 1754 Dr. Josiah Converse receipts for attendance and medicines for the Jones family £12 13s. He was probably not of Weston. Perhaps it would be safe to say that Dr. John Binney was the first physician who settled in Weston (about 1750). His widow married Daniel Adams, of Lincoln, in 1765.

Dr. Josiah Starr, born at Dedham in 1740, settled in Weston in 1762, and in that year married Abigail Upham, daughter of William Upham. He owned the Brookside Farm, now in the possession of heirs of Mr. Frederick T. Bush. His son Ebenezer, born in 1768, was a physician in Newton. Dr. Starr was practising medicine in Weston in 1781. The date of his death is not stated.

Ephraim Woolson, born in 1740, was graduated from Harvard in 1760; practised medicine in Weston, and died in 1802.

Dr. William Ward, of Athol, born December 8, 1750, settled in Weston about 1780, and in 1785 married Lucy Jones, daughter of Isaac Jones. He was physician of the town until 1791. He died in 1793.

Dr. John Clark was born in Halifax, N.S., May 14, 1778. His father was living at Halifax, having charge of the American prisoners. He married Jennett, daughter of Mrs. Ruth Mackey, of Weston, and would seem to have been in practice as a physician in Weston between 1802 and 1805, the latter being the year of his death at the age of twenty-seven.

Dr. Isaac Hurd, of Concord, practised largely in the north part of Weston. Dr. Bancroft studied medicine with him. He receipts to Deacon Isaac Hobbs for a Continental (Congress) certificate for $574 bequeathed him by Mrs. Abigail Jones, daughter of Isaac Hobbs.

Joseph Taft was probably of Lincoln, but practised in Weston. He makes out a bill to Isaac Hobbs, from "the beginning of the world to date," March, 1795, twelve shillings.

Dr. Amos Bancroft was widely known throughout Middlesex County. He was born in Pepperell in 1767, and was graduated at Harvard College in 1791. He studied medicine with Dr. Hurd of Concord, came to Weston about 1795, and remained until 1811, when he removed to Groton. He filled several offices of the town, and took a leading part in town affairs. He married Sally Bass, of Boston, in 1796. She died in Weston in 1799. Dr. Bancroft had an extensive practice, and at various times a considerable number of students under his charge. Among these was Dr. George C. Shattuck, who in 1811 married Eliza Cheever Davis, of Weston. During the winter, when the roads were blocked up with snow, he travelled on snow-shoes, and often he would be absent from home several days at a time. On one occasion he stopped at night at a tavern in order to see a patient. Passing through the bar-room, he noticed two evil-looking men, who eyed him in a suspicious manner. When he came out, the men had gone. The road from the tavern was lonely, and the place was three miles from the village. As the doctor had considerable money with him, he felt anxious, and not without cause, for, when he reached a secluded spot, these very men stepped out and tried to stop his horse. One of them snatched at the bridle, but missed it. The doctor, whipping the animal, left the men behind, but not before a bullet passed through the back of his sulky. While in Weston, Dr. Bancroft owned and occupied the Parson Woodward house, now Mrs. Dickson's. In 1848 he was one day crossing State Street in Boston, when he was knocked down and injured so severely that he died a few hours later. He was attended in his last moments by his old student, Dr. George C. Shattuck. He was seventy-seven years old at the time of his death.

Dr. Bancroft's son, Thomas Bigelow Bancroft, was graduated at Harvard in 1831, and studied medicine with Dr. Shattuck.

Dr. Benjamin James followed Dr. Bancroft as the physician of Weston in 1812, and remained its very popular and highly esteemed practitioner for over thirty-six years, until 1847 or 1848, when he removed to New Jersey, where he died. Dr. James filled different offices in the town, and was for many years town clerk, succeeding Isaac Fiske, Esq., in that office. He occupied for many years the house which stood adjoining the old Lamson store, where now stands the Cutting grocery. In 1814 Dr. James published a book on Dentistry, which was highly considered in its day.

Dr. Otis E. Hunt was born in Sudbury in 1822, and settled in Weston in 1848, where he remained until 1864, when he removed to Waltham, and now resides in Newtonville as a consulting physician. Dr. Hunt built the house now owned by Mrs. Sears.

Edgar Parker, of Framingham, followed Dr. Hunt in 1865. He was graduated at Harvard Medical College in 1863, and was assistant surgeon in the Thirteenth Regiment at the time of the war, and severely wounded in the battle of Gettysburg. He remained in Weston until 1867, when he relinquished his profession and became a portrait painter, and is now among the ablest of our artists. While in Weston, he was very popular both as a physician and for his social qualities, and his leaving was much regretted by the people. From 1867 to 1878 Dr. Parker was followed by three or four young men, whose stay was too short to leave much, if any, noticeable record. Dr. Parker died at Bridgewater in 1892.

In 1878 Dr. Mayberry followed Dr. Smithwick. Little is known of his antecedents. He remained in Weston until 1885, when he removed to Weymouth.

Dr. Frederick W. Jackson, born in Jefferson, Me., in 1858, studied medicine with Dr. Whittemore, of Gardiner, Me. He was graduated at the Long Island Medical School, and came to Weston in 1885. He built the house south of the church, and still continues to be the resident physician of the town.

No mention is made among the records of Dr. Wheaton, of Weston. The only mention made of him is in the Journal of Howe, who was General Gage's spy in Weston previous to the battle of Concord. Howe was secreted in Dr. Wheaton's house when the Liberty Men of the town gathered at Isaac Jones's tavern, the Golden Ball, carrying tar and feathers with which to decorate the spy, if caught in the house. Mr. Jones had, previous to their visit, sent him to the doctor's house, he being a Tory friend. Dr. Wheaton's house was that now owned by Mr. Ripley, then known as the Goldthwaite house, and later occupied by the inventor, Ira Draper.

XV.

The Taverns.

It has been found impossible at this late date to give what would otherwise be a highly interesting history of the old-time taverns that existed in such great numbers throughout Massachusetts previous to, and for many years after, the Revolution. It is often asked how it was possible for so many taverns to have been profitable in so close proximity to each other, as was the case in every village along main routes throughout New England. The main road through Weston was the most important thoroughfare in early days, connecting Boston with Connecticut, New York, Pennsylvania, and Washington. As late as 1835 the mail-coaches passed through Weston for Boston (about midnight). The mail agent, who accompanied each coach, was required by law to blow a horn as he passed through the towns, that heavy teams and other obstructions might be moved out of the way of the United States mails. The horn also gave notice to those desiring to take passage that they should be on the spot and not delay the mails. President Quincy gives an interesting picture of stage-coach travel at the close of the last century. He travelled frequently over our road on his way to New York, when he was engaged to a New York lady. Boston then had 20,000 inhabitants, and New York had only 30,000. Two coaches and twelve horses sufficed for the travel between the two commercial centres of our continent. The journey between the two cities was undertaken by few, and took as long to accomplish as it now takes a steamer to go to Europe. Mr. Quincy writes:—

The carriages were old, and the shackling and much of the harness made of rope. One pair of horses took the coach eighteen miles. Stopping-places for the night were reached at ten o'clock, and passengers were aroused between two and three in the morning, by the light of a farthing candle. Sometimes they were obliged to get out of the coach to help get it out of a quagmire or rut. They arrived at New York after a week's hard travelling, but wondering at the ease as well as the expedition with which the journey was effected.

> "Oh! the days are gone when the merry horn
> Awakened the echoes of smiling morn,
> As, breaking the slumbers of village street,
> The foaming leader's galloping feet
> Told of the rattling swift approach
> Of the well-appointed old stage-coach."

The country postmaster's duties in those days (particularly in winter) were of a more disagreeable nature than now, to say nothing of the small compensation then received from the government. There were then few newspapers, and what there were the postmasters were not required to mail. Their transmission over mail routes was done by the drivers of the coaches, who threw the papers out as they passed along their routes. The newspapers of that day were taken by clubs of three or four persons, and were passed from one to another, as is still the practice in some parts of England. This is probably one reason why so few old newspapers have been preserved. They were printed on very poor paper, usually manufactured at the printing-offices, and were consequently little calculated to stand the wear and tear of time and handling.

As stage routes increased and opposition lines were established, each had its tavern headquarters for the exchange of horses and for the entertainment of travellers. This business, together with the enormous amount of teaming from Vermont and New Hampshire, as well as from back towns of our State, and the large droves of cattle and hogs which passed over our road on their way to the towns of Brighton and Charlestown, was a great source of profit to the numerous taverns. The access to Boston for some years after the Revolution was not so easily accomplished as now. It was long and circuitous. All teaming and travel to that city from the interior was through Cambridge, over Winter Hill in Somerville to Charlestown on one side, and through Brighton and Roxbury on the other. In 1780 there was no bridge over Charles River. All communication was by ferriage. Isaac Jones, of Weston, provided timber for the Charles River bridge to the amount of £159 18s. 6d.

The oldest record of a tavern in Weston is that of Thomas Woolson, who settled in the town in 1660. In 1672 he purchased 250 acres of land of Richard Norcross, and in 1697 he bought the farm of John and Richard Coolidge. He was sentenced in 1685 to a fine of 20 shillings and costs and one hour in the stocks for selling drink without a license. He kept a tavern from 1685 to 1708, and died in 1713. He was a Selectman in 1699, 1700, 1702, and 1703. Thomas Woolson, his son, succeeded his father in the tavern. He was born in 1677. Thomas's daughter, Mary, married in 1724 Major Fullam, she being his second wife. In 1737 Isaac Woolson, who succeeded his father, Thomas, in the tavern, petitions the Court of General Sessions, praying that his license may be continued to him, as he has moved his house some distance from the original site. The Woolson stand was that now in possession of the heirs of Isaac Fiske.

The next tavern of which we have any record is that of Lieutenant John Brewer, who was born in 1669 in Sudbury, but moved to Weston in 1690. In 1693 he married Mary Jones. He died in 1709, leaving a farm and 216 acres of other lands, also a saw-mill and grist-mill. His nephew, Colonel Jonathan Brewer, Jr., commanded a regiment at Bunker Hill, and was afterwards a tavern-keeper in Waltham. In 1716 John Brewer's widow was licensed to keep a public house in Weston. Josiah Smith, son of William Smith, born in 1722, married Hepzibah Stearns, of Lexington, in 1744. It is presumed he kept the tavern, now the residence of Mrs. John Jones. His son Joel succeeded to the business at his father's death. He was a leading Liberty Man during the Revolution, and his tavern is spoken of in Howe's Journal just previous to the battle of Concord. This tavern was one of the most noted between Boston and Worcester. It has passed through many hands since the death of Joel Smith. Washington Peirce succeeded Joel in the tavern in 1817 on his marriage with a daughter of Joel, and continued to be its landlord for ten years. He was succeded by J. T. Macomber, Colonel Woods, and others, until the property was purchased by Colonel John Jones. The tavern of the Golden Ball, kept by Isaac Jones (born in 1728), is also mentioned in Howe's Journal. Mr. Jones was a noted Tory, and was reported to have kept General Gage informed of the arms and ammunition held by the Liberty Men throughout this section. Squire Barnes, of Marlboro, also mentioned in Howe's Journal, married a daughter of Mr. Jones, and was also a pronounced Tory. So dangerous and obstinate an opponent to the cause of liberty was Mr. Jones considered that he brought down on himself the following denunciation in the Worcester Convention in 1775:—

Resolved, That it be earnestly recommended to all the inhabitants of this county, not to have any commercial transactions with Isaac Jones, but to shun his house and person and to treat him with the contempt he deserves.

Mr. Jones died in 1813. The British officers were frequent guests at this tavern, driving out from Boston for suppers and sleighing parties. It was said that General Gage was also of these parties. Rebecca Baldwin, in her highly interesting diary, extending from 1756 to 1787, makes mention in 1773 of a dinner-party at Mr. Savage's at which her husband was invited to meet General Gage and his officers.

Captain Samuel Baldwin, who married for his second wife Rebecca Cotton, daughter of Rev. John Cotton of Newton, in 1762, succeeded Isaac Woolson in the tavern on the Isaac Fiske property. Captain Baldwin figures largely in town affairs throughout the Revolution. At the time of the Shays Rebellion in 1787 the troops from Boston, on their way to Springfield, bivouacked one night along our road, and the officers lodged at the Baldwin tavern. Here Dr. Gowen, of Weston, joined the forces as surgeon, and acted as such until the termination of the trouble. In 1806 Jonas Green kept this tavern, but in 1811 it became the property of Isaac Fiske.

The John Flagg tavern figures in history as the place where General Washington and suite passed the night in 1789, when on their way to Boston. A full account of this will be found in Chapter VII. of this volume. At what date Mr. Flagg began keeping this tavern has not been discovered. The first license on record is that of 1791; but he was the landlord before the Revolution, and continued to be such until 1812, when he sold the property to Thomas Stratton, taking up his residence on the prop-

erty now owned by Horatio Hews. Mr. Stratton kept the tavern
until 1823, when he sold the estate to Alpheus Bigelow, who leased
it to Lyman H. Hunter, J. T. Macomber, Dana Bruce, and William
Drake, who succeeded each other in rapid succession down to
1830, about which time Mr. Bigelow sold to Mr. James Jones.
Mr. Jones kept the tavern until his death, and was succeeded by
his son James Jones, at whose death it ceased to be a tavern, and
is now the property of Mr. Charles Emerson.

Benjamin Peirce, father and son, kept a tavern down to 1785
in what is now the house of Mr. Beals. The estate in that year
was sold by Colonel Samuel Lamson, executor of Mr. Peirce, to
Rev. Dr. Kendal for £490 3d.

Previous to the Benjamin Peirce tavern on the site of what is
now the Beals house, Mr. Peirce either built or owned a tavern
situated on a bridle road running through the present Perry farm,
which road connected Weston with Lexington and Reading.
The cellar of this old house may still be seen.

There were few houses of any importance in all these years that
had not first or last served as taverns. It was the most profitable business of all country towns along the main arteries of
travel. It was not unusual for fifty to one hundred teams to
be put up over night at a single tavern. The Lamson house
was also a tavern for a while, even down to the death of Colonel
Lamson in 1795. Benjamin Peirce, who married Mary Lamson,
died there in 1819.

Joseph Russell, son of Thomas Russell, who was born in 1745,
and in 1773 married Susannah Upham, kept a tavern for thirty-
one years, from 1791 to 1822. How many years before 1791 he
may have done so there is no record to show.

The Daggett tavern, so called, was built in 1821 by Charles
Wesson. Daggett kept this tavern for twelve years, until 1833,
when Davis succeeded him, but it was unoccupied when destroyed
by fire in 1844. This tavern was on the Concord road, on the
corner of the road to Lincoln. There was also an inn on the
opposite corner.

Charles Warren at one time kept the famous Punch Bowl
hostelry in Brookline, but sold out and returned to Weston in
1821, and assisted Wesson in building the Daggett tavern The

THE MARSHALL UPHAM HOUSE, ASH STREET.

Supposed to have been built about the year 1700, perhaps even earlier. It was torn down a few years ago by the Metropolitan Water Works, when their new water system was established.

THE FREDERICK T. BUSH HOUSE, SOUTH AVENUE.

Probably about two hundred years old, and originally known as the old Starr Farm. Formerly owned by Dr. Bowditch, by whom it was sold in 1856 to Frederick T. Bush, who extensively remodelled the house in 1858. It is still owned and occupied by the descendants of Mr. Bush. The photograph is of the old house.

property on both sides of the road is still owned by George W. and Cornelius Warren, of Waltham.

Isaac Train kept a tavern on the south side of the town, the estate now of Irving, near the Needham line. Train was landlord for eight years,—from 1802 to 1810.

Daniel Upham, Luther Robbins, Samuel Clark, Joseph Darrah, and T. A. Stone were also licensed innholders in Weston, but their several locations are not stated.

It is deeply to be regretted that much of the jovial and social life within these taverns has not been handed down to us. Gambling, or, perhaps more correctly speaking, card-playing, was before the Revolution, and for many years after, a common practice, not by any means confined to any one class of people, but prevailed generally among rich and poor, old and young alike. None would have thought it wrong to stake money or valuables upon the result of games of chance of any sort. In fact, no games were played without a stake, however small.

Lotteries both among individuals and towns, States and colleges, prevailed everywhere. In 1784 Weston petitioned the General Court for authorization to institute a lottery to raise £1,000 for the purpose of widening the great bridge at Watertown, and a committee was appointed by the town to dispose of the tickets. Isaac Jones would seem to have been the selling agent of these tickets. In 1790 the monthly State lottery was drawn in the chamber of the House of Representatives in Boston. In 1791 Thomas Hancock advertises State lottery tickets for sale, in halves, quarters, and eighths, for a prize of $10,000. Harvard College raised funds by lottery, and in New York State lotteries were instituted for every conceivable purpose, until finally they became so corrupt that the legislature prohibited them by statute. Private lotteries in churches and fairs have, however, continued down to our own day. About the year 1830 commenced the temperance and anti-card-playing crusade, resulting in 1838 in the first stringent laws against liquor selling, and especially against retailers. This movement led up to the famous "fifteen-gallon law," the result of which was that, from being obliged to have a large quantity of spirits on hand at one time, old topers were perpetually drunk.

With regard to card-playing and games of chance of whatever sort, the habit had become so general and firmly established that all manner of devices were resorted to for the purpose of concealment in taverns and public houses. Until within a few years there existed in the attic of Joel Smith's tavern a concealed room, not easily discovered by the uninitiated, in which was a table covered with a green baize cloth, where card-playing was continued as long as the house was a tavern. If report is true, the degenerate sons of early Bible-loving Christians were in the habit of resorting to this unhallowed spot even on the Lord's Day, and, while within reach of the preacher's voice across the way, would deal around the damning cards, now and again seeking to drown their quickening consciences in free potations of rum and sugar. While the names of some of these Sabbath-breakers are familiar to our people, suffice it to say, as a consolation to those who have forsaken the Calvinism of Dr. Watts or the strict letter of the Westminster Catechism, that many of those so unmindful of the ordinances of religion and propriety were, in after-life, overtaken with great worldly prosperity.

Although the taverns were gradually declining in their business, they continued to exist until about 1830, when the steamboats and railroads rendered stage routes unnecessary and competition unprofitable. Add to these obstacles the increasing restrictions on the sale of spirits, which finally broke down this once interesting and wide-spread business. So great has been the change in this respect in Weston that for more than thirty years there has not been an abiding-place for man or beast in the town outside of private hospitality. There are probably few other towns in the Commonwealth of which this can be said.

APPENDICES.

APPENDIX I.

Rev. Samuel Kendal's Letter of Acceptance.

(See Chapter I.)

Mr. Samuel Kendal's answer delivered in town meeting:—

My Christian Friends,—You having given me a call to settle with you in the gospel ministry may justly expect that I should consider it in a religious view, and give such an answer as may appear to me to be consistent with my duty. My answer is important to both you and myself, and to heaven have I looked for direction and earnestly desired to know wherein my duty consisted, with a disposition to conduct accordingly: I have likewise used the ordinary means for obtaining direction by consulting many friends, whose advice ought, as in such cases, to be taken and well considered. The first thing to be attended in the call is the minority of the people, this not so great as I could wish. Several whose friendship would afford me peculiar satisfaction, are opposed to my settlement, but, having conversed with the majority of them, I find that their objections are mostly founded upon misinformation and wrong apprehensions with respect to those things to which they object, and considering 'tis not probable the town will be better united in the choice of another, I can by no means suppose it to be my duty to give a negative answer, because some worthy men have not given their votes in favor of me, but I am sorry to say, that the measures taken by some amongst the nays, do, in some degree, lay me under a necessity to accept your call, and were there nothing further to be considered my answer would be affirmative, but it is no less a minister's duty to exercise prudence about those things that tend to his comfort and support, while he is engaged in his ministry, than it is for any denomination of men to provide for the comfort of themselves and families: and as the salary proposed is thought by all my advisers and by myself, insufficient for the support of a minister, and as the wood offered will not, in my opinion, and the opinion of those who judge from experience be sufficient to maintain the fires that are necessary in a family, I must decline accepting your invitation upon the terms offered. Your offers too being less than for years past you found necessary to the support of your late worthy pastor you can hardly suppose that I should be willing to accept the call under the present circumstances. I do not wish to burden the people more than to enable me to do my duty among them, nor would I dispute the generosity of this people more than that of any others, but those that better know than I do what is necessary to support a family do say that what you offer is not sufficient, and therefore you will receive this as a Negative answer, unless such alterations with respect to my support be made as may render it expedient for me to accept your invitation. This answer would have been given some months ago had it not been for the encouragement given me that the offer would be made better at the renewal of my call, so that you will not blame me for keeping you so long in suspense.

I am with love and respect your sincere friend and well wisher,

SAMUEL KENDAL.

The town, having considered Mr. Kendal's answer, voted to grant the sum of £10 in addition to the £80 heretofore granted, and also five cords of woods in addition to the fifteen cords of firewood, which makes in the whole £90 of money and twenty cords of firewood, upon which Mr. Kendal accepts the call.

APPENDIX II.

Rev. Joseph Field's Letter of Acceptance.
(See Chapters I. and IX.)

Boston, January 7th, 1815.

My Christian Friends,—The result of your last meeting, and the vote by which you express your desire of my becoming your pastor has been officially announced to me. When I consider the office I am thus invited to accept, the duties which you are calling on me to perform, the character which I am to assume, the relations in which I am to stand towards you, my mind is filled with anxiety and solicitude. I feel that it is no light matter to take upon me the load of a Christian minister. I feel that I am now called upon to decide a question the most important, the most interesting in its effects both to you and myself, whose decision involves subjects of the highest concern; consequences that extend beyond the grave. In forming a connection so lasting, so solemn, so intimate as that between a minister and people, perhaps more time than you have given might have been desired for reflection and consideration; but the peace and harmony with which you have acted and the unanimity which you have shown has prevented those difficulties which might otherwise have arisen on my mind, and by opening to me the prospect of being useful and successful in my calling has made the path of duty more plain and easy before me. In forming my determination, however, I trust that I have not acted with rashness, nor been influenced by any but the purest motives, and it is not without having first seriously considered the duties of the station and deeply and prayerfully reflected upon the importance of the subject, that I now, with the approbation of those whose opinions are ever to be valued by me, and impelled by the feelings of my own heart, solemnly accept in the presence of that being whose servant I am, and whose cause I am to defend, the invitation you have given me to exercise over you the pastoral charge. In doing this I am sensible of my inability to fulfill so perfectly as I would wish, the many obligations which arise out of the ministerial office, an office which I enter upon with more diffidence, when I reflect upon the ability and faithfulness with which he discharged its duties whose labors I am to continue. I tremble, indeed, at the great and awful responsibility of the station. But I put my trust in God, and look up to him for strength, for knowledge, for help. And I earnestly hope and trust your prayers, my brethren, may mingle with mine, in imploring our common father and friend, that he will make me sufficient for these things, that the connection in which we are about to engage may be mutually useful, and that having been faithful to each other on earth, we may hereafter meet in another and a better world, and enjoy forever the riches of divine love. With esteem and respect I subscribe myself yours,

JOSEPH FIELD, Jr.

At the period of the call and installation of Rev. Mr. Field to the church in Weston in 1815 the long and heated controversy between Orthodoxy and Liberal Christianity may be considered to a certain extent as having culminated in this town; and, upon Mr. Field's occupancy of the Weston pulpit, its Congregationalism ceased and Unitarianism became the prevailing creed, if so it can be called, of that church. It had become a rule at the latter part of the last century, when ministerial rates formed a part of the town taxes, and when the Baptist and Methodist churches were organized, to evade the taxes so levied for the maintenance of the ministry by declaring or "signing off" to other churches, and, by showing to the Selectmen of the town that they paid the tax for the maintenance of other churches, they were released from the town tax imposed for that purpose. By this means were removed in great part the doctrinal antagonisms which might otherwise have prevailed. That there should be still a sharp display of criticism from many quarters over the new departure in church doctrine was to be expected. One of these criticisms was the charge made against the Unitarians of practising an adroit concealment of the changes of opinions they had undergone in passing from Orthodoxy to Free Religion, the assigned motive for such concealment as stated being "to deceive an unsuspecting and confiding people" by "secretly undermining the prevailing faith" and "by working under covert towards a result which became too powerful for the people to resist." "Guilty silence had been practiced"; "insinuating methods had been used," etc. Dr. Morse, of Charlestown, published in 1815 a work in which all these explosive charges were made, and then war was indeed opened on the tented field of controversy. So far as Weston was concerned in all this war of creeds, the only remaining published record which interested the Weston church were the verses written by Henry Pason Kendal, son of Rev. Dr. Kendal, of Weston, in the Concord *Gazette* of 1830, and addressed to those who say "religion is not preached at the Unitarian church in Weston, and is not possessed by its members":—

Come! ye who deem yourselves so pure—
To Truth and Justice bow!
You've shown your zeal too long I'm sure—
Come! show your knowledge now!
Ye boldly say, it profits naught
To seek our House of Prayer;
Ye say, there's naught but morals taught—
There's no Religion there!
And say you this without a blush?
And of your neighbors too?
Henceforth let all our tongues be hush—
Religion dwells with you!
Then teach us your religious faith!
In charity impart;
O tell us what the Bible saith—
We'll learn it all by heart!
To say "Atonement should be taught,
But that's kept out of view;"
Not so! Christ's blood *Atonement wrought,*
Our Preacher says so too!
"He preaches Morals! nothing more,
Which are of small account;"
But are they not what Christ before,
Once taught upon the Mount!
Go! bring that sermon to your view!
Then say, are Morals naught?
I fear ye never read it through—
Or, maybe, have forgot!
"Judge not!" I think you can't deny,
Is in that sermon shown;
And never search your neighbor's eye,
Till you have cleans'd your own!
Some say, that plunging saves from harm—
Send sprinkled souls to hell!
We don't believe the quantum charm
Since tantum does as well!
Now comes a solemn charge! ye say,
There's no Religion there!
What is Religion? tell us, pray—
If James did not declare?
Religion pure and undefil'd
The Apostle says is this!
To visit every orphan child
And Widow in distress—

To show the world's deceitful ways,
And live unspotted here!
Exactly what our Preacher says,
In words distinct and clear!
And therefore, he must stand or fall,
With James th' Apostle sure!
If ye believe the Saint at all,
Our Preacher is secure!
He preaches pure Religion then!
And this ye can't deny;
Or else, his preaching's all in vain,
And James has told a lie!
There's one more charge I yet perceive—
Ye think a weighty one!
The Triune God we don't believe
Nor Christ—Eternal Son!
But surely we a Saviour need,
To wash our sins away!
A Mediator, who will plead
For such as go astray!
Our Heavenly Father answers well
As God of all supreme!
And Christ we cannot spare at all,
To make a God of him!
That Christ was sent to mediate,
Himself declares is true!
Is Christ your God! then plainly state
Who mediates for you!
And here I'll let the subject rest.
You feel fatigued I know!
You cannot answer now the test—
But will to-morrow though!
I wish I could believe that all
Your words were kindly meant;
The road was bad, and we might fall!
You spoke with good intent!
But much I fear 'tis no such thing!
I think I plainly see,
That these ill-natured charges spring
From want of Charity!
And when you find yourselves inclin'd
To censor us at all;
Just call the Saviour's words to mind
And let the weapon fall!

WESTON, January 18, 1830.

APPENDIX III.

Seating the Meeting-house, March 2, 1772.

First Seat Below.

	£	s.
Dea. Abijah Upham	178	–
Isaac Jones	178	10
Jonathan Stratton	178	–
Jonas Harrington	174	–
Jeremiah Whittemore	144	–
Joseph Garfield	143	10
William Upham	142	10
John Jones	140	10
John Allen	132	–
Isaac Hager	130	10
Edward Garfield	129	–

Second Below.

	£	s.
Elisha Warren	125	10
Samuel Train	124	–
Samuel Lamson	123	–
Jonas Harrington	122	–
Saml. Philipps Savage	120	10
William Whiting	120	10
James Merick	118	–
Samuel Severns	116	–
James Smith	115	10

First Seat Front Gallery.

	£	s.
John Merick	114	–
Samuel Child	112	–
John Lamson	112	–
Joseph Whitney	107	10
Isaac Harrington	110	10
Isaac Hobbs	105	10
Benjamin Peirce	105	–
Joseph Livermore	105	–

Third Seat Below.

	£	s.
Jeremiah Goodhue	104	–
Daniel Livermore	102	–
Jediah White	100	–
Benjamin Jones	97	10
Josiah Bigelow	96	10
William Lawrance	96	–
Nathaniel Coolidge	95	10
Thomas Rand	95	10
Joseph Peirce	95	–

Fourth Seat Below.

	£	s.
James Livermore	93	10
Thomas Russell	89	–
Joseph Lovewell	85	–
Thaddeus Spring	83	–
Lydia Goddard	80	–
John Bemis	79	10
Jonathan Underwood	79	10
David Stearns	79	–
Moses Harrington	79	10
Samuel Severns, Jr.	79	10

First Seat Side Gallery.

	£	s.
Benjamin Bond	74	10
Ebenezer Phillips	73	10
Elezebeth Hager	72	–
Tabatha Wheeler	71	–
Samuel Fiske	71	10
Jonas Sanderson	71	4
Jonas Peirce	70	10
Jonathan Spring	70	–
Joshua Peirce	67	–
James Stimpson	66	–
Israel Whittemore	63	7
Benjamin Fuller	63	10
Increase Leadbetter	60	–
Oliver Hastings	58	–
John Brown	57	–
Josiah Severns	56	–
Jonathan Stratton, Jr.	57	–
Joel Smith	57	–
John Flagg, Jr.	55	10

The Fifth Seat Below.

	£	s.
John Walker, Jr.	53	10
Timothy Bemis, Jr.	53	10
Abraham Sanderson	51	–
Uriah Gregory	50	–
Asa Smith	47	10
Benjamin Pollard	47	–
Nathaniel Bemis	44	–
Matthew Hobbs	43	–
Abraham Hews	39	–

Sixth Seat Below.

	£	s.
William Bond	36	10
Oliver Barber	35	–
Hezekiah Wyman	31	–
Josiah Cary	29	–

The second and third seat in the front left for the singers.

APPENDIX IV.

Town Clerks from 1721-1913.

1721, Benjamin Brown, Ebenezer Allen.
1722, Josiah Smith.
1730-31, Nathaniel Goddard.
1732-34, Josiah Livermore.
1734, James Mirick.
1735, Ebenezer Allen.
1738, Ebenezer Allen.
1754, Elisha Jones.
1755-58, Nathan Fiske.
1758-68, Braddyll Smith.
1768-69, Josiah Smith.
1770-74, Samuel Baldwin.
1775, Samuel Samson.
1776-77, Joel Smith.
1778, Samuel Lamson.
1779-80, Joel Smith.
1781-86, Isaac Hobbs.
1787, Samuel Lamson.
1788, Isaac Hobbs.

1789, Joseph Russell.
1790-93, Isaac Hobbs.
1794, Ebenezer Hobbs.
1795-98, Isaac Hobbs.
1799, Joseph Russell.
1800-03, Isaac Hobbs.
1804-08, Isaac Fiske.
1808-09, Isaac Hobbs, Jr.
1810-12, Isaac Fiske.
1813-15, Nathan Hager.
1817-18, Ebenezer Hobbs.
1819-21, Isaac Fiske.
1822-23, Daniel S. Lamson.
1824-27, Isaac Fiske.
1828-46, Benjamin James.
1847-63, Nathan Hagar.
1863-64 { Horace Hews. Benjamin F. Morrison.
1864-, George W. Cutting, Jr.

APPENDIX V.

Town Treasurers from 1754-1913.

1754, Elisha Jones.
1755, Nathan Fiske.
1756-57, Elisha Jones.
1758-68, Braddyll Smith.
1769-70, Jonas Harrington.
1771-73, Braddyll Smith.
1774-78, Samuel Lamson.
1779-82, Samuel Fiske.
1783, Isaac Hobbs.
1784-87, Samuel Lamson.
1788-90, Joseph Russell.
1791, Isaac Hobbs.
1792, Artemas Ward.
1793-97, Ebenezer Hobbs.
1798-99, Joseph Russell.
1800, Artemas Ward.

1801-06, Isaac Lamson.
1807-09, Isaac Hobbs, Jr.
1810-11, Isaac Train.
1812-15, Nathan Hager.
1816-18, Ebenezer Hobbs.
1819, Daniel S. Lamson.
1820, Nathan Fiske.
1821-23, Daniel S. Lamson.
1824-34, Isaac Hobbs.
1835, Charles Merriam.
1836-46, Benjamin James.
1847-58, Marshall Jones.
1859, Charles Dunn.
1860-89, Horace Hews.
1890-, Henry J. White.

APPENDIX VI.

Representatives.

Representatives from the town of Weston from the date of incorporation, 1712, to 1890:—

Francis Fullam, 1713 to 1720, 1722, 1724, 1729, 1730, 1731, 1736, 1737. He represented the town for fourteen years.
Josiah Jones, Jr., 1716, 1721, 1725, 1726.
Joseph Allen, 1727, 1728.
Ebenezer Allen, 1732, 1733, 1734, 1735.
Joseph Livermore, 1738, 1739, 1740, 1742, 1743, and 1749.
Josiah Brewer, 1741, 1744, 1745, 1746, 1747.
Abijah Upham, 1750, 1751.
Elisha Jones, 1752, 1753, 1754, 1756, 1757, 1758, 1760, 1761, 1762, 1763, 1773.
Braddyll Smith, 1774, 1775, 1776.
Abraham Bigelow, 1755, 1759, 1764, 1765, 1766, 1767, 1769, 1770, 1771, 1772.
Isaac Hobbs, 1777.
Joseph Roberts, 1778, 1780.
Josiah Smith, 1779, 1781.
Samuel Fiske, 1782, 1783, 1786.
Isaac Jones, 1784, 1785, 1787, 1788, 1789, 1790.
Amos Bigelow, 1791, 1792, 1793, 1794.
Town refused to vote for representative in 1795.
Artemas Ward, 1796, 1797, 1798, 1799, 1800.
John Slack, 1801, 1802, 1803, 1804, 1805, 1806.
Ebenezer Hobbs, 1807, 1809, 1810, 1811.
Isaac Fiske, 1808, 1812, 1813, 1814.
No representative sent in 1815, 1816.
George W. Smith, 1817, 1818, 1819, 1820, 1821, 1822.
Nathan Hobbs, 1823, 1824, 1826.
No representative sent in 1825.
Alpheus Bigelow, 1827, 1828.

Jonas Cutter, 1829, 1830.
Samuel Hobbs, 1831, 1832.
Abijah Coburn, 1833, 1834.
Henry Hobbs, 1835, 1836.
Jonas Hastings, 1837, 1838.
William Spring, 1839, 1840.
S. F. H. Bingham, 1841, 1842.
Edwin Hobbs, 1843, 1844.
Voted not to send, 1845, 1846.
Otis Train, 1847.
No vote recorded 1848, 1849.
Isaac Coburn, 1850, 1851.
John A. Lamson, 1852, 1853.
Voted not to send 1854, 1855.
Alpheus Morse, 1856, 1863.
Charles H. Fiske, 1867, 1871.
Edward Coburn, 1875.
Alonzo S. Fiske, 1878.
Henry J. White, 1883.
George W. Cutting, 1889.

APPENDIX VII.

SELECTMEN.

From second volume of Records, 1754:—
Elisha Jones, 1754, 1756, 1757, 1761, 1762.
Deacon Abijah Upham, 1754, 1755.
Captain Samuel Bond, 1754.
Samuel Seaverns, 1754, 1756, 1757.
Isaac Hager, 1754.
Nathan Fiske, 1755.
Abraham Bigelow, 1755, 1756, 1757, 1758, 1759, 1760, 1761, 1762,
    1763, 1764, 1765, 1766, 1767, 1768, 1769, 1770, 1771.
Ebenezer Hobbs, 1755, 1757.
Lieutenant Isaac Allen, 1755, 1756, 1757.
John Hastings, 1756.
Braddyll Smith, 1758, 1759, 1760, 1761, 1762, 1763, 1764, 1765,
    1766, 1767, 1768, 1769, 1770, 1771.
Henry Spring, 1758.
William Whitney, 1758, 1759, 1760, 1761, 1762.
John Warren, 1758, 1759, 1760, 1761, 1762, 1763, 1764, 1765, 1766.
John Allen, 1759.
James Stimpson, 1760.
Samuel Train, 1763, 1764, 1765, 1798, 1799.
Thomas Upham, 1763, 1764, 1765, 1766, 1774, 1775, 1776.
Josiah Smith, 1766, 1767, 1768, 1769, 1771, 1772, 1773, 1774, 1775,
    1777, 1778, 1779.
John Myrick, 1767, 1768, 1769, 1770, 1772, 1774.
Jonathan Stratton, 1767, 1768, 1772.
Abraham Jones, 1769, 1770, 1780.
Jonas Harrington, 1770.
John Lamson, 1771.
Josiah Whitney, 1771.   [1793.
Isaac Jones, 1772, 1778, 1779, 1784, 1785, 1786, 1787, 1788, 1789,
Joseph Whitney, 1772, 1773.
Thomas Russell, 1773.
Thomas Rand, 1773, 1774, 1775, 1776, 1777.
Benjamin Peirce, 1773, 1774, 1775, 1776.
Samuel Baldwin, 1775.

SELECTMEN

Israel Whittemore, 1776, 1777, 1778, 1779, 1780.
Jonathan Underwood, 1776, 1777.
Isaac Hobbs, 1777, 1782, 1783.
Samuel Fiske, 1778, 1779, 1780, 1781, 1782, 1783, 1784, 1785.
Joseph Roberts, 1778, 1779.
Nathan Hobbs, 1780.
Thaddeus Spring, 1780, 1781, 1782, 1783, 1786, 1787, 1788, 1789, 1790, 1791, 1792, 1794, 1795.
Isaac Fiske, 1781, 1808, 1810, 1811, 1812, 1813, 1814.
Samuel Lamson, 1781, 1782, 1783, 1784, 1785.
Uriah Gregory, 1781.
Jonathan Fiske, 1782, 1783, 1784, 1785.
Samuel Livermore, 1784, 1785.
Jonas Sanderson, 1786, 1787, 1788.
Nathan Hager, 1786, 1787, 1788, 1794, 1795, 1796, 1797, 1798, 1799.
Matthew Hobbs, 1786, 1787, 1788, 1789, 1790, 1791, 1792.
Joseph Russell, 1789, 1790, 1791, 1799.
John Coburn, 1789, 1790, 1793.
Amos Bigelow, 1790, 1791, 1792.
Joel Smith, 1791.
Artemas Ward, 1792, 1796, 1797, 1798, 1800.
Daniel Stratton, 1792.
Elisha Stratton, 1793, 1794, 1795, 1796, 1797, 1798, 1799.
Nathan Warren, 1793, 1809, 1810, 1812, 1813, 1814.
Joseph Nichols, 1793, 1794, 1795.
Abraham Harrington, 1794, 1795, 1796, 1797, 1798.
Samuel Train, Jr., 1796, 1797.
Alpheus Bigelow, 1799, 1806, 1807.
Isaac Lamson, 1800, 1801, 1802, 1803.
John Slack, 1800, 1801, 1802, 1803, 1804, 1805.
Nathan Fiske, 1800, 1801, 1802, 1803, 1804, 1805, 1808, 1815, 1816, 1817, 1818, 1819, 1820.
Ebenezer Hobbs, 1800, 1801, 1802, 1803, 1804, 1805, 1806, 1807, 1809, 1810, 1811.
Enoch Train, 1801, 1802, 1803.
Amos Harrington, 1804, 1805.
Abijah Fiske, 1804, 1805, 1806, 1807, 1811.
Moses Fuller, 1806, 1807.

Amos Bancroft, 1806, 1807, 1808.
Nathan Hobbs, Jr., 1808, 1809, 1810, 1811, 1821, 1822.
Josiah Hastings, 1808, 1809.
Reuben Carver, 1809, 1810.
Moses Fiske, 1811.
William Boyle, 1811.
Isaac Hobbs, Jr., 1812, 1813, 1814, 1815.
Thomas Bigelow, 1812, 1813, 1814.
Daniel Clark, 1812, 1813, 1814, 1815.
Nathan Hager, 1815, 1816, 1817.
Jedediah Thayer, 1815, 1816, 1817, 1818, 1819, 1820.
Jonas Coburn, 1816, 1817, 1818, 1819, 1825, 1827, 1828.
Amos Hobbs, 1816, 1817.
George W. Smith, 1818, 1819.
Washington Peirce, 1818, 1819, 1821, 1822.
Henry Hobbs, 1820, 1821, 1822, 1838, 1839, 1840, 1843.
Eliphalet Slack, 1821, 1822, 1823, 1824.
Luther Harrington, 1821, 1823, 1824.
Isaac Jones, 1822, 1823, 1824, 1825, 1826, 1837, 1843, 1844, 1845, 1846, 1847, 1848, 1849, 1850.
Isaac Brackett, 1823, 1824.
William Spring, 1823, 1824, 1836, 1837, 1838, 1839, 1840, 1841.
Benjamin James, 1825, 1826, 1827, 1828, 1829, 1830, 1831, 1832, 1833, 1834, 1835, 1836, 1837, 1838, 1839.
Abijah Coburn, 1825, 1826, 1827, 1828.
Sewell Fiske, 1825, 1826, 1830, 1831, 1832, 1833, 1834.
James Coburn, 1826.
Marshall Jones, 1827, 1828, 1829.
Benjamin Peirce, 1827, 1828, 1829, 1843, 1844, 1845, 1846, 1847, 1848, 1849, 1850, 1851.
Jonas Cutter, 1829, 1830, 1831.
Ld. W. Cushing, 1829, 1830, 1831, 1832, 1833, 1834.
John Jones, 1830, 1831, 1832, 1833.
Ezra Warren, 1832, 1833, 1834, 1835.
Converse Bigelow, 1834.
Charles Merriam, 1835.
Rufus Babcock, 1836.
Jesse Viles, 1837, 1838, 1839, 1840, 1841.

Samuel Hobbs, 1837.
Charles Warren, 1838, 1839.
Alpheus Bigelow, Jr., 1840, 1841, 1842.
Amos Warren, 1840.
Chester Dickinson, 1842.
Elisha Childs, 1842.
Edwin Hobbs, 1844, 1845, 1846, 1847, 1851, 1852, 1853.
Isaac Coburn, 1848, 1849, 1850, 1851, 1852, 1853.
William Hastings, 1851, 1852, 1853.
Nathan Barker, 1855, 1856, 1857.
Luther S. Upham, 1855, 1856, 1857.
Edward Coburn, 1855, 1856, 1857, 1867, 1868, 1869, 1870, 1871, 1872, 1873, 1874, 1875, 1876, 1877, 1878, 1879, 1880, 1881.
Benjamin Peirce, Jr., 1858, 1859, 1860, 1861.
Alonzo S. Fiske, 1858, 1859, 1860, 1861, 1862, 1863, 1864, 1865, 1866, 1867, 1868, 1869, 1870, 1871.
George B. Cutter, 1858, 1859.
Increase Leadbetter, Jr., 1860, 1861, 1862, 1863, 1864, 1865, 1866.
Simeon W. Brown, 1862.
Horace Hews, 1863, 1864, 1865.
Benjamin F. Cutter, 1866, 1867, 1868, 1869, 1872, 1873, 1874, 1875.
Abijah Coburn, 1870.
George W. Dunn, 1871, 1872, 1873, 1874, 1875, 1876.
Oliver R. Robbins, 1876, 1877.
George B. Milton, 1877, 1878, 1879, 1880.
Marshall L. Upham, 1878, 1879, 1880.   [1889.
Henry J. White, 1881, 1882, 1883, 1884, 1885, 1886, 1887, 1888,
Samuel Warren, 1881, 1882, 1883, 1884, 1885, 1886, 1887, 1888.
Nathan S. Fiske, 1882, 1883, 1884.
Arthur L. Coburn, 1885, 1886, 1887, 1888, 1889.
Henry J. Jennison, 1889, 1890, 1891, 1892.
Francis Blake, 1890, 1891, 1892.
Nathan S. Fiske, 1891, 1892.

[To the above list by Colonel Lamson may be added these: Selectmen 1892–99, Henry J. Jennison, Francis Blake, Nathan S. Fiske; 1900–09, Francis Blake, Nathan S. Fiske, Alfred L. Cutting; 1910–, Alfred L. Cutting, Nathan S. Fiske, Benjamin Loring Young.]

APPENDIX VIII.

THE SEPARATION FROM WATERTOWN AS A PRECINCT.

(From State House Records, June 14, 1698, O.S., June 24, N.S.)

The following order sent up from the Representatives, was read and concurred with.

Upon reading the report of a Committee of this Court upon the Petition of the Inhabitants of the West End of the Town of Watertown, praying to be a distinct Precinct for the setting up the publick worship of God among themselves:

Resolved and Ordered, That the Petitioners be and hereby are permitted and allowed to invite, procure, and settle a learned and Orthodox Minister to dispense the word of God unto them at the West End of the said Town of Watertown, viz., the farmers and inhabitants living on the West Side of Stony Brook, and that for that purpose they be a distinct and separate precinct, and their Bounds to extend from Charles River to Stony Brook Bridge, the Brook being the Bounds from said Bridge, containing all the Farm Lands to Concord Line, and from thence all Watertown Bounds to their utmost Southward Bounds and to Westward, and that all the present Inhabitants on the West Side of Stony Brook aforesaid, together with such as shall from time to time settle among them, have liberty to convene together to advise, agree upon and take such methods as may be suitable and convenient for the securing, encouraging, settling and support of a minister, qualified as aforesaid, and for the Building and furnishing of a meeting house according as shall be determined by a Major vote, and also to nominate and appoint a Committee of three or more persons amongst themselves to transact and manage that affair; and all the Inhabitants and Estates under their improvement, lying on the West Side of Stony Brook, within the precincts before mentioned, shall stand charge towards Building of the Meeting House, the Settlement and Support of the ministry in said place, in manner as the Law relating to the maintenance and support of

Ministers doth direct and provide, and be assessed thereto proportionately by two or more assessors as shall from time to time be elected and appointed by the Major part of the said Inhabitants for that purpose who may also nominate and appoint a Collector to gather and pay in the same as by warrant or order under the hands of such assessors shall be directed and ordered.

[Signed] WM. STOUGHTON.

APPENDIX IX.

LOCATION AND PRESENT OWNERSHIP OF HISTORIC BUILDINGS AND PLACES MENTIONED IN THIS HISTORY.

Page 4. "Sanderson's Hill."
Now owned by General Charles J. Paine, where his residence is located on Highland Street.

Page 5. "land of Nathaniel Coolidge, Sr."
Probably in vicinity of present high-school house.

Page 20. "old tavern on Ball's Hill."
Now demolished, the cellar being still visible on the northerly side of Stony Brook road from Waltham.

Page 44. "Richardson's farm-house."
Located back of the residence of George D. Pushee on Church Street and owned by him.

Page 65. "occupied by Mr. Richardson."
Residence on Church Street now owned and occupied by George D. Pushee.

Page 112. "now the residence of Mr. Emerson."
Estate of George H. Emerson on Central Avenue, the building having been destroyed by fire on November 6, 1902.

Page 113. "now of Oliver Robbins."
On Wellesley Street, now owned and occupied by William H. Hill.

Page 119. "Nicholas Boylston place."
On the north-east corner of South Avenue and Wellesley Street, now owned by General Charles J. Paine.

Page 124. "John T. Macomber's tavern."
On the Town Square, now owned by the heirs of John Jones.

HISTORIC BUILDINGS AND PLACES MENTIONED 213

Page 154. "the Minor property."
: On Central Avenue, now owned and occupied by Edward C. Green.
Page 154. "where now stands the Cutting house."
: Now the Town Library lot.
Page 154. "the present dwelling-house."
: Removed in 1899 to Church Street, and now owned by Charles H. Fiske.
Page 156. "the paint-shop of M. & J. Jones."
: Now demolished. It was located on Central Avenue in front of the present blacksmith's shop of M. E. Crouse.
Page 157. "the present school-house on Highland Street."
: Remodelled into a dwelling-house, and now owned by Mrs. Albert H. Hews.
Page 157. "the William Hastings house."
: On Central Avenue, now owned and occupied by Andrew B. Driver.
Page 157. "present Minor house."
: On Central Avenue, now owned and occupied by Edward C. Green.
Page 157. "owned by Mr. Bingham."
: Near Crescent Street, now owned by Charles A. Freeman, and used for a screen factory.
Page 158. "the double house."
: On North Avenue, now owned and occupied by George D. Abercrombie.
Page 159. "land now of Curtis Robinson."
: Taken in building overhead crossing on Church Street at Central Massachusetts Railroad station in 1912.
Page 159. "Dr. Kendal's study."
: Now located on estate of Charles A. Freeman on "Old Road," Pigeon Hill.
Page 162. "The Upham shop.
: Now demolished, formerly standing close to, and west of, the house on Central Avenue now owned and occupied by Arthur E. Upham.

Page 162. "the Daggett tavern."
> Now demolished. It was located on the southwest corner of North Avenue and Conant Road, on land now owned by George E. Byram. The cellar is still visible.

Page 162. "property of Abijah Coburn."
> On South Avenue, now owned by Bancroft C. Davis.

Page 163. "owned by Mr. Harrington."
> On North Avenue, near the Lincoln line, now owned by Frank T. Harrington.

Page 163. "store of Henry Fiske."
> Now demolished. It was located on North Avenue to the north of the house now owned by W. F. Schrafft.

Page 173. "erected in 1828."
> Destroyed by fire on December 31, 1899, and replaced by the present edifice built in 1900.

Page 184. "owned by Mrs. Sears."
> Removed in 1907 to the south side of Central Avenue, and now owned by Horace S. Sears.

Page 184. "house south of the church."
> On Central Avenue, now owned and occupied by Harry L. Bailey.

Page 190. "now the house of Mr. Beals."
> Estate on Central Avenue now owned by Mrs. Francis B. Sears, the house having been destroyed by fire on February 25, 1906.

_____, Shadrach 128

ABBOTT, John 38, Joseph 53, Nehemiah 48
ABERCROMBIE, George 213 94a
ABRAHAM, _____ 154
ABRAHAMS, Ralph 154 157
ADAMS, Buckley 90, Daniel 140 182, Elizabeth 173, J. W. 177, Jacob 36, John 48 113 116 62a, John Q. 148, John Quincy 145 146, Joseph 81 85, Samuel 70 71 83 96 114, Susannah 173, William 177, Zenas 176
ALDRICH, S. N. 147
ALLEN, _____ 51, Abbot 53, Abel 7 45 51 61, Abolm. 53, B. 61, Benjamin 48 53, David 35 36 51 120, Deacon 29 30, Ebenezer 7 10 42 44 45 47 51 55 60 163 167 202 204, Elezebeth 9, Elijah 80, Ephraim 111, Francis 9, Isaac 9 14 36 50 206, J. Senr. 61, John 9 36 51 74 93 94 201 206, John Jr. 79 86 90, Jonas 9 50, Joseph 7 10 15 38 40 42 53 61 204, Joseph Jr. 7, Josiah 38, Josiah Jr. 80, Nathaniel 28 50, Patience 9, Robert 9 Ruth 9, Samuel 40, Thankful 167, Zedakiah 9

AMHERST, Jeffery 35
ANDREW, John, 137 138 141
ANGIER, Rev. Mr. 4 5
ARNOLD, Robert 176
ASBURY, Thomas 176
ATKINSON, Kinsman 177
AUSTIN, Benjamin 74
AVERY, Ephraim 177, J. 74, Jonathan 96
AYER, John 139

BABCOCK, Rufus, 175 208
BACON, John 22
BADGER, Andrew 140
BAILEY, Harry 214, Samuel 88
BAKER, John 149, Thomas 48
BALDWIN, John 87, Mary 159, Rebecca 189, Samuel 38 72 189 202 206
BALLARD, Mary 107
BAMSHAM, Math 22
BANCROFT, Amos 116 183 208, Benjamin 79 87, Dr. 119 169 182 184 142a 174a, George 134, Thomas Bigelow 183
BANYEA, Edward 139
BARBER, Oliver 201
BARKER, Nathan 135 136 148 149 161 209, Nathan Jr. 150, William 154
BARNARD, John 45
BARNES, Squire 77 189

BARRETT, Luther 180, Major 74, Nathan 81 85 92
BARRY, William 141
BARTLETT, Enoch 107
BASS, Sally 183
BASSFORD, James 60
BATES, Isaac 133
BAYLEY, Samuel 92
BEALS, Mr. 190 214
BEAMAN, James 92
BELCHER, Andrew 18
BEMIS, Abigail 173, Abijah 127, Abraham 173, Charles 111, Daniel 80 87 90, Elizabeth 173, Emory 175, Jacob 94, James 88, Jedediah 80, Jeduthun 88 90 92 95, John 35 37 38 48 50 79 87 90 92 94 201, Jonas 173, Lot 111, Mary 173, Nathan 87, Nathaniel 201, Tabitha 173, Thomas 94, Timothy 37 65, Timothy Jr. 201
BENJAMIN, Daniel 80 87 90, Jonathan 37
BENNETT, Mr. 157
BENNY, Thomas 38
BENSON, Alonzo 180
BENTON, Sanford 177
BERNARD, John 22
BESSON, Nicholas 141
BETTY, Adam 65
BIDWELL, Ira 177
BIGELOW, Abraham 14 37 68 109 110 111 126 160 204 206, Abram 158a, Alpheus 14 80 90 110 111 132 154 157 190 204 207, Alpheus Jr. 209, Amos 160 204 207, Anna 91, Convers 79, Converse 87 128 162 208, Deacon 122, Dr. 14, Elias 80 87, Ephraim 30a, Francis Edwin 128, Frank 139, George 155, Isaac 14 162, Jacob 91, James 38, John 95, Jonathan 40, Joseph 37, Joshua 9, Josiah 80 201 126a, Mr. 166, Nathaniel 37, Roger 79 87, Thomas 12 87 111 162 208 126a, Timothy 118 119, William 79 111
BIGLO, James 53 61, Jonathan 55 60, Joshua 53 60
BIGLOE, Abraham 51, Benjamin 51, Jonathan 51, Joseph 50, Nathaniel 51
BIGULAH, John 22
BILLINGS, Jonas 111, Nathaniel 94
BINGHAM, _____ 213, Mr. 158, S. F. H. 205, Samuel 133 178
BINNEY, Ames 177, John 36 49 182
BINNY, Jonathan 38
BIRD, Francis 148
BLACKMER, William 177
BLAKE, Francis 209
BLANCHARD, Luther 81
BOGLE, William 111
BOLYSTON, Nicholas 65

BOND, Benjamin 36 50 167
201, Henry 36 88,
Samuel 48 90 206,
William 36 38 50 80 86
90 201, William Jr. 79
BONNEY, Isaac 176
BOUTWELL, Gov. 147
BOWDITCH, Dr. 190a
BOWDOIN, Gov. 108 110,
James 95 96 97
BOWEN, Mr. 158
BOWMAN, Jonas 36 64,
Joseph 56
BOYCE, Park 162
BOYLE, William 208
BOYLSTON, Nicholas 119
178 212, Rebecca 178,
Nathaniel 80
BRACKETT, David 111
162, David Jr. 162
BRACKETT, Eben 79, Isaac
208
BRAMAN, William 177
BRATTLE, Mr. 5
BREWER, John 6 160 162
188, Jonathan Jr. 188,
Josiah 9 43 44 204, Mary
162 163
BRICKETT, Gen. 91
BRIGGS, George 134 135
BRIGHT, John 22 160
BRITTEN, Sefroy 140
BROCETT, Samuel 157
BROMFIELD, Edward 18
BROOKS, Col. 90
BROOKS, Col. 92, Eleazer
74 81 85 86, J. 63, James
48, John 110, 112, Joseph
40 48 63, Joseph Jr. 48,
Joshua 48, Luke 14a,
Nathan 128
BROWN, Adolphus 128,
Anna 9, Benj. 61,
Benjamin 10 12 38 40-45
48 51 52 54 56 59 163
167 202, Benjamin Jr. 9
48 65 66, Deacon 56,
Edward 158 162,
Ephraim 175, Henry 140,
James 63, John 54 68
201, Jonas 81, Jonathan
36, Joseph 63, Marshall
128, Mr. 57, Nathan 48,
Nathl. 60, Simeon 157
209, Timothy 63, William
54
BROWNE, Abraham 2
BRUCE, Dana 190, John 60
BRUMLEY, David 176
BRYANT, Mrs. 179
BULL, Jacob 64
BULLARD, ___ 45, Benj.
61 63, Benjamin 45 53,
Ebenezer 111, Isaiah 79,
Jacob 22, Jonathan 28 36
51 54 60 72 90, Jonathan
Jr. 54 60, Joseph 54 60
BULLOCK, Alexander 145
BURGOYNE, Gen. 91
BURRAGE, A. S. 180 181,
F. C. 181, Mrs. 180
BURTON, Charles 141
BUSH, Frederick 182 190a
BUTLER, Benjamin, 137
150
BUTTRICK, Major 78
BUXTEN, William 51
BYRAM, George 214

CABOTT, Edward 87
CADWELL, John 177
CAMBELL, Giles 177
CAPEN, Christopher 36 38 64
CAPRON, Ephraim 94
CAREY, Isaac 140
CARNES, William 141 142
CARTER, Amos Jr. 143 174, Daniel 43 50, William 141-143, William Henry 139
CARVER, Reuben 119 178 208
CARY, Josiah 87 201 Peter 80 87 88 92 95 Samuel 37 William 79
CASE, J. W. 176 James 149, James Mrs. 32
CASWELL, Jane 157, Mr. 163
CAVANAUGH, Mchl. 141
CHADWICK, Charles 54 60, John 22
CHAFLIN, William 145 146
CHANDLER, Joy 141, William 141
CHENEY, Amanda 151, George 139
CHILD, Nathan 111, Richard 160, Saml. 65 79, Samuel 36 72 111 201, Solomon 111
CHILDS, E. F. 143 174, Elisha 209, Franklin 143 174 175, Isaac 111, Shubal 50

CHUBB, Mary 64, Silence 64
CLARK, Daniel 208, E. O. 150 155, Hobart 16, Jennett 182, Jeremiah 48, John 95 182, Judah 43 48, Percival 64, Samuel 191, William 139
COBURN, ____ 162, Abijah 162 205 208 209 214, Arthur 209, Edward 135 149 150 205 209, Isaac 136 137 145 150 205 209 78a, James 208, John 98 108 207, Jonas 111 208 78a, Joseph 87, Thomas 94a
COGGSHALL, Samuel 177
COGGSWELL, James 90
COGSWELL, James 86 87
COLLEDGE, Josiah 50
CONANT, Mary 48
CONNERS, John 141
CONVERSE, Josiah 182
COOK, Daniel 58, David 139, Mr. 59
COOKE, Mr. 57
COOLEDGE, Paul 87
COOLIDGE, Daniel 35, John 188, Jonathan 5, Josiah 40 65, Nathaniel 5 7 10 53 54 201, Nathaniel Jr. 212, Nathl. 61, Paul 80, Richard 188
COOPER, James 140
COREY, Benjamin 63, E. 63, Isaac 86, Jonathan 63, Josiah 79, Thomas 79
CORLISS, Samuel 140

CORNELL, Mrs. 119
CORNWALLIS, Lord 97
CORY, Ebenezer 56, Isaac
   37 50 79, Samuel 38,
   Samuel Jr. 36, Thomas 56
   63, William 38
COTTON, John 10 189, Mr.
   167, Peter 91, Rebecca
   189
COUGHLIN, John 140
COX, Artemas 87, Elisha 37
   38, Sarah 91
COY, Nehemiah 176
CRAME, Origen 180
CROSBY, George 141
CROUSE, M. E. 213
CUMMINGS, Joseph 161
CURTIS, Oliver 79 87 90
CUSHING, C. 135
Cushing, J., 28, Ld. W. 208,
   Thomas 96 97
CUTER, Mr. 65
CUTLER, Ebenezer 48
CUTTER, ____ 157,
   Alpheus 126 14a,
   Benjamin 144 209,
   Charles 140, Edmund
   142, Edward 140, Elisha
   63, Ezekiel 158, George
   209, Jonas 63 205 208,
   William 100
CUTTING, ____ 184 213,
   Alfred 209, G. W. 155,
   George 129 142 149 154
   205, George Jr. 161 202,
   James 22, John 158 142a,
   Mr. 154 155 157
CUTTLER, Ebenezer 48

DAGGETT, ____ 190, 214,
   Charles 111, Milton 175
DAGSBURG, Ferdinand
   140
DAKIN, Samuel 48
DAMMSON, J. 98
DANA, Francis 112, Richard
   128, T. W. 74
DANFORTH, Samuel 87
DARRAH, Joseph 191
DAVIS, Bancroft 214,
   Daniel 88, Eliza Cheever
   183, Gen. 110, H. F. 180
   181, Isaac 81 134 138,
   John 133 171, N. F. 180,
   Randall 163
DAY, Henry 140, John 177
DERBY, Capt., 82, Gen.
   162, Martha 151, Samuel
   124
DEVENS, Charles 141
DEWING, Nathaniel 36 45
   51
DEXTER, Samuel 20 116
DICKINSON, Capt. 159,
   Chester 209, Mrs. 14 183
DILL, George 22
DIX, Jonas 80
DOAN, Joseph 61
DOANE, John 141
DOLBEAR, Benjamin 36 38
DRAKE, Benj. 140, William
   190
DRAPER, Ira 185
DREW, John 139
DRIVER, Andrew 213
DRURY, Leonard 134
DUDLEY, Benjamin 86, J.
   19, Joseph 18

DUNBAR, Asa 72 73
DUNHAM, H. C. 175,
  Howard 177
DUNN, Andrew 170,
  Andrew 179, Charles 136
  203, George 144 149 150
  156 209, John 179,
  Joseph 53
DURFEE, Michael 141
DYER, S. O. 177

EASTABROKE, Daniel 18
  19
EASTERBROOK, Daniel 60
EATON, brothers 30a,
  Daniel 168, Ebenezer 168
EIRE, Simon 2
ELLIS, George 126a,
  Lucinda 14a
EMERSON, Charles 190,
  George 212, Mr. 112
EMORY, Nathan 176
EPES, Daniel 18
ESTABROOK, Daniel 54
EVERETT, Edward 127

FAHEY, Thomas 139
FAIRBANK, George 176
FAIRFIELD, James 140 142
FALGHAW, Michael 61
FALSHAW, Michael 53
FARRAR, George 88
FARRER, George 90
FAULKNER, A. 87, Francis
  74 81 85
FAYBIEN, Joseph 141
FELCH, Ebenezer 9, John 45
  51, Nathaniel 32 37 45 51
  88

FIELD, Charles 139, Dr. 16
  126, Joseph 197 198,
  Joseph Jr. 15 122 123,
  Rev. Dr. 46a 132, Rev.
  Mr. 133
FILMORE, Daniel 177
FINNEGAN, John 176
FISHER, Charles 139,
  Ebenezer 133
FISK, Capt. 90, Jonathan 86
  91, Nathan 29 32 37 88
  90, S. 175, Samuel 91 93,
  William 54 60
FISKE, A. S. 143, Abijah
  207, Alonzo 144 145 149
  150 163 205 209 110a,
  Augustus 142a, C. H.
  148, Capt. 113, Charles
  145 205 213 174a, 62a,
  Deacon 113, Ebenezer
  111, Henry 163 214,
  Isaac 14 118 121 122 124
  125 136 138 169 184 188
  189 202 204 207,
  Jonathan 36 79 85 111
  168 207, Moses 208, Mr.,
  174, Nathan 14 50 65 110
  111 202 203 206 207
  209, Samuel 12 80 98
  100 201 203 204 207,
  Sewell 111 163 208,
  Thaddeus 14 163
FITCH, Charles 141, John
  40
FLAGG, Benoni 51, Capt.
  95, Daniel 111, David 38,
  Elisha 38, Enoch 111,
  Henry 157, Isaac 79 86
  90, John 72 80 100 189,

John Jr. 201, Mary 32,
Michael 22, Thomas 7 38
50 53 61 63
FLETCHER, D. 63
FLINT, Abel 86, Edward 48,
Ephraim 48 89, John 79
FLOYD, Andrew 139,
George 140
FOSTER, Richard 46,
Richard Jr. 56
FOX, Eli 150
FREEMAN, Charles 213
FRENCH, Merrill 150
FROST, John 79
FULHAM, Francis 18 19
FULLAM, Capt. 52 63, Col.
30 50, F. 60, Francis 6 7
25 29 45 47 51 204,
Jacob 22 40, Justice 45,
Major 188, Sgt. 23,
Squire 22 59
FULLER, A. 74, Benjamin
201, David 79, Ella 180,
F. T. 180, Jeremiah 37,
Moses 207, Thaddeus 80
86, Thomas 36
FULLUM, Elisha 37
FURBUSH, Elisha 111

GAGE, Gen. 82 188 189,
General 75 77, Robert 48,
Susannah 64
GALE, Abraham 32 51 65,
Elisha 37, Henry 37
GARDNER, Henry 74 95
GARFIELD, ___ 162,
Benoni 40 42 163,
Cooper 111, Edward 201,
Enoch 63, John 48,
Joseph 37 201, Thaddeus
80, Thomas 43 44 48 61,
Thomas Jr. 48
GASTON, William 149 150
GAY, Ebenezer 172
GEARFIELD, Benj. 61,
Benjamin 54 59, Benoni
10 54 61, Daniel 37,
Edward 50, Ephraim 22,
Samuel 37, Thomas 54
GENET, French minister
116
GEORGE, John 80
GERRY, Elbridge 112
GIBBS, Mr. 5
GILL, Moses 119 178,
William 94
GLOVER, Gen. 91
GODDARD, Edward 166,
Lydia 201, Mr. 95,
Nathaniel 44 50 202
GOLDTHWAITE, ___ 185
GONORANS, Samuel 54
GOODHUE, Jeremiah 201
GOODING, Samuel 36 64
GOODNOW, Jeremiah 64
GOOKIN, Nathaniel 6
GORDON, H. 74, R. F. 181
GORE, John 48 63, Jonathan
48
GORHAM, Nathaniel 112
GOULD, John 80
GOURGAS, John Mark 14a
GOVE, John 176
GOWELL, William 150
GOWEN, Dr. 157 189,
Hannah 113 161
GOWING, Mr. 158

GRANT, Caleb 54 55 60 , Gen. 83
GRAVES, Thomas 95
GRAY, Harrison 74, William 124
GREEN, Edward 213, Isaac 91, Jonas 189, Samuel 108
GREENLEAF, Enoch 100 108 157
GREGORY, Abijah 143 174, Abraham 51, Elijah 36 37, Isaac 37 50 87 92, Louisa 151, Uriah 86 125 179 201 207 158a
GRIFFIN, Leonard 177
GROOM, Jonathan 40

HAGAR, Benjamin 37, Hannah 32, Jonathan 37, Nathan 79 78a, Simeon 36
HAGER, Benjamin 49, Brother 175, Ebenezer 201, Isaac 37 50 201 206, John 50 86-88 90 94, Nathan 86 88 112 134 135 141 159 202 203 207 208, Nathan Jr. 159, Phineas, 80 87 90, Wm. 22
HAINES, John 23
HALE, John 128
HALL, Joshua 176
HAMMOND, Ebenezer 50
HANCOCK, ____ 191, Gov. 112, John 73 74 83 95 96 97 112
HANNAH, Corey 48

HARRINGTON, ____ 161, Abraham 14 79 114 207, Amos 90 207, B., 60, Benj, 60, Benjamin 50 52 55, Daniel 89, Elisha 100, Frank 214, George 22 51 176, Isaac 9 50 201, Isaac Jr. 90, J. Q. A. 135, Jabez 37, Joel 88 90 131, John 137, Jonas 36 45 50 51 94 100 118 201 206, Jonas 3rd 79, Joseph 50 100, Joseph Jr. 72, Justin 178, Luther 111 125 162 208, Moses 36 100 201, Mr. 160 163, Quincy 162, Robert 5, Stephen 35 36 38, Thankful 9, Thomas 87, Tyler 128, William 111
HARRIS, Amos 180
HARVEY, Moses 109
HASTINGS, Edward, 37 Elezebeth 9, Francis 163 180 181 110a 126a, Frank 126 159, James 86 178, John 9, John 13 22 28 45 51 206, John Jr. 107, Jonas 205 110a, Josiah 111 208, Mary 13 151 180, Mr. 162 163 164 176, Oliver 107 132 178 201, William 157 209 213
HAYDEN, Lewis 128
HAYWARD, Caleb 157 James 81
HAYWOOD, Caleb 116

HAZELTINE, Benjamin 176 177
HEADLEY, John 43 48
HEATH, Frederic 180, William 73 87
HELY, Nathaniel 22
HEMPSTEAD, Henry 177
HENRICK, Indian sachem 35
HENZY, William 139 142
HEWS, A. H. 181, Abraham 15 79 82 111 156 161 201, Albert 213, Charles 111, Frederick 139 142, Horace 136 141 142 145 202 203 209, Horatio 137 190, Marshall 15 140 145 156, Mr. 179, Samuel 15
HILL, Abraham 167, Benjamin 176, John 173 176, Lucius 140 142, Nathan 176, Thomas 90, William 212 174a
HINDS, Orlando 176
HINKLEY, Harry 180
HIRTLE, E. J. 180 181, G. A. 181, George 180
HOADLEY, J. 63
HOAR, Mr. 125, Samuel 89
HOBART, Wm. 79
HOBBS, Albert 65, Amos 111 208, Ebenezer 38 50 109 122 158 159 202-204 206 207, Edwin 134 135 137 143-145 149 174 205 209, Elisha 79, George 140, Henry 111 158 159 205 208 94a, Isaac 12 15 37 65 66 87 89 92 98 100 111 114 122 158 159 183 201-204 207 94a, Isaac Jr. 202 203 208 78a, John 162, Josiah 46 50 158 167, Mary 66, Mary Ann 159, Mathew 85 79 87 95 159 201 207, Nathan 111 124 158 204 207, Nathan Jr. 208, Reuben 79 86 87, Samuel 71 158 205 209 94a, William 90 109 110, Wm. 86
HODGES, Joseph 179 180
HODGKINS, Thomas 37
HOOK, Elias 163, George 163
HORNBROOKE, ____ vi, Francis 16
HOSMER, Abner 81, Amos 90, William 91
HOW, Edward 2, Estes 94
HOWARD, Nathaniel 86
HOWE, ____ 184 188 189, British Spy 30a, John 75 76, Oliver 177
HOYT, Benjamin 176
HUBBARD, Reuben 176
HULL, Elias 176, J. Mervin 180, Stephen 176
HUNT, Ebenezer 48 52, Ebenr 60, Ephraim 18, Otis 136 142 161 184, Samuel 51
HUNTER, Lyman 190
HURD, Abijah 64, Dr. 183, Isaac 182
HUTCHINSON, Charles 180, Eliakim 18, Elisha 18, Gov. 110

ILLINGSWORTH, H. 140
INGRAHAM, D. G. 157

JACKSON, Edward 56,
  Frederick 184, John 63,
  Jonathan 43 44, Major
  112
JACOBS, David 159
JAMES, Benjamin 118 124
  125 134 184 202 203
  208, Dr. 126, Isaac 46a
JAMESON, Nathaniel 50
JANSEN, Louis 177
JAY, John 116
JEFFERSON, Thomas 115
JENISON, Saml. 65
JENKINS, Thomas 175
JENNISON, Henry 209,
  Isaac 177, John 45,
  Joseph 80, Joshua 86,
  Josiah 88, N. 98,
  Nathaniel 37 45, Peter
  154 182, Robert 182
JOHNSON, Byron 155,
  Charles 154, Josiah 80,
  Saml. 140
JONES, ___ 182, Aaron 36,
  Abigail 34 183, Abijah
  143 174, Abraham 36 65
  89 206, Amos 79,
  Benjamin 37 201, Capt.
  30 50 52 59 60 107 112,
  Charles 145, Daniel 14,
  Elias 112, Elisha 202,
  Elisha 28 29 32 36 38 50
  68 71 73 98 152 203 204
  206, Francis 37, Isaac 37
  65 72 77 100 108 111

116 126 128 132 151 152
154 157 168 179 182 185
187 189 191 201 204 206
208, Isaac Jr. 90, Israel
36, J. 213, James 10 40
42 53 61 63 79 163 190,
John 40 45 50 60 77 125
133 155 161 162 170 188
201 208 212 30a,
Jonathan 36, Jones 54,
Joseph 7 36 38, Josiah 6 7
9 12 18 19 34 39 40 53
61, Josiah Jr. 7 204,
Lemuel 87, Lewis 139,
Lucy 64 182, M. 213,
Marshall 111 134 136
156 161 162 175 203
208, Martha 172, Mary
73 188, Moses 50, Mr.
153, Mrs. 91, Nathan 37,
Nathaniel 53, Nathl. 61,
Ralph 138 139 142, Saml.
61, Samuel 26 36 38 53,
Solomon 80 86, Stephen
14 126 William 80, Wm.
Pitt 111
JORDAN, Jabez 177

KENDAL, Dr. 119 125 159
  198 213 142a, Frank 156,
  Henry 198, Mr. 13 98
  168, Rev., 39, Rev. Dr.
  122 156 190 94a, Rev.
  Mr., 107, Samuel 14 15
  16 100 116 118 170 179
  195 196 14a, Samuel
  Rev. Dr. 11
KENNEY, Oliver 161
KENNY, Oliver 149

KENY, William 65
KEYES, Daniel 140
KIBBY, Epaphras 176 177
KILBURN, David 176
KING, Elias 150
KINGSBERRY, Elijah 79 86
KINSMAN, A. B. 177
KIRKLAND, President 15
KNIGHT, Jonathan 64

LACOUNT, William 177
LAFAYETTE, Gen. 111
LAMBORD, Benjamin 177
LAMSON, ___ vi 127 156 184, Alvan 14, Amos 64 111 113, Clarissa 154, Col. 125, D. S. 78 138, Daniel 111 124 125 139 154 155 162 202 203, Daniel S. v, E. T. 78 155 156, Ebenezer 48, Isaac 105 122 154 155 157 160 203 207, John 37 40 44 50 65 80 89 135 148 154 162 201 205 206, Major 85 87 92, Mary 190, Patience 125, Samuel 37 44 78 79 81 85 86 95 97 100 110 154 157 168 190 201-203 207 209, Samuel Jr. 111
LANE, Job 81
LAWRANCE, Jonathan 80, William 36 50 72 80 201
LAWRENCE, Amos 137, Daniel 80, Samuel 37
LEADBETTER, Henry 38 128, Increase 36 38 79 107 144 201, Increase Jr. 209, Jacob 178, Swift 128
LEAR, Mr. 112
LEARNARD, Thomas 41
LEARNED, Isaac 22
LEE, Woodis 36
LEUB, James 180
LEVERETT, John 25
LIENSMOUTH, Daniel 61
LINCOLN, Caleb 140, Gen. 108, Levi 124, Pres. 83
LINDSEY, John 177
LINSEY, John 176
LIVERMORE, Abijah 36, Abijah 38, Daniel 28 51 53 72 85 87 94 201, David 79 90, Ephraim 111 113, Isaac 50, J., 60, James 37 65 201, John 7 52, Jonas 45, Jos. 60, Joseph 7 9 36 45 50 52 201 204, Josiah 7 37 85 157 202, Lieut. 95, Marshall 157, Mary 9, Nathaniel 36 50, Saml. 65, Samuel 89 94 207, Samuel Jr. 115, Silas 86 90, William 111
LIVINGSTON, Beulah 151
LLOYD, James 14a
LOCKE, Isaac 176, Joshua 111
LONG, John 150
LOOMIS, A. A. 177
LORING, J. Q. 136
LOTHROP, Solomon 84
LOV, Samuel 55 60
LOVE, Samuel 55
LOVEL, Joseph 45

LOVELL, Joseph 51 54
LOVEWELL, Capt. 22 23, Jos. 80, Joseph 37 54 60 201·
LOWELL, Joseph 7
LYND, Joseph 58
LYNDE, Joseph 3 18

MACKEY, Jennett 182, Ruth 182
MACOMBER, J. T. 188 190, John 124 212
MADAB, John 40
MADOB, Daniel 55, Daniel Jr. 54, Isaack 53
MADOC, Isaac 53
MANN, Horace 65
MANSFIELD, James 36 38, Theophilus 32 37 49
MARBLE, Elias 176
MARRIAM, Charles 136
MARSH, Elisha 56 57 58
MARSHALL, ___ 133, Col 112 107, James F. B. 62a 94a, Miss. 148, Thomas 91 98 100 116 62a
MARTIN, Arthur 141, James 36
MASON, Capt. 22, Hugh 22, Thaddius 46
MASTERS, John 3
MASTICK, Joseph 87 88 90
MATHER, Rev. President 5
MATHIAS, Abner 90
MAYBERRY, Dr. 184
MAYHEW, Thomas 2
MCDONALD, John 180
MCINTOSH, Royal 156
MCKEE, J. W. 176

MCPHERSON, Hugh 154
MEDUB, Daniel 51
MEREDITH, William 177
MERRIAM, Amos 48, Charles 125 126 143 144 155 156 203 208
MERRICK, James 201, John 201
MERRILL, Abraham 177, John 177, William 177
MEYER, Philip Jr. 139
MIDDLESEX, Mrs. 119
MILLER, Samuel 46
MILLS, Charles 81
MILTON, George 149 150 209
MINOR, ___ 154 157 213
MIRICK, James 28 38 43 50 202, John 36 50 72, Josiah 38
MIRRICK, Jacob 72
MIXOR, John 55 60
MODOB, Isaac 63
MODOCK, Isaack 53
MODUB, Daniel 49
MODUP, Daniel 60, Daniel Jr. 60, Isaac 61
MONROE, B. 63, Benjamin 48 63
MOODY, Charles 150
MOORE, Ezekiel 153
MORRIS, Robert 128
MORRISON, Benjamin 142 202
MORS, Joseph 5 6 Mr. 17 166
MORSE, Alpheus 128 137 205, Charles 111, Dr. 198, George 140

MORTON, Fuller 140 142,
Marcus 127 133, Perez 74
MOULTON, Bathsheba 32
64
MUDGE, Thomas Hicks 177
MUNNIMONT, B. 63
MUNSON, N. C. 147
MYRICK, John 206

NELSON, Thomas 48
NEWBURY, Edwin 150
NICHOLS, Joseph 207
NICKLIN, Charles 177
NILES, Samuel 74
NOON, Rev. Mr. 175,
Samuel 177
NORCROSS, Isaac 35 ,
Jeremiah 2, John 79,
Joseph 35 36 38 51,
Nathaniel 56, Noah 35
38, Richard 40 54 165
166 188, Richd. 61,
William 36, Wm. 35
NORMAN, John 91
NUTTING, Samuel 79 90

O'CONNELL, John 141
O'CONNER, James 141
OBER, Henry 141
OLIVER, Chief Justice 72
OME, Azor 96
OSBORN, Vanransalear 176
OSGOOD, Abraham 177,
Rev. Dr. 122
OSTANDER, Daniel 176
OTHEMAN, Bartholomew
176
OTIS, Erastus 176, Harrison
153, James 70 153

PAINE, Charles 149 212
62a, Paine 176
PALMER, James 140,
Samuel 177, Thomas 139
PARKER, Clement 176,
Edgar 184, Theodore 128
PARKHURST, ____ 113,
Amos 80, Deacon 29 30
51, George 45 49, John 7
12 22 45 53 61, Joseph
51, Josiah 37 38, Lois 64,
Nathan 36, Nathaniel 64
80 87
PARKS, Charles 111, Danl.
65, Eleazer 90, James 89,
John 40 162, Joseph 48
111, Josiah 90, Richard
55 60 162, Whitten 162
PARMENTER, Jacob 79,
Jonas 90, Major 78,
Nathaniel 88, Solomon
90
PARRIS, Samuel 166
PARTRIDGE, Thomas 32
PATCH, Samuel 144,
Samuel Jr. 139
PATTRICK, Daniel 2
PEABODY, Oliver 25
PEACOCK, Cuffee 36,
James 90
PEIRCE, Abel 90 94, Abijah
89 163, Amos 90 111
Benjamin 14 37 72 79 80
134 156 168 190 201
206, Benjamin Jr. 86 94
209 126a, Benjamin Sr.
30a, Edward 86, Epm. 65,
Francis 7 60, George 48,

Isaac 87 111, Jacob 40
60, John 80 86, Jonas 48
80 94 201, Joseph 43 48
55 60 80 201, Joseph Jr.
48, Joshua 86 201, Moses
80, Thaddeus 88 95 111,
Tho. 65, Thomas 45 51,
Washington 160 188 208
PENDLETON, Bryan 2
PENNOCK, ___ 32
PERKINS, Jared 177
Thomas 147
PERRY, ___ 190, Dan 176
PETERSON, Whitman 175
PHILIPPS, Saml. 61
PHILIPS, Ebenezer 90,
Samuel 50 53
PHILLIPS, Eben 80,
Ebenezer 37 201, John 3
18, Samuel 73 126a,
Wendell 146, William
124
PICKERING, Francis 175,
George 176 177
PIERCE, Benjamin 208
PIKE, Simeon 87 94
PIORI, Jacob 54
PIPPS, William 3
PIRRICO, Francis 54
PITCAIRN, Major 78
PITMAN, Robert 148
PITTS, John 74
PLYMPTON, Ralph 156
POLLARD, Benjamin 201
POMEROY, Seth 73
PONTAS, John 158a
POOLE, Francis 140
POOR, Mary 180, Voluny
180

POWELL, Joseph 74
POWERS, John 139
POWNALL, John 80
PRATT, Panamuel 90,
Samuel 86 107, Simeon
71
PREBLE, Jedediah 73
PRENTICE, Thomas 41
PRESCOT, James 121
PRESCOTT, Abel Jr. 81,
James 96, Oliver 74 85
PRIEST, Mary 64
PRIOR, Wm. Jr. 22
PUSHEE, George 212
PUTNAM, ___ vi, Israel 35

QUINCY, President 186

RAMSDELL, Hezekiah 177
RAND, Benjamin 9 14 79 86
87 163, Daniel 87 88 163,
George 140, Thomas 37
79 89 93 95 98 201 206,
Thomas Jr. 79 86
RAVLIN, Thomas 176
REED, David 48
REVERE, Mr. 11, Paul 91
115
RICE, Abel 158, Alexander
149 150, Solomon 103
RICHARDSON, ___ 44 65
78 212, Henry 139,
Herbert 140, John 90,
William 90
RICHIE, Peter, 141
RIPLEY, Francis 174a, Mr.
77 185
RISLEY, John 177

ROBBINS, Benj 56,
  Chandler 16, Luther 191,
  Mrs. 154, Oliver 113 209
  212, Richd. 60, Saml. 61
ROBERTS, Benjamin 179,
  Charles 139, J. 98, John
  90 94, Joseph 92 93 100
  107 204 207, Walker 140
  141, William 62a, Wm.
  140
ROBIER, Thomas 166
ROBINS, Richard 53,
  Samuel, 53
ROBINSON, ___, 141,
  Curtis 159 213, Geo., 60,
  Geo. Jr. 60, George 7 54
  55, John 87 139 141-143,
  Keen 87 88 92, Oliver 36
  38
ROBY, Luther 76
ROPES, Timothy 179 180
RUSSELL, ___, vi, Abner
  111, Charles 16, Deacon
  89, Elmore 111, James 3,
  Joseph 80 86 91 169 190
  202 203 207, Thomas 12
  37 49 50 80 98 100 190
  201 206, Thomas Jr. 86
  87
RUTTER, ___, 20

SABIN, Elijah 176
SAGARD, Ephraim 48
SALES, Henry 155
SAMSON, Samuel 202
SANBORN, Jacob 177
SANDERSON, Abraham 80
  201, Amos 111, Daniel
  87, David 79, George
  177, Jacob 111, John 91,
  Jonas 4 7 88 111 122 201
  207, Mary 158
SANGER, Nathaniel 22,
  Samuel 132
SAVAGE, Deborah 179, Mr.
  71 189 126a, Samuel 14
  98, Samuel Philipps 201,
  Samuel Philips 68 98 100
SAWIN, Francis 56, John 55
  56 60, Manning 56,
  Thomas 56
SAWTELLE, Enoch 22
SCARRETT, Isaac 176
SCHRAFFT, W. F. 110a
SCHRAFT, W. F. 214
SCHWARTZ, ___, 65,
  John 180
SEARS, Edmund 16, Francis
  14 214 14a, Horace 214,
  Mrs. 184 214, Rev. Dr.
  16
SEAVERN, Joseph 113
SEAVERNS, Abijah 86,
  Joseph 178, Josiah 79 85,
  Samuel 206, Samuel Jr.
  100
SERGEANT, Peter 18
SEVERANCE, Saml. 63
SEVERANS, Josiah 201
SEVERENCE, Saml. 65
SEVERNS, Joseph 107,
  Josiah 107, Samuel 7 50
  201, Samuel Jr. 107 201
SEWALL, Justice 4 6,
  Samuel 3 18
SEWELL, Judge 25
SHARPE, Hugh 141

SHATTUCK, Benjamin 166,
    George 183 142a, Mr. 85,
    Samuel 161
SHAW, Judge 128
SHAYS, Daniel 108
SHED, Oliver 154 157,
    Reuben 64
SHEPHARD, Noah 51
SHEPPHERD, Jonathan 36
SHERBURNE, Oliver 150
SHERMAN, John 2, Lucy
    180
SHIRLEY, William 47
SIBLEY, ___, 126, Mr. 161
SIMPSON, James 201
SLACK, Eliphalet 208, John
    119 204 207
SMITH, ___, 20, Adam 45
    51, Adoniram 139, Albert
    37, Asa 35 72 201,
    Braddyll 32 37 38 50 73
    74 82 202-204 206,
    Clarissa 11, Col. 76 89,
    Daniel 36 51, Elbridge
    179, George 154 155 204
    208, Henry 36 38,
    Hepzibah 188, Jabez 140,
    James 37 201, James Jr.
    80, Job, 61, Joel 77 80 96
    106 113 129 154 160 188
    192 201 202 207 30a,
    John 53, Jonathan 22,
    Joseph 22 139, Josiah 32
    38 65 73 88 96 111 188
    202 204 206, Julius 136,
    Lemuel 139, Marshall
    175, Nahum 136, Nathan
    21 80, Simeon 79 86,
    William 37 50 188 30a,
    William Jr. 51, Zebediah
    48
SMITHWICK, Dr. 184
SNELLING, Joseph 176,
    Samuel 126a
SOULE, Joshua 176, Nathan
    177
SOUVERANS, Samuel 60
SPARHAWK, George 14a
SPAULDING, Nathan 177
SPEEN, John 25
SPOONER, William 74
SPRAGUE, Peleg 133
SPRING, Elezebeth 9, Elijah
    36, Elisha 38, Henry 36
    50 206, Jonathan 65 107
    201, Mary 9, Nathan 111,
    Thaddeus 36 38 65 107
    114 201 207, Thomas 51
    53 61 95, William 133
    205 208
SPRINGS, Henry 38
ST. CLAIR, Gen. 91
STANLEY, Ichabod 35 36
    38
STARK, Gen. 91, John 35
STARR, ___, 190a,
    Ebenezer 14 182, Josiah
    111 113 182
STEADMAN, Abijah 36 79,
    David 86, Ebenezer 80
    86, Jos. 80, Joseph 32 86,
    Josiah 79
STEARNS, Abijah 163,
    Daniel 143 174, David 37
    201, Ephraim 173,
    Habakkuk 173, Hepzibah
    188, Jonathan 154

STEDMAN, Abijah 86,
  Jonathan 36
STEEL, Joel 177
STERNS, Habakkuk 123
STICKNEY, Warren 139
STIMPSON, Benjamin 86,
  Daniel 14, James 32 54
  60 65 107 206, John 79
  86 87, Jonathan 51 53 61,
  Jos. 74, Lemuel 80 86 87,
  Nathaniel 51, Phineas 90,
  Samuel 65, William 142,
  Wm. 139
STIMSON, Andrew 37,
  James 38 51, James Jr.
  49, Jonathan 37, Joseph
  37 38, Nathaniel 38,
  Samuel 36 38
STODDARD, Isaac 176
STONE, A. T. 191, Joseph
  88 90 94, Nathaniel 165,
  William 177
STORRS, Joseph 90
STOUGHTON, William 3,
  Wm. 211
STOWE, F. V. 110a
STOWELL, John 141
STOWERS, John 2
STRATTON, ____, 20,
  Charles 111, Daniel 80
  173 207, Dexter 106,
  Elisha 79 207, Henry
  111, Jonathan 36 50 72
  79 86 98 107 201 206,
  Jonathan Jr. 201, Lieut.
  94, Martha 173, Thomas
  189 190
STREETER, Elisha 176
STRONG, Gov. 121

STURGIS, Rev. Dr. 180
SULLIVAN, Gen. 4 88
SUTHERLAND, George
  177
SWEET, Charles 147
SWEETZER, ____, 145
SYMMES, Thomas 5
TAFT, Joseph 183
TALBOT, Thomas 150
TAYLER, William 18
TAYLOR, Samuel 80
TAYNTOR, Joseph 22
TEEL, Abner 140
TENNEY (?), William 65
THAYER, Jedediah 208
THOMAS, Jane 32, John 73
THORNDIKE, Samuel
  Lothrop 126a
THRASHER, E. H. 177
TIBBETTS, John 91
TINKHAM, John 176
TITCOMB, Moses 34
TODD, Capt. 91
TOPLIFF, C. H. 136 138
  139 144 145, Calvin 180,
  Rev. Mr. 141
TOWER, Ambrose 48
TOWNSEND, M. A. 98,
  Penn, 18
TOZER, Simon 53 61
TRAIN, Charles 14 178 179,
  Deborah 179, Enoch 207,
  Isaac 111 191 203, John
  45 50 56 65, Joshua 65,
  Otis 128 135 205, Saml.
  65, Samuel 38 45 72 87
  100 179 201 206, Samuel
  Jr. 80 107 128 178 207,
  widow 50, William 65

TROWBRIDGE, Edward 28 29
TUCKER, Ebenezer 139 162, George 139 142 143, Henry 139
TUFTS, Thomas 6
TWITCHELL, Samuel 79
UNDERWOOD, Jonas 79 86 90, Jonathan 201 207, Joseph 65, Saml. 79, Samuel 86
UPHAM, A. M. 180, Abigail 182, Abijah 28 40 51 56 128 162 201 204 206, Arthur 213, Benjamin 86, Daniel 191, Deacon 29 30 89, Edwin 140, George 162, Henry 150, James 113, Joel 135 162 168, Josiah 45, Luther 135 150 209, Marshall 209 190a, Nathan 50 111 162 180, Phineas 90 162, Phinehas 72, Susannah 190, Thomas 12 37 40 51 72 206, widow 113, William 51 65 182 201
VANNEMAN, John 176
VARNUM, Joseph 118
VAUGHN, John 141
VICKORY, John 176
VILES, David 111, Jesse 44 111 208, John 173
VINTON, Porter 177
WAIGHT, John 54 60, Joseph 22 54, Thomas 54 60
WALKER, Isaac 79 86 94, John 28 29 32 37 46 50, John Jr. 79 92 201, Jonathan 36 38, Joseph 90, Nathaniel 50, William 133
WARD, Artemas 73 74 112 114 116 168 203 204 207 30a, Artemas Jr. 110, Daniel 95, William 182
WARK, Charles, 150
WARREN, ____, 51 126a, Abijah 79 91, Amos 132 209, Charles 190 209, Cornelius 191, Cynthia 142a, Daniel 53 56 60, Daniel Sr. 22, Deacon 50 122, Dr. 9, Elisha 91 92 201, Ezra 132 208, George 136 191, Harriet 180, J. 60, Jedidiah 88, John 12 32 36 40 50 55 59 61 87 89 98 100 206, John Jr. 54 79 61 86 87, John Sr. 142a, Jonathan 79 86 162 110a, Josiah 50, Mehitable 9, Micah 79, Michael 86, Mirick 112, Nathan 12 90 111 207, Nathaniel 112, Nehemiah 111, Philemon 88, Rufus 110a, Samuel 209, Sarah 50, Silas 14
WASHBURN, Albert 140, William 148 149
WASHINGTON, Gen. 84 85 112 189, George, 83 116, 62a
WATSON, ____, 84
WATTS, Dr. 192
WEBBER, Daniel, 141

WEBSTER, Daniel 20,
  Moses 177, Walter 141
WEELSON, Joseph 37
WELCH, James 141
WELLINGTON, Henry 155,
  J. 63, John 54 61, Jon. 48,
  Josh. 50, Palsgrave 59 61
WENDELL, Oliver 74
WESSON, Charles 190,
  Stephen 48, Timothy 48
WESTON, Daniel 90,
  George 174 175, Nathan
  80
WHEATON, Dr. 77 184 185
  174a
WHEELER, Abijah 37 50,
  Asabet 87, Jedediah 80,
  Solomen 38, Solomon 36,
  Tabatha, 201, Thomas 48,
  Timothy 47
WHIDDEN, C. C. 176 177
WHITE, Deacon 5, Henry
  113 148 149 150 172 203
  205 209, Jedediah 64,
  Jediah 201, John 48
WHITEHEAD, Daniel 97,
  Elisha 97, John 80
WHITING, Joseph 61 201,
  Josiah 90, Saml. 60,
  William 201, Wm. 60
WHITMAN, Joseph 175 176
WHITNEY, Abijah 111,
  Abraham 37 50, Elisha
  131, John 2 22 40 48 50,
  Joseph 37 50 53 63 80
  206, Josiah 206, Moses
  22, Mr. 94a, Nathaniel
  52, Phineas 14, Samuel

52, William 37 38 50 52
  74 80 206
WHITTEMORE, Aaron 78a,
  Capt. 94, Dr. 184, H. A.
  140, Isaac 36, Israel 74
  80 95 108 201 207,
  Jeremiah 38 201, Nathan
  50
WICKER, Joel 176
WILLARD, Dr. 110, M. 64,
  Mr. 6
WILLIAM, Williams 11
WILLIAMS, Col. 36 38,
  Ephraim 34 35 153,
  Hannah 10, John 163, Mr.
  13 29 45, Nathaniel 38
  167, Nemiah 65, Rev.
  Mr. 49, Thomas 79 86,
  William 6 7 10 14 42 50
  153
WILLIS, Samuel 175
WILSON, Capt. 81, Thomas
  6
WINDHAM, John 22
WINSLOW, Isaac 18
WINTHROP, Adam 3 25,
  Gov. 2 20
WOLLSON, Joseph 52,
  Thomas 55
WOOD, John 58
WOODS, Col. 188, Henry
  147
WOODWARD, Abigail 14
  109, Miranda 14, Mr. 13
  30 168, Parson 78 183,
  Rev. Dr. 142a, Rev. Mr.
  96 97 156, Samuel 11 12
  14 29 31 80 88 92,

Samuel Rev. 38, Sarah
156, Wareham 156
WOOLSON, Asa 36,
Ephraim 14 182, Hannah
9, Isaac 188 189, Jos. 60,
Joseph 7 9 29 40 50 167,
Mary 9 188, Mr. 52,
Nathan 37, Thomas 60
188, Thomas Jr. 55 60
WRIGHT, Elizur 128, John
48 54 79 86, Joseph 54,
Thomas 7, widow 110a
WYMAN, Artemas 87,
Danl. 65, Hezekiah 80,
Hezekiah 100 201, Jesse
90, Nathaniel 92
YOUNG, Benjamin 209

www.ingramcontent.com/pod-product-compliance
Lightning Source LLC
Chambersburg PA
CBHW070244230426
43664CB00014B/2401